Writing Women in Late Medieval and Early Modern Spain

University of Pennsylvania Press
MIDDLE AGES SERIES
Edited by
Edward Peters
Henry Charles Lea Professor
of Medieval History
University of Pennsylvania

A listing of the available books
in the series appears at the
back of this volume

Writing Women in Late Medieval and Early Modern Spain

The Mothers of Saint Teresa of Avila

Ronald E. Surtz

University of Pennsylvania Press

Philadelphia

Publication of this volume was assisted by a subvention from the Program for Cultural Cooperation Between Spain's Ministry of Culture and United States Universities.

Cover stamp: La Vida de Santa Magdalena, Valencia, Juan Joffre, 1505

Library of Congress Cataloging-in-Publication Data
Surtz, Ronald E.
    Writing women in late Medieval and early modern Spain : the mothers of Saint Teresa of Avila / Ronald E. Surtz.
        p.   cm. — (Middle Ages series)
    Includes bibliographical references and index.
    ISBN 0-8122-3292-5
    1. Spirituality—Spain—History.   2. Spirituality—Spain—History—16th century.
3. Spirituality—Catholic Church—History.   4. Christian literature, Spanish—Spain.
5. Catholic literature—History.   6. Spanish literature—Classical period, 1500–1700—
History and criticism.   7. Nuns as authors.   8. Catholic Church—Spain—History.
9. Spain—Church history.   I. Title.   II. Series.
BX1584.S87   1995
282'.46'082—dc20   95-5353
                                                                                              CIP

Para mis compañeras de viaje:

Aurora

Barbara

María

y para siempre

Nora

Contents

Acknowledgments

In the preparation of this book I have received help and encouragement of many kinds. First and foremost, Nora Weinerth was a scintillating confidante, critic, and collaborator in all stages of the writing of this study. Travel grants from the Princeton University Committee on Research in the Humanities and Social Sciences enabled me to carry out research in Spain. Princeton University also provided a partial subvention for publication. Particular thanks are due to Father Teodoro Alonso Turienzo of the Escorial Library and to Father Josef Metzler of the Archivio Segreto Vaticano as well as to the staff of Firestone Library. I am very grateful for the hospitality of Doña Amalia Serrano Camarasa, María del Valle Vaquero Serrano, and María Carmen Vaquero Serrano of Toledo. Jodi Bilinkoff was unstinting in her advice and encouragement. I would also like to thank my editors at the University of Pennsylvania Press and my two readers, E. Ann Matter and Anne Cruz. My student assistants, especially Beatriz de Alba-Koch, provided invaluable help and much good humor. Finally, I dedicate this study to a group of friends who were my special traveling companions through time, space, and mind.

A Note on Texts

For the sake of consistency, in transcribing or quoting medieval and Golden Age Spanish texts, I have expanded abbreviations and added accent marks, punctuation, and capital letters in accordance with modern usage. I have regularized the use of *u/v* and *i/j/y* and transcribed as *r* initial *rr-* and *-rr-* after a consonant. I use *e* to represent the Tironian sign.

In transcribing or quoting medieval Latin texts, I have expanded abbreviations and added punctuation and capital letters in accordance with modern usage. I have regularized the use of *u/v*, and I use *et* to represent the Tironian sign.

Unless otherwise indicated, English translations of medieval Latin and Spanish texts are my own.

Quotations from the Bible are taken from the revised version of the Douai-Rheims English translation of the Latin Vulgate (New York: Benziger Brothers, 1944). I therefore follow the Vulgate numbering of the Psalms.

Abbreviations

Glossa ordinaria	*Biblia latina cum Glossa ordinaria. Facsimile Reprint of the Editio Princeps: Adolph Rusch of Strassburg 1480/81*, 4 vols. (Turnhout: Brepols, 1992).
Golden Legend	Jacobus de Voragine, *The Golden Legend*, trans. William Granger Ryan, 2 vols. (Princeton, N. J.: Princeton University Press, 1993).
Patrologia Latina	*Patrologia cursus completus: series latina*, ed. J.-P. Migne, 221 vols. (Paris: Migne, etc., 1841–1864).

Introduction

Despite received opinions to the contrary, sixteenth- and seventeenth-century Spain had a wealth of female authors. Even a cursory perusal of a biobibliography like Manuel Serrano y Sanz's *Apuntes para una biblioteca de escritoras españolas* reveals that hundreds of women were writing in early modern Spain.[1] These women are all but unknown for several reasons. Nearly half of them were nuns whose works were written largely for "in-house" consumption and never intended for publication.[2] Often these religious women wrote not out of personal motivation but because they were required to do so by their confessors in order that their experiences could be examined for their orthodoxy.[3] Such was the genesis of surely the best known of these spiritual autobiographies, Saint Teresa's *Vida*. Teresa never lived to see her works in print; they were published posthumously in 1588, six years after her death.[4] The writings of most other nuns remained in manuscript form and were never published, not even in our century. Notwithstanding the consistent interest aroused by Saint Teresa's *Vida*, modern readers are unlikely to consider the spiritual biography as particularly galvanizing reading. And yet, the fact remains that whether these female authors are known or not, whether their works are read or not, such women wrote and their writings are extant.

However, if we look at the period prior to Saint Teresa (1515–1582) and her contemporaries, we find a rather different state of affairs. In stark contrast to the prevalence of writing women in the second half of the sixteenth century and the entire seventeenth century, the fifteenth and early sixteenth centuries can boast of but a handful of female authors.[5] Nearly all are nuns, Leonor López de Córdoba[6] and Florencia Pinar[7] being the notable exceptions. Thus, Castile is scarcely different from other regions of medieval Europe, for writing was an activity in which women—whether lay or religious—hardly ever engaged.

The status of women in Spain in the Middle Ages, as in the rest of Europe, was at best ambiguous.[8] If in general women occupied an inferior position socially and legally, there were always exceptions. Indeed, in some ways conditions in Castile were propitious for an enlarged role for women, at least in the earlier period. For example, in her study of municipal charters of the twelfth and thirteenth centuries, Heath Dillard concludes that women "gained status, meaning a highly respected position in municipal society, as the responsible custodians of their household's and town's material, as well as reproductive, assets."[9] Townswomen, she goes on to observe, enjoyed substantial rights and protections. Daughters were able to inherit most kinds of municipal wealth on an equal footing with their brothers, and towns were solicitous of a woman's property rights (215). The abbess of the Cistercian convent of Las Huelgas enjoyed quasi-episcopal jurisdiction over the towns and churches subject to her monastery. She could confer benefices, establish new parishes, hear matrimonial and criminal cases, approve confessors, and issue licenses to priests to say Mass in her churches.[10] She and other Cistercian abbesses in Burgos and Palencia also believed that they had the right to bless their own nuns, hear confessions, and preach in public. If in 1200 a bull of Innocent III prohibited these latter practices,[11] it did not affect the rights of jurisdiction exercised by the abbess of Las Huelgas, which remained intact until 1874.[12] Nonetheless, the attempts to curb the abbesses' powers constitute a salutary lesson regarding the status of women, namely, that what may have been valid in frontier Spain or in the early Middle Ages did not necessarily hold true in later periods. And what was applicable to certain Cistercian abbesses was not the case for the abbesses of other religious orders. We must also be careful to distinguish between different categories of women. What was true for the nobility may not have been so for the lower classes. What was valid for nuns may not have been valid for laywomen. Moreover, while roles for women may have expanded in some areas, certain roles were more acceptable than others. Owning and administering property was one thing; authoring books was quite another.

What does make Castile different from other European countries is that, even if we allow for a certain number of lost texts, the tradition of women writing, be it in Latin or in Castilian, is a relatively late, namely, fifteenth-century, phenomenon. This is in sharp contrast to medieval Germany, which produced a Hrotsvitha in the tenth century and a Hildegard of Bingen in the twelfth, or to medieval France, with its Héloïse and Marie de France in the twelfth century.

In dealing with the writings of nuns, the question of the degree of female literacy is of obvious importance. In medieval Castile, as was the case elsewhere in Europe, female education was often viewed as undesir-

able. The Castilian poet Carvajal, who was active at the Neapolitan court
of Alfonso V between 1457 and 1460, wrote:

Amad, amadores, muger que non sabe,
a quien toda cosa paresca ser nueva;
que quanto más sabe muger, menos vale
segund, por exiemplo lo hemos de Eva,
que luego comiendo del fructo de vida,
rompiendo el velo de rica inocencia,
supo su mal e su gloria perdida.
Guardaos de muger que ha plática e sciencia.[13]

(Love, ye lovers, an ignorant woman to whom everything seems a
novelty, for the more a woman knows, the less she is worth as, for example, in the case of Eve, who after eating the fruit of life, destroying
the veil of splendid innocence, became cognizant of her error and her
lost glory. Beware of a woman who has experience and learning.)

Likewise, in the treatise that Martín de Córdoba wrote for Princess Isabella (the future Isabella the Catholic), the author uses an anecdote from
Varro concerning classical Athens to justify the exclusion of women from
the world of learning. Nonetheless, he makes an exception for highborn
ladies, like Saint Catherine of Alexandria and Isabella herself, to whom
education is permitted.[14]

In the case of female religious communities, it appears that at least
some nuns were given an education appropriate to the activities that they
were expected to perform. The constitutions that Saint Dominic wrote in
1212 or 1213 for the convent of San Sisto in Rome stipulate that to avoid
idleness the nuns should engage in manual labor whenever they are not
otherwise occupied in singing the Divine Offices or learning to read.[15] The
constitutions drafted in 1249, probably by the master general Humbert
of Romans, for the French convent of Montargis recommend learning to
read as a means of deriving greater spiritual benefits from chanting the
Divine Offices.[16] Nonetheless, when in 1259 Humbert revised the constitutions for Dominican nuns, he removed the specific mention of instruction
in reading.[17] On this issue the constitutions for nuns end up being strik-
ingly different from the constitutions for friars, which call for a *magister
studentium* and specify what kinds of books are to be read.[18] In his study
of Humbert's attitude toward the Second Order, Edward Brett concludes

that Dominican nuns were not required to be literate and that the master general assumed that most of them would not understand the meaning of the Latin words they were singing.[19] In more general terms, Anne Bagnall Yardley notes that literacy among nuns was invariably linked to singing the liturgy.[20] Thus, the fourteenth-century Catalan translation of the rule for Poor Clares envisions two sorts of nuns: the educated, who can sing and read the Divine Offices, and the unlettered, who are relegated to saying Our Fathers while their literate sisters sing the hours.[21] However, in the case of intelligent youngish nuns, the abbess is directed to find a suitable instructor to teach them to sing the Divine Offices (223). Obviously, different religious orders at different times and in different places called for varying attitudes and possibilities regarding the education of female religious.[22] There is some evidence that literacy in Latin for nuns may have increased somewhat in the late fifteenth century, for Isabella the Catholic, who set the example by learning Latin at a relatively mature age,[23] encouraged the learning of Latin by nuns as part of the program of religious reform she and Ferdinand fostered under the aegis of Cardinal Cisneros.[24] When in 1500 the queen was in the process of founding a convent in Granada, Isabella sought to secure the profession of a young woman literate in Latin so that she could teach Latin to the other nuns.[25]

Paul Saenger distinguishes between two types of literacy. The phonetically literate were able "to decode texts syllable by syllable and to pronounce them orally. . . . Although the reader often had from extraneous sources a general appreciation of the sense of the text, he was not competent to comprehend its precise grammatical meaning." Comprehension literacy was "the ability to decode a written text silently, word by word, and to understand it fully in the very act of gazing upon it."[26] In the light of this distinction, it is likely that many nuns were phonetically literate in Latin and perhaps comprehensively literate in the vernacular. It is pertinent to note in this regard that the fact that a nun—or anyone else for that matter—quotes and even translates Latin phrases is at best an ambiguous criterion for literacy in Latin. For example, Pedro Ruiz de Alcaraz, who did not know Latin, was nonetheless able to quote memorized biblical passages in Latin and then supply the Castilian translation.[27]

As M. T. Clanchy has pointed out in the case of England, reading and writing were independent skills in the Middle Ages. The fact that someone could sound out a written text, be it in the vernacular or in Latin, did not mean that the person was able to write in one or the other of those languages.[28] This phenomenon was also related to the question of gender, for the Chevalier de La Tour Landry, in the book he wrote in 1371–1372 for the education of his daughters, opines that they should learn how to read but that there is no need for them to know how to write.[29] In any case, being unable to write did not prevent a person from composing letters or literary works, for literary composition was most commonly associated with the practice of dictation to a scribe.[30] Thus, the ability to write as such was not a sine qua non for nuns who produced texts. Indeed, the degree of literacy of María de Santo Domingo and Juana de la Cruz is open to question. Both were probably illiterate or nearly so, and the words pronounced during their mystical ecstasies were taken down by those who witnessed the nuns' extraordinary experiences. For this reason modern critics have sometimes questioned whether such visionaries are to be considered the authors of the texts they dictated. This is, of course, ironic, for at least in the early Middle Ages, few male writers were also their own scribes.[31] Does anyone question that Saint Jerome and Saint Gregory the Great are the authors of the works they probably dictated to secretaries?

Literacy simply meant possessing the skills necessary for producing texts. For women, however, actually writing or dictating texts meant overcoming severe psychological barriers to written expression. Saint Paul's injunction that women keep silent (I Corinthians 14:34) was extrapolated to include writing. Indeed, writing was viewed as a more serious infraction than speaking because of its obvious public dimension—manuscripts were circulated—and because writing was considered a task appropriate only to the male gender. Even when it was thought advisable that women learn to read and write, female writing was never intended to leave the private sphere of the home or the convent, for the public world of men was off-limits to the writings of women. While the traditional justification for female silence is the notion that Eve's words led Adam to sin, the Virgin Mary, that is, the anti-Eve, was also used as a model for cultivating the virtue of silence.[32] Thus, Saint Bonaventure observes that the Bible records but seven occasions on which the Blessed Virgin spoke.[33] In the pictorial arts, the Virgin Mary was depicted as learning to read, but she was hardly ever portrayed writing.[34] Due emphasis was given to the biblical verse in which Mary, after witnessing and participating in the marvels of the Nativity, "kept all these words, pondering them in her heart" (Luke 2:19).[35] It would have been unseemly for the Virgin to publicize such happenings through writing, for that was the task of the four evangelists, who were, of course, males.[36]

The question of authority is central to medieval literature. In producing their texts, writers derived their own authority from the authority enshrined in the preexisting texts of the recognized authors who preceded them. Needless to say, the written links in this chain of authority were all forged by males, whose textual male-bonding stretched diachronically back in time to classical antiquity as well as to the revealed Word of a male God. Women were excluded from this chain of authority, at least as far as the presence of any female authors endowed with authority is concerned. Of course, some women appropriated this form of patriarchal authorization in their writings. Teresa de Cartagena, for example, foregrounds her use of "male" authority by announcing that she is quoting a given biblical verse as "esta buena abtoridat." [37] Elsewhere, however, she links her female status to a lack of authority, stating that what she says has little authority because of her uncultivated female intellect. [38] This means that women writers had to develop textual strategies designed to make up for their lack of authority. Teresa de Cartagena used her own personal experience as an alternative means of authorizing her texts. [39] Other nuns claimed that their utterances were divinely inspired, thus effectively parenthesizing not only the ecclesiastical establishment, but also the entire system of written authority and the masculine space of writing that medieval constructions of gender had allotted to males.

Ecclesiastical tradition and medieval canon law excluded women from the priesthood and therefore from positions of authority in the male-dominated clerical establishment. This meant that if women were to achieve any sort of power or status through religion, it had to be in ways that circumvented the patriarchal Church hierarchy. [40] One way to authority was through visionary experiences that could be understood to come directly from God. The possibility of visions as an alternative to the priesthood for women was recognized even by the Church establishment. For example, Saint Thomas Aquinas argues that, although women may not be ordained, they may be prophetesses:

> Prophecy is not a sacrament but a gift of God. Wherefore there it is not the signification, but only the thing which is necessary. And since in matters pertaining to the soul woman does not differ from man as to the thing (for sometimes a woman is found to be better than many men as regards the soul), it follows that she can receive the gift of prophecy and the like, but not the sacrament of Orders. (Supplement, Q. 39, art. 1) [41]

However, what Aquinas permits with one hand, he takes away with the other. He allows women to receive the gift of prophecy, but not to reveal their prophecies in public:

Speech may be employed in two ways: in one way privately, to one or a few, in familiar conversation, and in this respect the grace of the word may be becoming to women; in another way, publicly, addressing oneself to the whole church, and this is not permitted to women. (II–II, Q. 177, art. 2)

Aquinas's caveat notwithstanding, medieval women received visions and prophecies and communicated them to their confessors and to others. Indeed, such phenomena serve to distinguish male and female spirituality in the Middle Ages. As a result of their statistical study of medieval and early modern saints, Donald Weinstein and Rudolf Bell conclude that visions, signs, prophecies, and demonic visitations are considerably more prominent in the lives of female saints than in those of their male counterparts.[42]

The nuns themselves were conscious of the fact that they did not possess the learning, and thereby the written authority, of men, and sought therefore to defend their own brand of infused knowledge. At the beginning of her sermon for the Feast of Saint Francis (1509/1510), Mother Juana de la Cruz claims that Christ, speaking through her, observes that the Father often hides his secrets from the lettered and the learned while revealing them to the humble and lowly:

Padre mío poderoso, graçias te fago porque ascondiste tus escondidos e altos secretos a los letrados e sabios e los revelaste a los sinples e despreçiados e humilldes.[43]

(My powerful Father, I give you thanks because you hid your secret and profound mysteries from the lettered and the wise and revealed them to the simple and despised and humble.[44])

Although in the sermon the Lord is referring to Saint Francis, it is nonetheless to be understood that Mother Juana herself, the recipient of the revelation, is yet another of these simple and humble souls.[45] In like vein, the prologue that a cleric wrote for his edition of the *Libro de la oración* (ca. 1518) of Juana's contemporary, María de Santo Domingo, contains the following observation:

Sus palabras de doctrina tan alta y tan provechosa, siendo mujer sin letras y aldeana, es gran confusión para los hombres y mucha mayor para los letrados, los quales contra ellos pueden mejor dezir por ella lo que Sant Augustín contra sí por Sant Antón: "Levántanse los indoctos y arrebatan el cielo y nosotros con nuestra sciencia çapuzámonos en el infierno." Digo, señor, indoctos por sciencia acquisita, porque de la sciencia infusa el Spíritu Sancto le dio tanta a esta su sierva quanta a otra.[46]

(Because she is an unlettered village woman, her words of sublime, beneficial teaching throw men into much confusion and even more so learned men.
Against the latter, let others say through her what St. Augustine said against
himself through St. Anthony: "The unlettered rise up and grasp Heaven while
we with our learning sink into Hell." I maintain, your Grace, that the unlettered are those with acquired learning and that in terms of infused learning,
the Holy Spirit bestowed as much on this His handmaid as on any other.[47])

Once again, the infused knowledge associated with the visionary experience of women is contrasted with the book learning of the scholar.

Nonetheless, I do not want to overemphasize the dichotomy between
a "masculine" formal acquisition of knowledge and a "feminine" infused
knowledge, for both popular wisdom and learned tradition extolled the
intuitive knowledge of the unlettered, whether male or female. The *Libro
de los doze sabios* of circa 1237 advises the sovereign never to disdain the
counsel of the uneducated, for God sometimes and unexpectedly inspires
the humble.[48] Writing in the mid-fifteenth century, Martín de Córdoba observes that peasants have an instinctual knowledge that the learned cannot
comprehend. Likewise, women's increased intuition compensates for their
being less rational than men.[49] In his sixteenth-century gloss of the saying, "A los bobos se apareçe la Virgen María" ("The Virgin Mary appears
to fools"), Sebastián de Horozco first offers a worldly interpretation, ex-
plaining that the simple and virtuous person often acquires more wealth
than the wise and industrious person.[50] Horozco then adds a spiritual interpretation, declaring that God often esteems and rewards those whom
the world disdains.[51] In his 1611 dictionary, Sebastián de Covarrubias criti-
cizes those who interpret the proverb in the sense that fortune favors fools
and insists on the interpretation that the Virgin often chooses to manifest
herself to the humble.[52]

Certain religious reform movements similarly deprecated the sterile
ratiocinations of the schools and extolled a less intellectual approach to religion. In fifteenth-century Spain, the writings that emanated from reformed
Franciscan congregations attest to a prejudice against too much bookish
knowledge. Alleging the authority of Saint Francis himself, Pedro de Villacreces excluded grammar and the other liberal arts from the friars' program
of study.[53] Writing in 1460, Lope de Salinas recalls that his spiritual master, Pedro de Villacreces, said that he learned more from weeping in the
darkness of his cell than from studying by candlelight in Salamanca, Tou-
louse, and Paris. Furthermore, he would prefer to be a simple old woman
with her love of God and of her neighbor than to be an expert in the

theology of Saint Augustine or Duns Scotus. Brother Pedro would therefore begin to teach his disciples by telling them to weep and to avoid the study of the liberal arts.[54] Noteworthy here is the appropriation by a male reformer of traits usually associated with female spirituality, a spirituality that is portrayed as a blind faith, happy in its ignorance of bookish learning. Nonetheless, if Brother Pedro was opposed to superfluous erudition for his friars, he could scarcely have approved of anything beyond the rudiments of reading for nuns, let alone their possessing sufficient instruction to compose books.

Because private revelations were believed to come directly from God, thereby sidestepping the Church hierarchy, they were viewed with suspicion, and not only in the case of visions experienced by women. Franciscan reform movements in fifteenth-century Castile were extremely mistrustful of revelations. At one point Lope de Salinas denounces as an abuse any revelations whatsoever. No matter how much they may seem of divine origin, he says, "son de escupir" ("they should be spat upon").[55] In another work, addressed to both men and women, Brother Lope appropriates the criteria of Abbot Isaac of Syria, warning that many pseudo-prophets will appear before the coming of the Antichrist. The devil will seek to inspire false revelations, especially in those of little formal education and in those who consciously seek after them out of pride. True revelations come as a gift from God with no human effort. Therefore, no one should allow pride to lead him to desire to have revelations, and any revelation should be scrutinized to see if in any way it leads to notions that contradict the teachings of the Church.[56] Likewise, Dominican spirituality was suspicious of revelations. Chapters XIV and XV of Saint Vincent Ferrer's *Tractatus de vita spirituali* (1394?) are devoted to overcoming the temptations that arise from diabolical suggestion. Such temptations can be avoided by never desiring visions and revelations and thus never incurring the charge of pride and vain curiosity. Further, one should avoid the company of persons who claim to have had such visions or revelations, especially if they seem to contradict the Scriptures or the teachings of the Church.[57]

Since it was essential to distinguish genuine revelations from diabolical illusions, alleged visionaries needed to be examined with great care. Medieval misogynist traditions conspired to make female visionaries automatically suspect, for the female sex was considered particularly susceptible to diabolic deception.[58] When such famous and influential female visionaries as Catherine of Siena and Bridget of Sweden became involved in Church politics, the polemic between their supporters and detractors foregrounded the need to develop criteria to determine the genuineness of their revelations.[59] Jean Gerson, the celebrated chancellor of the University of Paris, supported Joan of Arc, but was suspicious of Bridget of Sweden and probably of Catherine of Siena.[60] Significantly, his *De probatione spirituum* (1415) arose from the controversies surrounding the revelations of Saint Bridget, whose divine inspiration Gerson denied. Although the *De probatione spirituum* purports to set forth the criteria for examining the supernatural experiences of both sexes, women end up being the object of particular scrutiny. Gerson observes that people new in the service of God are more easily led astray, and even more so in the case of "the young and in women whose enthusiasm is extravagant, eager, changeable, uninhibited, and therefore not to be considered trustworthy."[61] Later on in his treatise, Gerson returns to the need to examine women visionaries with particular care:

> If the visionary is a woman, it is especially necessary to learn how she acts toward her confessors or instructors. Is she prone to continual conversations, either under the pretext of frequent confession or in relating lengthy accounts of her visions, or by any other kind of discussion? . . . Even if nothing more detrimental occurred than a great waste of precious time, it would give abundant satisfaction to the devil. Also, you must realize that a woman has something else: an unhealthy curiosity which leads to gazing about and talking (not to mention touching). . . . Moreover, the abiding peace of God is in quiet. Consequently no one will be surprised if such people, having embraced false teachings, turn aside from truth. All the more is it true if these women, itching with curiosity, are the kind whom the Apostle describes: *Silly women who are sin-laden and led away by various lusts: ever learning yet never attaining knowledge of the truth.* (36–37)

In his *De examinatione doctrinarum* of 1423, Gerson begins by evoking Eve's role in the Fall, and then observes:

> Every teaching of women, especially that couched in solemn word or writing, is to be held suspect, unless it is first diligently examined according to one of the six rules we have mentioned above, and much more thoroughly than the teaching of men. Why is this so? The reason is obvious, for not only human but also divine law forbids such as they. Why? Because women are too easily seduced, because women are obstinate seducers, because it is not suitable for them to be privy to divine wisdom.[62]

Underlying both passages are such traditional misogynist clichés as female loquacity, curiosity, and dangerous sexuality.

Although the reception of mystical revelations was a typical manifestation of female spirituality in the Middle Ages, in Castile women mystics flourished only in the late fifteenth century. Indeed, before that time the bellicose religiosity of a Castile devoted to the Reconquest against the Muslims did not provide a congenial setting for mysticism of any sort. In a speech that the Hieronymite Juan Serrano is said to have delivered before the pope in 1428, his fellow Castilians are portrayed as neglecting the more gentle aspects of religion[63] as a result of their continuing struggle against the Muslims.[64] In contrast, the messianic atmosphere of the late fifteenth-century Spain of Ferdinand and Isabella was especially propitious for all sorts of extraordinary religious phenomena.[65] Under the aegis of Cardinal Cisneros (1436–1517), revelations, and especially female revelations, were encouraged.[66] In fact, when Cisneros sponsored the printing of a Castilian translation of Saint Vincent Ferrer's *Tractatus de vita spirituali*, the translation omitted the chapters in which the saint warned against the temptation to seek after visions and revelations. Significantly, the vernacular version of the *Tractatus* was appended to the Cisneros-sponsored Castilian translation of the *Book* of the female mystic, Angela of Foligno.[67] Female visionaries fortunate enough to live in the Spain of Cardinal Cisneros found in him a champion ready to defend not only mystical experiences in general but also female spirituality in particular.[68] Among the spiritual works published at Cisneros's expense were a Castilian translation (1502–1503) of the *Vita Christi* of Ludolph the Carthusian, and both a translation (1504) and the Latin text (1505) of the *Ladder of Divine Ascent* of Saint John Climacus. With regard to works of female spirituality, Cisneros sponsored the publication of a Castilian translation of the letters and prayers of Saint Catherine of Siena (1512), a translation of Raymond of Capua's *Life of Saint Catherine of Siena* (1511), the Latin text of Mechtild of Hackeborn's *Liber spiritualis gratiae* (1505), and both the Latin text (1505) and a Castilian translation (1510) of the *Book* of Angela of Foligno.[69]

The prologue that the translator added to the Castilian version of Angela's *Book* probably reflects Cisneros's own ideas on the question of female spirituality. The prologue establishes a dichotomy between two types of knowledge: that acquired through formal studies by the educated, that is to say, by males, and the infused science closely associated with women. It appears, observes the translator, that what is hidden from males blinded by their carnal ways has been clearly manifested through this strong woman.[70] He goes on to remark that for the greater scorn and embarrassment of sinful males, God has sometimes ordained that women should teach men. In this respect Angela resembles the Old Testament prophetess Holda (IV Kings 22:14) to whom the people had recourse, much to the shame and disgrace of men and doctors of the law. Because the male sex had broken God's commandments, the gift of prophecy was transferred to the female sex.[71] In Antonio de la Peña's prologue to the Castilian translation of the life of Saint Catherine of Siena, the translator begins by observing that the celestial Jerusalem is to be populated not only with men but also with women. Eve was created from Adam's rib while he was in rapture contemplating the secrets of God, and we should therefore duly value God's creation of woman amid such mysteries. As compensation for their feminine weakness, God has given some women the gift of prophecy.[72] Christ further honored womankind by choosing to be born of a woman, and he was incarnated to redeem both men and women. After the Resurrection, he chose to reveal himself first to women. De la Peña then attacks those who deny that women will be resurrected with their female bodies at the Last Judgment (sig. a 3ᵛ). The translator goes on to praise the virgin-martyrs as well as the holy women of the Bible (sig. a 4). Finally, he observes that Divine Providence sometimes sees fit to empower weak women in order to deflate the pride and presumptuousness of men, especially men who consider themselves wise (sig. a 5ʳ).

Late fifteenth-century Castile thus offered a propitious atmosphere for the flowering of extraordinary religious phenomena, especially those experienced by women. However, what the visionary nuns present as a revelation was not born Minerva-like through divine inspiration as a result of the mystical experience. To the extent that an extraordinary spiritual experience is often translated into a series of visual or verbal images, such revelations were conditioned by verbal and iconic texts with which the nuns were familiar.[73] As Carl A. Keller observes:

> The few studies that do exist concerning visionary experience in Christianity, Islam, and Ancient India tend to prove that there is a close relationship between the acquired language and thought habits of the human subject, and the contents of the visions he may have. Visions are a kind of language which runs parallel to the spoken language and to the conceptual framework of the visionary's daily life. In brief, the Christian sees Christian symbols: the Cross, Christ, the Virgin, and so forth; the Muslim perceives Arabic letters and non-figurative designs; the Buddhist contemplates Buddhas sitting on lotus thrones. Visions appear, then, as interior projections or visualizations of the respective community's myth-dream which the subject has chosen, consciously or unconsciously, as his own personal myth-dream.[74]

Indeed, one of the striking characteristics of the female visionaries is their familiarity with the Bible, saints' lives, apocryphal traditions, and major currents of medieval spirituality. This phenomenon is especially note-worthy because many of these women came from peasant backgrounds and were illiterate or nearly so. How, then, did they acquire their familiarity with such traditions?

It is important to note that illiteracy did not necessarily block ac-cess to written culture, for reading almost always meant reading aloud and thereby sharing the contents of a book with a circle of listeners.[75] In an effort to make every moment count, one member of a religious community would read aloud to her companions during meals.[76] In the first half of the fourteenth century at the Benedictine convent of San Clemente de Toledo, miracles of the Virgin were read during Advent, Saint Jerome's *Lives of the Fathers* during Lent, and the *Gesta Salvatoris* during Holy Week.[77] In the case of the Cistercian convents of Avila, recommended mealtime readings in a manuscript of 1485/92 included, among other texts, the Bible, saints' lives, the *Moralia* and *Dialogues* of Saint Gregory the Great, Francesc Eixi-menis's *Vida de Nuestro Señor Jesucristo*, the letters of Saint Jerome, and various works of Saint Augustine. All these texts were to be read in the vernacular.[78] The 1510 inventory of the convent of San Francisco in Toledo lists the books that are to be read aloud to the nuns during meals: a volume of the Gospels and epistles of the liturgical year, various works attributed to Saint Bonaventure, the *Vita Christi* of Ludolph the Carthusian, the *Con-temptus mundi*, and the *Mirror of the Cross* of Domenico Cavalca.[79] The official biography of Mother Juana de la Cruz records an occasion when the *Floretus* of Saint Francis was read to her, apparently shortly after she took the veil in 1496.[80] In a later vision her guardian angel advises her companions to read the *Flos sanctorum*.[81]

The recommendation of the Bible as one of the texts to be read aloud in the refectory is of crucial interest because the nuns discussed in the pages that follow demonstrate their familiarity with a wide range of biblical texts. Indeed, the Scriptures are central to the spirituality of these women, as can be seen in their rewriting of key biblical episodes, or in their quoting or paraphrasing of specific verses. Such an intimate knowledge of the Bible would seem to contradict received notions that vernacular versions of the Scriptures were not widely available in the Middle Ages. Nonetheless, a number of translations circulated in medieval Castile,[82] and readers of the Bible must have included laywomen whose households could afford to pur-chase books or religious communities that would have had a copy in their library. When Alfonso Martínez de Toledo seeks to make fun of women's acquisitiveness, he enumerates the objects he might have expected to find in their jewel cases, items that include a Psalter in the vernacular.[83] Teresa de Cartagena relates how she found considerable consolation in reading the Psalter.[84] The 1331 inventory of the library of the Benedictine convent of San Clemente de Toledo includes a Bible.[85]

In any case it appears that the first law prohibiting Castilian translations of the Bible was not promulgated until after the expulsion of the Jews in 1492. Even then, it was not because translations were deemed dangerous for the laity in general, but specifically because recent converts from Judaism might be tempted to backslide if vernacular translations of the Old Testament were readily available.[86] Moreover, even that prohibition was not all-inclusive, for institutions of learning, religious foundations, and noblemen beyond suspicion were exempted.[87] Partial translations were permitted, at least for a time, especially if they were accompanied by a commentary. Thus, in 1493 Gonzalo García de Santa María published a Castilian translation of the *Postilla super epistolas et evangelia* (1437) of the Dominican William of Paris. This book made the Gospels and epistles for Sundays and proper of the Mass available in the vernacular, for as its colophon says, the work is intended for those who do not know Latin so that they can read the Gospels in the privacy of their own home.[88] Later, Ambrosio Montesino revised this translation of the Gospels and epistles, publishing his version in 1512. A second edition, published in 1525, included a series of explanatory sermons. The Inquisitorial Indexes of 1551 and 1559 allowed this work to continue to be read with the proviso that all editions contain the accompanying sermons.[89] Large sections of the Bible in the vernacular were also available in translations of medieval best-sellers such as the *Vita Christi* of Ludolph the Carthusian.[90] The *Vita Christi* contains quotations from all four gospels, nearly every epistle, and a majority of the books of the Old Testament, as well as exegetical glosses that incorporate quotations from the writings of the Fathers and medieval commentators.[91]

Sermons were another channel for the diffusion of biblical quotations as well as patristic and medieval interpretations of those texts. Medieval sermons were fixed in form and were invariably centered on a single biblical verse, the *thema*. Normally, three aspects of the *thema* were singled out for development through authorizing quotations and exemplary tales.[92] As Francisco Rico has pointed out in the case of the sermons of Saint Vincent Ferrer (14), in developing the *thema* the preacher would adopt the conventionalized methods of biblical exegesis, using such standard tools as the

Glossa ordinaria, Peter Comestor's *Historia scholastica*, and the writings of the Fathers. Through sermons the faithful became familiar with Latin quotations from the Bible—together with their juxtaposed vernacular translations—and with excerpts from standard commentaries on the Scriptures. When the visitor of the convent of Poleteins criticized Marguerite d'Oingt (d. 1310) because one of her writings concerning the Passion contained an episode not found in the Scriptures, Marguerite countered that she had heard it from a sermon preached by a Franciscan friar.[93] Teresa de Cartagena recalled hearing a preacher quote Peter Lombard in order to bolster his arguments.[94]

A significant factor informing the content of visions is the tradition of affective and participatory meditation on the life of Christ, codified in the anonymous Franciscan work, the late thirteenth-century *Meditationes vitae Christi*. Significantly, the book is addressed to a woman, a Franciscan nun, who is warned in the prologue that not all the episodes on which she is to meditate will be found in the Scriptures:

> However, you must not believe that all things said and done by Him on which we may meditate are known to us in writing. For the sake of greater impressiveness I shall tell them to you as they occurred or as they might have occurred according to the devout belief of the imagination and the varying interpretation of the mind.[95]

The *Meditationes* invites the pious reader to participate imaginatively in various episodes of Christ's life, as when at the Nativity, for example, she is exhorted to imitate the angels and shepherds who knelt in adoration of Christ:

> You too, who lingered so long, kneel and adore your Lord God, and then His mother, and reverently greet the saintly old Joseph. Kiss the beautiful little feet of the infant Jesus who lies in the manger and beg His mother to offer to let you hold Him a while. Pick Him up and hold Him in your arms. Gaze on His face with devotion and reverently kiss Him and delight in Him. (38)

The pious soul is invited not only to participate imaginatively in sacred history but also to follow the model of the author of the *Meditationes* in meditating on possible and probable episodes not contained in the Scriptures. By the end of the fifteenth century this sort of imaginative visualization was no longer an exclusively Franciscan phenomenon but was part of a widespread tradition of affective spirituality.[96] This helps to explain why the novelization of the Scriptures is one of the ways in which the mystic experience is translated into a concrete message or revelation, for holy women were presumably accustomed to perform such visualizations in the course of their daily meditations.

Iconography could also be an important didactic tool for nuns, for religious women—and others as well—lived in a world in which they were surrounded by religious images. An anthology of reminiscences recorded by the companions of Mother Juana de la Cruz mentions some thirty-one statues or paintings to be found in her convent, either because the religious figures spoke to her from the image or because the image was believed to have the power to grant indulgences.[97] Iconographic conventions were so fixed that the average Christian knew exactly what Christ, the Virgin, and the saints looked like. One of Saint Catherine of Siena's first biographers recounts that she had a vision in which she saw Saint Peter, Saint Paul, and Saint John "just as she had seen them painted in the churches."[98] As Chiara Frugoni has pointed out, to the extent that iconographical conventions represent a language common to the visionary, her scribe or confessor, and her eventual readers, the images that such conventions supply turn out to be a particularly suitable means for translating the experience of the divine.[99]

It is likely that the sermons they heard and the devotional works read aloud to them during meals familiarized nuns with the major trends in scriptural interpretation codified by the Fathers of the Church and medieval commentators. For that reason I have not hesitated to treat those exegetical works as significant intertexts, not necessarily because the nuns had a direct knowledge of specific texts, but because such commentaries indicate the broad context of scriptural exegesis that nurtured the nuns' spirituality. However, even if we restrict those intertexts to the principal commentaries, it does not mean that the sisters knew only such mainstream traditions of biblical interpretation. One of the visions received by Juana de la Cruz contains instructions for the performance of an Assumption play.[100] A perplexing aspect of the resulting play is the presence of an obscure motif, which juxtaposes the exaltation of the Virgin, the Fall of Lucifer, and the Immaculate Conception.[101] The question is less how Juana came to be familiar with that theme than what the implications were of the presence of such a recondite motif in the utterances of a supposedly unlettered nun. Perhaps the spiritual education of female religious, however random and inconsistent, for those very reasons could turn out to be more sophisticated than we might believe.

Fifteenth-century Castile was the site of a vigorous *querelle des femmes* in which the attackers of women had recourse to nearly every misogynist cliché, while the champions of women sought to defend them with the appropriate arguments. Jacob Ornstein has neatly mapped out the major participants in the polemic.[102] Although the seminal antifeminist text in the debate seems to have been the "Maldezir de mugeres," a poem composed around 1440 by Pere Torrellas, it is Alfonso Martínez de Toledo's *Corbacho* (1438) that most cogently sums up the misogynist traditions. According to the *Corbacho*, women are avaricious, envious, fickle, conceited, garrulous, and mendacious. Among the texts that seek to defend women is the *Triunfo de las donas* (1443) of Juan Rodríguez del Padrón, who offers fifty reasons why woman is superior to man. For example, Padrón argues that woman was created in paradise and is more beautiful, cleaner, more pious, more loving, and more merciful than man. Padrón even attempts to rehabilitate Eve, arguing that Satan tempted her out of envy of her beauty, and also that Eve sinned out of ignorance and because she was deceived by the serpent. Alvaro de Luna's *Libro de las virtuosas y claras mugeres* (1446) seeks to publicize the virtues of female saints and of illustrious women from the Old Testament and classical antiquity. Martín de Córdoba's *Jardín de las nobles doncellas*, dedicated to Princess Isabella, the future Isabella the Catholic, is both a mirror for princes, or rather, princesses, and a treatise praising the virtues of women. By defending women, Martín de Córdoba defends Isabella's fitness and even her right to rule. The pro-feminist debate is important for contextualizing the nuns discussed in this study, for the polemic ranged over the lifetimes of most of them. Although the debate had somewhat the character of a literary game, it did nonetheless serve to foreground in a contemporary literary setting centuries of misogynist and pro-feminist arguments. More specifically, to the extent that many nuns identified with celebrated biblical figures who provided positive role models for women, the debate was relevant to women writers because both they and the pro-feminist male authors used such figures to defend women.

As mentioned above, the visionary experience and the transmission of that experience through language are two different things. The experience itself is essentially ineffable, while the translation of that experience into a concrete verbal text cannot but draw upon other verbal or iconic texts familiar to the visionary. What the visionary draws upon hints at concerns that go beyond the ineffable experience and suggests, instead, rather practical considerations. As William Christian has observed with regard to Marian apparitions: "What people hear the saints say, or the way they see the saints, reveals their deepest preoccupations."[103] While sometimes such messages consist of traditional spiritual verities (the need for penitence, Christ's infinite love for humankind, and so forth), in other cases visions reveal more personal preoccupations. For example, because visions in general, and especially visions received by women, were viewed with suspicion unless validated by the ecclesiastical authorities, such supernatural phenomena often incorporate into their verbal message a defense of the authenticity of the experience that generated them. While sometimes such a defense consists merely in the assertion that the message is divinely inspired, in other cases the visionary incorporates into the vision what we might now call rhetorical strategies, that is, more sophisticated tactics designed to persuade the audience of the genuineness of the divine message the vision purports to convey.

This book will concern itself with late medieval Castilian nuns and specifically with those few religious women who preceded Saint Teresa as authors and/or mystics.[104] A common received notion is that in the Middle Ages the convent was merely a prison for unwanted females. While this may have been true in some cases, personal statements from other nuns evidence true vocations and what we would now call a positive self-image. In her study of French nuns from the eleventh to the thirteenth centuries, Penelope Johnson argues that medieval society held nuns in special reverence and that such religious women tended to project a self-image as worthy people.[105] Indeed, the religious life afforded many women a measure of freedom that might otherwise have been denied them in the secular world. The cases treated in this study show an entire gamut of possibilities.

Constanza de Castilla was born in the prison where her father languished and eventually died, and Constanza herself might have suffered a similar fate. In any case, the politics of late fourteenth-century Spain made it dangerous for her to live in the secular world, and entering the convent may have saved her life or, at least, the quality of her life. Being a nun did not prevent Constanza from maintaining close contact with her royal relatives, nor did it preclude her from taking considerable pride in her exalted lineage. Presumably, Constanza received an education appropriate to her royal station, and for half a century she was the prioress of a very important religious community. There is no evidence that Constanza was in any way criticized for writing or even that the fact that she wrote was deemed out of the ordinary. Despite the official pose of humility she adopts in her works, the problem of authority hardly manifests itself in them. It appears that in a sense she never stopped being a princess and had no need to defend her actions, even if her actions included writing.

Teresa de Cartagena came from a prominent and prosperous middle-class family that had produced several notable scholars. Teresa was stricken with deafness at an early age and may have been placed in the cloister by relatives unwilling to take care of her. Her writings mix personal experiences with the citation of the appropriate authorities, be they biblical or patristic. When Teresa was severely criticized for performing the "masculine" task of writing a devotional treatise, she responded by penning a spirited defense of her appropriation of an activity that most considered suitable only for males.

María de Ajofrín, Juana de la Cruz, and María de Santo Domingo came from lower-class families, and their formal education was probably limited. It is likely for that reason that they used their mystical experiences to authorize their writing.[106] María de Ajofrín and Juana de la Cruz decided to become nuns at a very early age and did so, despite the opposition of their relatives. María de Ajofrín had difficulty in proving the validity of her supernatural experiences, but once her authority was established, she was in a position to sermonize the male ecclesiastical hierarchy of Toledo. Juana de la Cruz had a major conflict with the superiors of her order over a question of ecclesiastical jurisdiction, resulting in her removal as prioress. Nonetheless, she was so renowned for her visionary experiences that, although she was the daughter of peasants, such important personages as Cardinal Cisneros and Emperor Charles V came to hear her ecstatic utterances. Criticism of her life-style led María de Santo Domingo to be examined four times by the superiors of her order, but thanks to her powerful protectors, she was never disciplined. Indeed, one of her patrons, the duke of Alba, was so impressed by her spirituality that he founded a convent especially for her. Among the issues that María raises in her writings is the resistance of a hostile male audience to accept spiritual messages received by women.

Although the nuns in this book can be considered to be Teresa's precursors, I expressly decided to avoid a teleological approach, that is, to view the nuns who wrote—or were written about—before Teresa as interesting only to the extent that they foreshadowed her. Rather, I aimed to see and to present them as individuals reacting to individual circumstances in individual ways. The nuns who anticipated Teresa worked in isolation; it is extremely unlikely that they even knew about one another. In a sense, they had neither "mothers" nor "sisters," if by that we mean other women writers whose works were familiar to them. The ways in which they created authority and the ways in which they compensated for their ignorance of models of female writers will be the focus of the chapters that follow.

1. The New Judith: Teresa de Cartagena

Most of what is known about Teresa de Cartagena must be gleaned from her works, since Teresa's status as female and as nun marginalized her as far as historical records are concerned. Francisco Cantera Burgos conjectures that she was born between 1420 and 1435.[1] She was already a nun in 1453, when she is mentioned as such in the will of her uncle, Alonso de Cartagena.[2] Considerably more is known about Teresa's relatives, for she was born into a distinguished family of converts from Judaism. Her grandfather, Salomon Halevy, was chief rabbi of Burgos. After his conversion in 1390, he adopted the name Pablo de Santa María and became bishop of Burgos. He was both a poet and a celebrated writer of exegetical treatises. Teresa's great-uncle was the chronicler Alvar García de Santa María. Her uncle, Alonso de Cartagena, was bishop of Burgos, a translator of Cicero and Seneca, and the author of didactic treatises in both Latin and Castilian.[3] Teresa's father, Pedro de Cartagena, was a distinguished member of the town council of Burgos and an important political figure under Juan II and Enrique IV. Teresa's family was thus both socially and intellectually distinguished.

Teresa went deaf at an early age,[4] an experience she describes as a "cloud of human and earthly sadness that cloaked my entire life and carried me off in a dense whirlwind of suffering to an island called 'The Reproach of Men and the Outcast of the People.'"[5] The progress of her infirmity seems to have been gradual, for she remembers a time when she was able to hear sermons preached.[6] Teresa was probably a Franciscan nun,[7] and Cantera Burgos supposes that she lived in a convent in either Salamanca or Burgos (541). Lewis J. Hutton conjectures that her family placed her in a convent in order to rid themselves of her care.[8] Teresa herself observes that relatives not only scorn those afflicted with illness,[9] but also try to dispatch them from their homes.[10] Teresa claims that she studied at the University of Salamanca,[11] but it is not clear what she meant by that declaration, since women were barred from attending such institutions.[12]

In her writings Teresa reveals how her sense of isolation was only increased when she was in the company of others because she could not hear their speech (39). The act of writing became a means of both self-consolation and communication.[13] According to Cantera Burgos (546), it is likely that Teresa's first extant work, the *Arboleda de los enfermos*, was composed between 1453 and 1460. Some time after the *Arboleda* began to circulate in manuscript, Teresa was criticized for having written a spiritual treatise, an activity deemed appropriate only for men. In response, she penned a spirited defense of her right to literary expression, the *Admiraçión operum Dey*. The *Admiraçión* is not only what some might now call a feminist text,[14] but also, as Alan Deyermond observes, a rare example in medieval Spanish literature of "a writer's reflections on the creative process, an indication of how it feels to be a writer."[15]

Both the *Arboleda* and the *Admiraçión* are addressed to a female dedicatee, who is explicitly identified in the case of the *Admiraçión* as the noblewoman Juana de Mendoza, the wife of the poet and important political figure Gómez Manrique.[16] In the dedication of the *Admiraçión* to Juana de Mendoza, Teresa expresses the hope that God will inspire her to compose the subsequent treatise (112) and claims that her patroness asked her to write the work (111). Teresa thereby not only shields her work with the authority of her dedicatee's aristocratic social status, but also implies that her self-defense was not written of her own free will but rather out of obedience to her patroness.[17] This also means that the immediate motivation to write the *Admiraçión* was an earthly, and more specifically, a female authority.

This chapter will focus on the *Admiraçión operum Dey*, highlighting the strategies that Teresa uses to defend her writing. To begin with, she invokes tactics that had become rhetorical commonplaces for medieval women writers. If on one hand she refers to her own weakness and unworthiness,[18] on the other hand she suggests that God will inspire her writing. Even Hildegard of Bingen, whose intellectual powers were far superior to those of Teresa and of most of the men of her time, nonetheless invoked formulas of unworthiness and self-deprecation.[19] Similarly, the claim of divine empowerment was employed by numerous women writers in the Middle Ages to justify their transgression of Saint Paul's injunction that women should keep silent. Nevertheless, Teresa's most notable strategy was the creation and re-creation of certain key images. This chapter will concentrate on three of those images: the bark/pith image, the biblical Judith, and the blind man on the road to Jericho. It will also address the question of Teresa's feminism and, more concretely, the limits of that feminism. But before considering the *Admiraçión*, it is useful to give some idea of the nature and contents of the *Arboleda de los enfermos*, that is, the work whose negative critical reception occasioned the writing of the *Admiración*.

The *Arboleda de los enfermos* is intended to demonstrate the spiritual benefits of bodily infirmities. The motif of illness, which is used as a metaphor by other writers, is both literal and figurative for Teresa, since she uses her own deafness as an example for her readers or listeners.[20] The *Arboleda* is thus notable for its integration of personal experience and devotional commonplaces, for Teresa supports her observations by invoking the authority of both her own experience and written sources, largely biblical and patristic.

The main idea of the *Arboleda* is that the suffering born of sickness is in reality beneficial because, through the cultivation of the virtue of patience, bodily illness can lead to spiritual health and thereby to salvation. Thus, Teresa considers her deafness a blessing because it has prevented her from hearing worldly noises, which were drowning out the healthy doctrines of the Lord (40). In her allegorical introduction, Teresa says that for a long time she has lived in exile on a desert island, but with the help of the Lord she has been led to understand that her isolation is actually a blessing. By planting the island with groves (*arboledas*, hence the title of the treatise) of solid doctrine and spiritual consolations, she has transformed the painful solitude of earthly chatter into the company of virtuous behavior. Alone on her island, Teresa will write the *Arboleda* in order to combat idleness (38–39).

The treatise proper is fundamentally a commentary on Psalm 44:11 ("Hearken, O daughter, and see, and incline thy ear; and forget thy people and thy father's house") and Psalm 31:9 ("Do not become like the horse and the mule, who have no understanding. With bit and bridle bind fast their jaws, who come not near unto thee"). Thus, Teresa must listen with the ear of her soul and abandon both her father's house (sinfulness) and her people (earthly desires). Further, the bit (reason) and the bridle (temperance) must constrain the jaws (vain desires). More specifically, it is Teresa's illness that has served as both bit and bridle by preventing her from eating foods harmful to her spiritual health (49).

Continuing with the alimentary imagery[21] and re-creating the biblical parable of the great supper (Luke 14:16–23), Teresa observes that, while God has invited everyone to his heavenly banquet, the sick and suffering are in a sense forcibly dragged to the feast by their very afflictions. Here Teresa rejects traditional allegorical expositions of the parable, which usually identified those compelled to attend the supper with the heathen,

the Jews, and the heretics.[22] Instead, she personalizes her source by interpreting the parable literally: she associates her own physical affliction with
the crippled, the blind, and the lame mentioned in the Bible (55). Teresa
goes on to mix architectonic and alimentary images, comparing her deafness to God's cloistering her hearing. Those who are ill can be said to have
professed in the convent of the suffering (58), whose abbess is the virtue of
patience (64). The convent of the suffering is blessed, for it enables those
who profess in it to join in the Lord's banquet. Next, Teresa defines two
degrees of patience. Suffering with prudence characterizes the first degree
of patience, but when suffering leads to spiritual blessings, it makes for an
even more perfect form of patience (67–69). Drawing on her own experience and re-creating the biblical parable of the talents (Matthew 25:14–30),
Teresa asserts that the afflicted receive five coins from God and then go
on to earn five more through their suffering (69–70). Teresa discusses each
one of the allegorical coins, giving special attention to the second, suffering itself, which she expounds by means of a medical image: Christ the
physician gives the spiritually ill the bitter medicine of suffering, which,
paradoxically, makes the body sick and the soul healthy (75). Concretely,
suffering is a medicine that cures the seven fevers (the seven deadly sins)
that afflict the soul (76).

Seeking an appropriate authority to support her assertions, Teresa recalls hearing a sermon in which the preacher invoked the authority of Peter
Lombard, the Master of the Sentences. She, however, will invoke Job,
whom she dubs the "Master of the Patiences" (96–97). In so doing, Teresa
rejects the standard patriarchal form of authority based on the writings of
learned men in order to invoke the authority of experience, personified in
the sufferings of Job.[23] Teresa ends her treatise by observing how perfect
patience entails not only the virtue of prudence, but all the other cardinal
as well as the theological virtues.

As previously mentioned, the negative reception accorded the *Arboleda* motivated the writing of an apology, the *Admiración operum Dey*. In
her introduction, Teresa stresses the theme of divine grace, for it was only
with the help of God that her otherwise weak female intellect was able to
compose the *Arboleda* (113). Her treatise, she observes, caused great wonderment, not because of its contents, but simply because it was written by
a woman.

As the *Admiración* proper begins, Teresa asks why some things cause
more amazement than others, if everything the Creator has done is worthy
of our admiration. The answer, she believes, lies in the fact that the things

wrought by God, which we see every day, seem so natural to us that they do not cause us to marvel. Applying this observation to her own situation as a writer, Teresa postulates that men were amazed by a woman's writing such a treatise precisely because erudite activities are normally performed by men, not by women (115). Nonetheless, she argues, God is omnipotent and can just as well grant wisdom to a woman as to a man.

Men's intellectual abilities, she reminds her readers, are not inherent to their male status but are rather a divine gift. If God granted certain boons to the male sex, it was not because he wished to favor that sex with greater grace but for his own secret purposes (116). Although God made the male sex strong, brave, and daring, and the female sex weak and cowardly, human nature is one. In fact, the differences between the sexes are divinely ordained in such a way that each one complements the other. To illustrate the complementarity of the sexes, Teresa uses a simile taken from Nature; she compares the strong male and the weak female to the tough bark (*corteza*) that covers the soft pith (*meollo*) of plants and trees. Just as both bark and pith are necessary for the preservation of the plant, so the strong male and the weaker female are necessary for the preservation of the human species:

> E si queredes bien mirar las plantas e árboles, veréis cómo las cortezas de fuera son muy rezias e fuertes e sofridoras de las [ten]pestades que los tienpos hazen, aguas e yelos e calores e fríos. Están así enxeridas he hechas por tal son que no paresçen sino un gastón firme e rezio para conservar e ayudar el meollo qu'está en[cerc]ado de dentro. E así por tal horden e manera anda lo uno a lo ál, que la fortaleza e rezidunbre de las cortezas guardan e conservan el meollo, sufriendo esteriormente las tenpestades ya dichas. El meollo así como es flaco e delicado, estando incluso, obra interiormente, da virtud e vigor a las cortezas e así lo uno con lo ál se conserva e ayuda e nos da cada año la diversidá o conposidad de las frutas que vedes. E por este mismo respeto creo yo qu'el soberano e poderoso Señor quiso e quiere en la natura umana obra[r] estas dos contraridades, conviene a saber: el estado varonil, fuerte e valiente, e el fimíneo, flaco e delicado. (117)

> (And if you are willing to look closely at plants and trees, you will see how the outer bark is very tough and strong and forbearing of seasonal storms, rain and frosts and heat and cold. It is thus grafted and formed in such a way that it seems but a strong and firm setting to preserve and succor the pith that is enclosed within. And thus in such a way and arrangement the one works with the other, for the strength and toughness of the bark protect and preserve the pith, enduring on the outside the storms already mentioned. The pith, since it is weak and delicate, being enclosed, works on the inside, gives strength and vigor to the bark. And thus the one preserves and succors the other and every

year gives us the variety or mixture of fruits that you observe. And I believe that in this same respect the supreme and powerful Lord willed and wills to effect in human nature these two opposites, which is to say: the masculine status, strong and brave, and the feminine, weak and delicate.)

The strength and courage of males preserve and guard that which is exterior; men govern and defend the fatherland and conserve their wealth. Women, weak and timid and unable to endure the rigors and dangers inherent in government and defense, are enclosed within their houses, where they help by devoting themselves to domestic tasks:

> Ca los varones con su fuerça e ánimo e sufiçiençia de entendimiento conservan e guardan las cosas de fuera, ⟨e⟩ así en procurar e tratar e saber ganar los bienes de fortuna, como el regir e governar e defender sus patrias e t[i]erras de los enemigos, e todas las otras cosas que a la conservaçión e provecho de la replúbica se requiere, e por consiguiente a su[s] particulares haziendas e personas; para lo qual, mucho conviene [y] es menester que sean robustos e valientes, de grande ánimo e aun de grandes e de muy elevados entendimientos. E las fenbras, así como flacas e pusilánimis e no sofridoras de los grandes trabajos e peligros que la procuraçión e governaçión e defensión de las sobredichas cosas se requieren, solamente estando inclusas o ençercadas dentro en su casa, con su industria e trabajo e obras domésticas e delicadas dan fuerça e vigor, e sin dubda non pequeño sobsidio a los varones. (117–118)

> (For men with their strength and courage and capable intellect preserve and guard exterior things, both in accumulating and dealing in and knowing how to obtain material possessions as well as in managing and governing and defending their countries and lands from their enemies, and all the other things necessary for the preservation and well-being of the state and thereby their personal wealth and persons, for which it is very important and necessary that they be strong and courageous, of great valor, and even of great and lofty intellect. And women, since they are weak and timorous and unable to tolerate the extreme hardships and dangers necessary for the accumulation and management and defense of the above-mentioned things, just being enclosed and contained inside their houses, with their industry and effort and delicate domestic labors give strength and vigor, and doubtless no little help to men.)

Thus, concludes Teresa, the privileges that God has given men are not to the detriment of women, nor are female weakness and timidity a sign of male superiority. Rather, these oppositions (*contraridades*) form part of God's providential plan for the preservation of the species (118).

The arboreal image posits a set of oppositions: outside versus inside, hard versus soft, public versus private, protecting versus nurturing, and, by extension, dry versus moist. In so doing, the image appears to appropriate and reinforce a series of traditional stereotypes regarding gender roles. Thus, for example, Saint Isidore of Seville asserts that *mulier* ("woman") is derived from *mollities* ("softness," but also "weakness") precisely because the principal difference between males and females lies in the respective strength and weakness of their bodies.[24] Likewise, *vir* ("man") is derived from *vis* ("strength") because men are stronger than women.[25]

Teresa's arboreal image and the corresponding gloss contrast the inside and the outside, the private and the public, privileging the house as the proper sphere of female activity.[26] Similarly, in handbooks for brides and married women, moralists and would-be moralists warned against the dangers of leaving the home and sought to restrain women to the private sphere. For example, the fifteenth-century poet Fernán Pérez de Guzmán defines the space outside the house as the space of men and the inner space ("puerta adentro") as the appropriate space for women:

> Así como es propio al varón ganar,
> por arte, o çiençia, o cavallería,
> por agricultura, o mercadería,
> fuera de la casa, por tierra o por mar—
> así las mugeres regir e guardar
> de la puerta adentro es muy grant ayuda,
> que por mucha agua que traya el açuda,
> en alverca rrota no puede durar. (vv. 433–440)[27]

> (Just as it is characteristic for man to earn a living outside the house by the arts or erudition or knighthood, by agriculture or commerce, on land or at sea, so it is a very great help for woman to supervise and watch over the home, for no matter how much water a water wheel may raise, it cannot last in a leaky reservoir.)

The inner-outer dichotomy extended even to the sexual differences between men and women. Following the Aristotelian and Galenic notion of the inverse similarity between the male and female organs, medieval medical writers discovered parallels between the vagina and the penis. The *Anatomia Vivorum* notes:

> God created the uterus to be the instrument and the place of generation in women. Its neck is to be compared with the penis, and its internal cavity to the *oschium* or scrotal pouch. . . . The female organ is inverted, or turned inward; the male is everted or turned outward.[28]

Different authors attributed different meanings to such anatomical characteristics. According to one view, woman's enclosed and therefore hidden genitalia were a sign of feminine superiority.[29] Medieval medical treatises further associated women with liquids and moisture, asserting that woman had a moister nature than man.[30] In Teresa's image, the pith plays the traditional female role of feeding and nurturing ("dan fuerça e vigor") from within, as if nursing the bark with its sap.

It is difficult to judge the extent to which Teresa's botanical image is original. In any case, it does not appear to be traditional. A more important question is the use that Teresa makes of the image and the way in which it simultaneously reasserts and undercuts stereotyped male/female categories.[31] The standard biological model for gender roles in the Middle Ages is that of the human body, codified by Saint Paul in Ephesians 5: 22–24: "Let women be subject to their husbands, as to the Lord. Because the husband is the head of the wife, as Christ is the head of the church. He is the saviour of his body. Therefore as the church is subject to Christ, so also let the wives be to their husbands in all things." Head and body working together assure the smooth functioning of society, provided, of course, that the body remains subordinate to the head. Needless to say, the Pauline image perpetuates stereotyped views of male superiority and female subservience: man is associated with the higher rational faculties, woman with the lower corporal faculties. Although Teresa mentions the subordination of woman to man,[32] she does not at all dwell on that notion, and the biological image she chooses to express the male-female relation belies the concept of subservience, for the bark is not more important than the pith nor is the pith more important than the bark.

Teresa's insistence on the complementarity of gender roles is especially striking when viewed in the light of such patriarchal codifications of female subordination as the *Summa theologica* of Saint Thomas Aquinas. Commenting on Genesis 2:18 ("And the Lord God said: It is not good for man to be alone; let us make him a help like unto himself"), Aquinas reduces woman's role as helpmate to a strictly biological function: "It was necessary for woman to be made, as the Scripture says, as *a helper* to man; not, indeed, as a helpmate in other works, as some say, since man can be more efficiently helped by another man in other works; but as a helper in the work of generation" (Part I, Q. 92, art. 1).[33] Aquinas then contrasts the case of perfect animals (including human beings), in which the active power of generation belongs to the male sex and the passive power to the female, with the case of plants, which possess the active and passive generative power together by means of their seeds (1:466).[34] Aquinas here incorporates a medieval scientific commonplace, and the fact that plants were known to reproduce without the subordination of one sex to the other has significant implications for Teresa's choice of images. In electing a botanical image, Teresa is able to avoid the issue of active versus passive roles in reproduction and thereby to parenthesize patriarchal notions of female subordination while highlighting the notion of man and woman as complementary helpmates.

In introducing the arboreal image, Teresa states that the tough bark is grafted and formed so as to constitute a firm setting or mounting to protect the soft pith. *Enxerir* ("to graft") is a word that appears in other passages in Teresa's works, some of which are relative to the image under discussion. At the beginning of the *Admiraçión* proper, Teresa observes that the composition of learned treatises is taken for granted as a typical activity for the male gender, but is considered something quite extraordinary in the case of women. Nonetheless, the same God who can "graft" knowledge onto the male intellect can likewise "graft" it onto the female intellect, and that despite women's small aptitude for such matters (115). Later, Teresa refers once again to the divine action of "grafting" knowledge onto the intellect of men (128). We can observe two things here. First, the horticultural image corresponds aptly with the concept that the privileges of men are a divine gift that can be bestowed ("grafted"), should God so desire it, on women as well. Second is the notion that Almighty God can graft together unlikely or dissimilar combinations, be it special wisdom in the case of a woman or the male/female elements that comprise the model of human society defined by the bark/pith image.

The use of the botanical image is a good example of the limits of Teresa's feminism. She accepts traditional gender roles for men and women and prefers to portray the miraculous nature of her own empowerment to write a book as an exception to the rule. Teresa is nonetheless capable of moments of subversion, however ambiguous, in her acceptance of the status quo. The bark/pith (*corteza/meollo*) metaphor is often used in medieval Spanish literature to contrast the surface meaning of a text with its hidden didactic content.[35] Teresa manipulates to her own advantage her readers' familiarity with this rhetorical commonplace, for in her botanical image the essential part, the *meollo*, corresponds to the female element, while the superficial interpretation, the *corteza*, corresponds to the male. Teresa thereby invites her readers to look beyond the surface *corteza* of her image in order to seek out the hidden *meollo* of female superiority.

In expounding on the arboreal image, Teresa introduces another image

that likewise undermines her portrayal of the complementary relation between the two genders. Teresa states that the hard bark resembles a firm
gastón (the setting or mounting for a jewel) that protects the soft pith. If
the male element in her simile is the setting for the jewel, then the female
element must be the jewel itself. Although at face value Teresa insists on
the complementarity of the sexes, her choice of images undermines that
assertion, for by implicitly comparing woman to a jewel presumably more
precious than its setting, she slyly suggests female superiority over the male.

It is evident that in the *Admiraçión* Teresa wishes to portray the writing of the *Arboleda* as an extraordinary manifestation of divine grace. This
constitutes a retrospective reading of the previous treatise, for in the *Arboleda* itself Teresa does not claim that it is divinely inspired. Aside from the
criticism her treatise evoked, to what extent was she aware of the transgressive nature of the act of writing in the case of a female author? Teresa herself
provides a partial answer to that question in a passage that arises from the
bark/pith discussion in which she compares her divine empowerment to
wield the pen to Judith's divine empowerment to wield the sword. God,
says Teresa, has given certain privileges to man; woman by her very nature
is weak and fearful and lacking in courage ("flaca e temerosa e de pequeño
coraçón"). Nonetheless, from time to time God can endow woman by
his divine grace (*graçiosamente*) with the same privileges with which he
has endowed man innately (*naturalmente*), causing her to realize actions
that cause wonderment. Thus, says Teresa, people would marvel to see an
otherwise weak and timorous woman take up the sword and defend her
fatherland from its enemies (119).

Punctuating her discussion with an instance of direct address to her
patroness,[36] Teresa poses the rhetorical question: What man so strong and
valiant and courageous could be found in olden times, and even in present
times, who dares to bear arms against Holofernes? Nonetheless, a woman
did not fear to confront him. Men, says Teresa, will argue that this was
brought about by the special grace and cleverness that God gave to the prudent Judith. Teresa agrees with this argument, adding that divine grace and
wisdom are greater than the natural strength given to men, for that which
an entire army of men could not accomplish was effected by the grace and
cleverness of a single woman. Nonetheless, Teresa's own case pales beside
that of Judith:

> Que manifiesto es que más a mano viene a la henbra ser eloquente que no
> ser fuerte, e más onesto le es ser entendida que no osada, e más ligera cosa

le será usar de la péñola que del espada. Así que deven notar los prudentes varones que Aquél que dio industria e graçia a Iudit para fazer un tan maravilloso e famoso acto, bien puede dar industria o entendimiento e graçia a otra qualquier henbra para fazer lo que a otras mugeres, o por ventura algunos del estado varonil, no s[ab]rían. (120)

(For clearly it is more within reach for a woman to be eloquent than to be strong, and more decorous for her to be intelligent than daring, and easier for her to wield the pen than the sword. Thus, let prudent men note that he who gave grace and cleverness to Judith to perform a marvelous and celebrated action can well give any other woman wisdom or understanding and grace to perform actions that other women—and even some men for that matter— would not be able to perform.)

Previously, by means of the bark/pith image Teresa all but reduced sexual differences to male strength and female weakness. If God empowered Judith with the superior physical strength usually associated with the male gender, Teresa argues, surely he can empower Teresa to write, an activity requiring no great corporal might. While elsewhere Teresa associates intellectual endeavors with the masculine sphere of action, she fails to do so in the context of her discussion of Judith, perhaps suggesting that the exercise of the intellect is not all that inappropriate an activity for a woman. She is thus able to argue that it is more proper and less remarkable for a woman to write than to wield a sword. By casting swordplay by a woman as a particularly improbable and astonishing instance of female empowerment, her own empowerment to write, while likewise divinely ordained, appears nonetheless to be less transgressive of expected norms of comportment.

One might further argue, observes Teresa, that her own situation is not really similar to that of her biblical predecessor, for Judith's virtue and sanctity made her worthy of such a divine gift. Other women are not necessarily so deserving. Nonetheless, she argues, God bestows his blessings on whomsoever he chooses, regardless of his or her merits. The fact that he does so but rarely, and even less frequently in the case of the female gender, is all the greater cause for admiration. Thereupon, punctuating her argument once again with a direct address to her patroness, Teresa returns to her point of departure: men have marveled at her treatise simply because writing books is so rare in the female gender (120–121).

Judith, the woman whom Teresa adopts as a sort of personal emblem, is first and foremost a biblical figure. Why did Teresa choose Judith? There are, to be sure, a number of parallels, some superficial, others less so, between the two women. The Bible calls attention to the fact that the widowed Judith lived in chastity.[37] Teresa, as a nun, has made a vow of chastity. Judith was a Jew; Teresa is of Jewish lineage. Judith saw herself as the humble instrument of God's will.[38] Teresa portrays her act of writing as the product of divine grace. The high priest Joachim praised Judith for having acted "manfully" (Judith 15:11).[39] Teresa, in performing an activity deemed the prerogative of men, has similarly acted as a man.

Both Judith and Teresa were empowered to wield typically masculine—and even phallic—instruments.[40] What can be said of Judith's usurping of the phallic sword and Teresa's usurping of the phallic pen? When Teresa is discussing the privileges with which God endowed the masculine gender, she singles out the fact that he made man strong, brave, and daring, while woman is weak, cowardly, and timorous. Sooner will a man face a fierce bull than a woman would face the mouse that darts among the folds of her skirts. And should women see a naked sword, their natural timidity will cause even the sight of such a weapon to instill extreme fear in them (116–117). Thus, the sword becomes an emblem of masculinity, carefully distanced and disassociated from the world of women.[41] Given Teresa's overall strategy of emphasizing the supernatural nature of her empowerment to write, it is now possible to see how she manipulates her readers' expectations and exploits their familiarity with the story of Judith. First, she establishes the sword as a prerogative of the masculine gender. Then, she calls attention to the exceptional nature of Judith's action, emphasizing the theme of divine empowerment and highlighting the sword as the instrument of that empowerment. Finally, by establishing the equivalence of Judith's sword and her own pen, she is better able to call attention to what she would have her readers believe is yet another exceptional case of divine empowerment, namely, her composition of a learned treatise.

Centuries of exegesis had transformed the biblical Judith into a complex figure with many connotations. Judith was viewed as a prefiguration of the Virgin Mary or of the Church. Thus, the triumph of Judith over Holofernes was interpreted as the triumph of the Church over its enemies.[42] As Holofernes came to represent Sin, Judith's victory over him became a prefiguration of the victory of the Virgin over Satan. Iconographically, the violence of Judith's action found its counterpart in representations of the Virgin piercing Satan with a spear.[43] In its contrast between Judith's chastity and Holofernes's concupiscence, the story came to be read as a warning against the dangers of lust. Nonetheless, as Marina Warner has observed, "the moral about virtue triumphing through the hand of a woman could so easily be collapsed upon itself and taken the other way round."[44] Thus, in the pictorial arts Judith was sometimes depicted as a wanton whose female sexuality entrapped Holofernes. Although the Vulgate specifies that when Judith bathed and perfumed herself and put on her best garments, "all this dressing up did not proceed from sensuality but from virtue" (Judith 10:4), those actions could nonetheless be interpreted as exemplifying feminine wiles. Moreover, in certain sixteenth- and seventeenth-century paintings Judith is assimilated to Salome: Judith holding the head of Holofernes resembles Salome holding the head of John the Baptist.[45] The lesson that equated female sexuality with sin and death could not be clearer. In any case, although the end was taken to justify the means, there was no getting around the fact that the means involved lying, seduction, and murder, and thus the story of Judith could be read as yet another allegory of female duplicity.

The preceding discussion manifests that medieval biblical exegesis and iconography developed a whole gamut of interpretations of the story of Judith, interpretations that ranged themselves between the two polar models for women in the Middle Ages: the virgin and the whore. This is not to suggest that Teresa saw herself as a latter-day Virgin Mary or as a femme fatale. Rather, Teresa's appropriation of the biblical figure, when placed in the context of the reception of the story of Judith in the Middle Ages, gives some appreciation of the motives behind what modern readers may perceive as an overreaction to her act of writing on the part of her male contemporaries. In the light of the various interpretations of the biblical personage outlined above, Teresa's choice of Judith as an emblematic figure has ambiguous ramifications. If, for Teresa, Judith represents a significant instance of divine empowerment of the otherwise weak female gender, a male audience may have been equally inclined to see in Judith an instance of the transgression of the boundaries of acceptable female behavior.[46]

Teresa's epoch had strictly circumscribed the areas in which women were permitted to act. Certain activities were deemed appropriate to the female gender, others—writing among them—were not. Despite the exaggerated critical reaction to the composition of the *Arboleda de los enfermos*, it is worth noting that Teresa's detractors apparently found no doctrinal errors in that treatise. The brouhaha seems to have revolved around the simple fact that the work was composed by a woman. If Judith's decapitation of Holofernes can be read as a symbolic castration,[47] then Teresa's taking up the pen to write a spiritual treatise must have seemed as threatening to male readers as if she were brandishing a sword precariously close to their genitals. Nonetheless, in choosing Judith as her spiritual mother in the *Admiración*, Teresa expresses the hope that, as her biblical predecessor triumphed over the forces of evil, so will she herself triumph over her critics by successfully defending her right to write.

The Judith episode is followed by a passage in which Teresa employs further rhetorical strategies to defuse the negative reception accorded her *Arboleda*. If her treatise occasioned astonishment, she argues, it was because that which is out of the ordinary causes wonderment. Nonetheless, Teresa cautions that there are two kinds of amazement, one good, the other bad. The gift of grace, she reminds her readers, comes from God. "Good" amazement is that which is properly directed at the source of all grace, God himself. "Bad" admiration occurs when we express wonderment at the human recipient of divine grace instead of at its source (124). Teresa thus attempts to manipulate the critical reception of her treatise through a sort of literary blackmail: readers who do not wish to be guilty of "bad" admiration should not focus on Teresa herself (should not criticize her?) and should concentrate instead on God's manifestation through her. In so doing, Teresa also defuses any allegation that she wrote for personal glory.

Next, Teresa asserts that the learned contents of her treatise are considerably less remarkable than the fact that it was written by a woman (126–127). Indeed, what is the value of learning if many wise men have been damned and many ignorant men saved? True wisdom, says Teresa, is learned in the school of the constant recollection of the blessings of God (128), for her own work is not really a philosophical or theological tract but rather a record of God's gifts and hidden favors (129). In contrasting the possibly dangerous book learning of men with her own infused wisdom, in one stroke Teresa assails the potential vanity of male erudition and extols the divine origin of her own empowerment to compose a learned treatise.

Teresa prepares to close the *Admiración* with a final defense of the *Arboleda*. She begins by answering two specific charges that had been leveled against her: that she had consulted learned men in order to write the treatise and that she had copied from other books. Teresa responds by asserting that God was her only teacher: "He alone consoled me, and he alone taught me, and he alone read to me."[48] Moreover, as Deyermond has pointed out, Teresa's critics are here guilty of imposing a literary double standard, for in the Middle Ages "the incorporation of material from *auctores* was considered an enhancement of a literary work."[49]

Teresa then compares her intellect, which God inspired to write the *Arboleda*, to the blind man whom Christ met on the road to Jericho (Luke 18:35–43). If at first Teresa relates in the third person how her intellect called upon the Son of David to have mercy, she suddenly injects herself into the biblical narrative, shifting to the first person and imagining herself calling out to Christ from the side of the road to Jericho:

> E como mi çiego entendimiento sintió por las señales ya dichas qu'el Salvador venía, luego començó a dar secretas bozes diziendo: "Ave merçed de mí, Fijo de David." E los que ivan e venían increpavan a este ya dicho çiego entendimiento mío que callase. E sin dubda puedo dezir que ivan y venían muchos desvariados cuidados e gran turbamulta de respetos tenporales humanos, de los quales mi entendimiento era increpado e aun costreñido a callar, ca como yo estava en el camino çerca de Jericó, que se entiende puesto todo mi cuidado en la calle d'este mundo, e más çerca mi deseo de las afecçiones umanas que de las espirituales, no era maravilla si los pensamientos que ivan y venían e pasavan por mi entendimiento eran vezinos de Gericó, conviene a saber, más familliares del siglo que no de la religión cuyo nonbre usurpava por estonçes. Así que estos ya dichos pensamientos e movimientos umanos increpavan a mi çiego entendimiento que callase, mas él, con el grand deseo que tenía de ver luz, más y más multiplicava sus secretas bozes diziendo: "Ave merçed de mí, Hijo de David." (132)

> (And as my blind intellect perceived by the aforementioned signs that the Savior was coming, it thereupon began to utter secret cries, saying: "Have mercy on me, Son of David." And those who were coming and going admonished this aforementioned blind intellect to keep silent. And I can say without doubt that many foolish cares and a great throng of human temporal concerns were coming and going, which reprimanded and even forced my intellect to keep silent, for since I was along the road near Jericho, that is to say, I had fixed my entire mind on the highway of this world and my will [was] closer to human affections than to spiritual ones, it was no surprise that the thoughts that came and went and passed through my understanding were inhabitants of Jericho, that is to say, servants more of this world than of the religious order whose name I had usurped at that time. And so these aforementioned thoughts and human motions admonished my blind intellect to keep silent, but it, with the great desire that it had to see the light, multiplied even more its secret voices, saying: "Have mercy on me, Son of David.")

In the allegorical interpretation that follows, Teresa explains that just as he cured the blind man, Christ the true physician cured her and permitted her to see the light. Therefore, let those who doubt that she wrote the *Arboleda* abandon their disbelief and instead marvel at the power of the Lord (133–134).

Obviously, medieval Bible commentaries depended greatly on the skill, ingenuity, and personal circumstances of the individual commentators, and for that reason it is difficult to speak of a standard interpretation of a given passage. The gospel story of the blind man became one of the read-ings for Quinquagesima and was therefore incorporated into the Roman Breviary with the pertinent patristic gloss, in this case portions of Saint Gregory the Great's homily on Luke 18: 31–43. To the extent that this com-mentary occupies a privileged position, due precisely to its enshrinement in the Breviary, it is possible to use it as a touchstone for Teresa's own inter-pretation. For Gregory, the blind man represents humankind who, driven out of paradise, must suffer the blindness of its condemnation. Nonethe-less, through the presence of its Redeemer, humankind recovers its sight so that it can see the delights of the interior light and walk with steps of good deeds along the path of life.[50] Another standard commentary is furnished by the *Glossa ordinaria* on Luke 18:35, which likewise interprets the blind man as representing humankind.[51]

Teresa makes surprising use of the gospel story, surprising most of all because that which Gregory and the *Glossa ordinaria* interpret in a collec-tive sense (the blind man represents all humankind),[52] Teresa interprets in a personal sense (the blind man represents Teresa). Indeed, it is perhaps inaccurate to speak of interpretation; rather, we should speak of an appro-priation, for Teresa personalizes the gospel story to such a degree that she becomes the blind man. As Christ miraculously enabled the blind man to see, in empowering her to write the *Arboleda*, God performed a miracle for her alone. In addition to its value as an emblem of divine grace, the appropriation of the role of the blind man is a sign of Teresa's social and spiritual isolation. Just as she chooses not to defend the right of all women to write, preferring instead to privilege herself as a special case, so she re-jects a collective interpretation of the biblical episode, preferring instead to emphasize its relevance to her alone.

Some comment needs to be made on Teresa's use of Latin in the course of her recasting of the biblical miracle. Concretely, she appropriates from the Gospel of Saint Luke the words of the blind man according to the Vulgate text. When Christ asks: "¿Qué quieres que faga a ti?" ["What wilt thou that I do to thee?"], her intellect responds: "Domine, Domine, ut videam lumen" ["Lord, that I may see"]. In the lengthy Castilian gloss that follows, Teresa amplifies the biblical text, begging that the rays of light of the Lord's prudence illuminate her dark, feminine ignorance.[53] Christ answers in Latin with but a single word: "Respice" ["Receive thy sight"]. And at that, says Teresa, the veil of darkness that had blinded the eyes of her intellect was torn away and it saw and followed the Savior, glorifying God (133). It is impossible to say if Teresa knew Latin or not, for her quotations of biblical passages in Latin could have been learned by rote or copied from florilegia, which might have included verses from the Vulgate with the corresponding Castilian translation. We should not, however, exclude the possibility that she did know how to read and perhaps even how to write Latin. If that was indeed the case, then she consciously chose to write in the vernacular, the mother tongue, and not in Latin, the sex-linked patriarchal tongue.[54]

In any case, what is important here in the Jericho episode of the *Admiración* is that Teresa "speaks" Latin. Her arrogation of the Latin phrase spoken by the blind man goes beyond the canonical use of Latin authorities to defend or support a line of argument, for she places the biblical text in her own mouth. It could be argued that in both cases it is a question of scriptural quotation, but it is one thing to authorize a text through "third-person" citation and quite another to appropriate in the first person a scriptural quotation, casting oneself in the role of a biblical character. It is useful to recall here Walter Ong's view of Latin instruction as a male-centered Renaissance puberty rite, due in part to the distancing of its segregated male world from the maternal space of the home, where women were present and the vernacular tongue prevailed. This meant that, "in general, girls, who were educated at home and not in schools, could be quite literate without having any effective direct access at all to the learned world, which was a Latin-writing, Latin-speaking, and even Latin-thinking world."[55] Teresa thus uses a language associated with a masculine world from which she is excluded and uses it in a treatise intended to circulate, not in a private, women's space, but in the public—and thereby male—space of the world at large. Did Teresa's male readers consider her appropriation of the words of the gospel in Latin an unseemly arrogation of a "male" language, a threatening incursion into an all-male intellectual territory?

Furthermore, the appropriation of the episode of the blind man can be read as an allegory of Teresa's writing. When the blind man first cried out to the Lord as he passed, the crowd "rebuked him, that he should hold his peace" (Luke 18:39). Nonetheless, the blind man continued to cry out, and it is then that Christ noticed him and the miracle took place. The biblical episode thus poses the question of speaking versus silence. This was, of course, a particularly burning issue for medieval women writers in the light of the scriptural injunction that women should keep silent: "But I suffer not a woman to teach, nor to use authority over the man, but to be in silence with all subjection. For Adam was first formed, then Eve.

And Adam was not seduced, but the woman, being seduced, was in the transgression" (I Timothy 2:12–14).[56] Silence was often cited as a sign of feminine virtue, and the biblical prohibition was invoked as the justification for confining women to the private sphere, limiting their access to education, and suppressing their self-expression through writing.

Like the blind man, Teresa does speak. Technically, the equivalent of the miraculous healing of the blind man is Teresa's original empowerment to write the *Arboleda*. Nonetheless, I think that one can extrapolate and see her invocation of the biblical story as a justification to continue to speak and thus to validate and authorize the writing of the *Admiración*. Teresa could well have interpreted the negative critical reaction to the *Arboleda* as a sign that she should keep silent in the future. But like the blind man, Teresa refused to heed the crowd of her detractors. She chose to speak out, to defend herself, and to write the *Admiración*, perhaps suggesting to her readers that just as the blind man's speech was rewarded with a miracle, so too will her own speaking out find approval on the part of the Lord.

Teresa's choice of personal emblems has important ramifications for the consideration of the way in which she sees herself. In choosing Judith, Teresa chooses a female who is unlike her naturally weaker sisters, for she is made strong by divine grace. In choosing the blind man, Teresa chooses a male who is unlike his naturally strong brothers, and that weakness is remedied through divine grace. Both figures represent Teresa to the extent that together they express the tensions underlying her conception of herself as woman and writer. Judith, Teresa, and the blind man are all exceptional cases that in some way frustrate the expectations created by their gender. Teresa establishes early on in the *Admiración* that women are naturally weak and men naturally strong. Nonetheless, God in his mysterious ways occasionally chooses to empower the weak. Thus, Judith was after all a feeble woman but was marvelously empowered to perform a wondrous deed. The blind man was "unnaturally" weakened by his infirmity but was made strong when Christ restored his sight. Like Judith, Teresa is a weak woman. Nonetheless, she is divinely empowered to perform a deed that is—in her own eyes—as wondrous as that of the slaying of Holofernes.

The man on the road to Jericho is blind; Teresa is deaf. God does not cure Teresa's deafness as such, but as she explains in the *Arboleda*, her deafness turns out to be a boon, for it makes possible the small miracle of the turning to God of her interior ear and eventually the even greater wonder of the composition of a book. Teresa reiterates this connection shortly after the episode of the blind man when she observes that the Lord closed the doors of her ears and opened the eyes of her understanding and she saw and followed the Savior.[57] This passage is in the first person and its last phrase appropriates the verse from the gospel story in which the blind man is actually cured: "And immediately he saw and followed him, glorifying God" (Luke 18:43). If blindness and deafness are signs of weakness, then bodily infirmities turn out to be empowering. Teresa's deafness is both a physical handicap and a sign of her weakness as a female, that is, the very weakness that makes possible the astounding transformation of that weak woman into a "manly" writer of treatises.

The empowered Judith performs the "manly" and active deed of killing the enemy of her people. The blind man, his sight restored, performs the relatively passive action of praising God. Teresa, who has already established that the fact of her writing is more important than the substance of her treatise (127), ends up increasing her own prestige as the recipient of divine empowerment by reducing the composition of her *Arboleda* to a manifestation of God's power and reducing its contents to a record of divine favors received. Paraphrasing once again the conclusion of the biblical episode of the blind man, Teresa describes how her blind understanding saw and followed and continues to follow the Savior, glorifying God.[58] She goes on to say:

> E quando escreví aquel tractado que trata de aquesta inteletual Luz e sobredicha çiençia, la qual es alabança e conoçer a Dios e a mí misma e negar mi voluntad e conformarme con la voluntad suya, e tomar la cruz de la pasión que padesco en las manos del entendimiento interior, e ir en pos del Salvador por pasos de af[l]içión espiritual, e manificar a Dios por confisión de la lengua, dando loor e alabança al su santo Nonbre, recontando a las gentes la igualeza de la su justiçia, ⟨de⟩ la grandeza de su misericordia, e la manifiçençia e gloria suya. (138)

> (And when I wrote that treatise that deals with this intellectual Light and aforementioned knowledge, which is praise and knowing God and myself and denying my will and conforming myself to his will, and taking up the cross of the malady from which I suffer with the hands of my interior understanding, and following the Savior with steps of spiritual suffering, and glorifying God with the confession of the tongue, giving praise and laud to his holy Name, telling people the equity of his justice, the greatness of his mercy, and his magnificence and glory.)

Her book is not important because she, Teresa, has something to say. Its significance lies in the fact that its author, a feeble woman, has marvelously belied her weak female status by performing a "manly" action.

Teresa thereby reduces herself and her writing to a mere sign of divine might, for in her view the *Arboleda* is less a treatise with a didactic message than an icon that denotes the power of the Almighty to empower the weak. Thus, Teresa ends up sharing the fate of the blind man. Just as his reaction to the miracle is to magnify the glory of God, so Teresa's reaction to her own small miracle is to magnify God's glory by writing, not writing as content or writing as self-expression, just writing as a manifestation of God's power to occasionally upset traditional gender expectations. By identifying with cases of divine empowerment of both a weak female and a weak male, Teresa undercuts her own received notions concerning the supposed physical and intellectual superiority of the male gender. She sees herself—as she sees Judith—as a special case among women, much as the blind man's infirmity makes him a special case among males.[59] Just as Teresa stresses the uniqueness of Judith, she rejects traditional collective interpretations of the episode of the blind man, casting herself in the role of the personal recipient of Christ's miraculous empowerment. Thus, Teresa's appropriation of the roles of Judith and the blind man turn out to be emblems of her splendid isolation.

2. Constanza de Castilla and the Gynaeceum of Compassion

Princesses were a valuable commodity in the Middle Ages, for the royal blood that ran through their veins made them significant objects of exchange in strengthening domestic or international alliances. Royal daughters could be expected to live a pampered life and then marry a foreign prince or a noble member of one of the first families of the realm.

For Constanza de Castilla, fate decreed otherwise, for the political disasters of fourteenth-century Spain rendered her status as princess a liability. In 1354, Constanza's grandfather, King Pedro I, considering void his marriage to Blanche of Bourbon, married Juana de Castro. Informed of a plot against him, Pedro abandoned Juana the day after the wedding, leaving her pregnant with Constanza's future father, Prince Juan. Pedro was never to see his abandoned wife Juana again.[1] Meanwhile, the Castilian civil war of the mid-fourteenth century pitted Pedro against his bastard half-brother Enrique. In 1369 Enrique, who had already proclaimed himself King Enrique II, murdered Pedro, thus placing the illegitimate Trastámara dynasty on the throne of Castile. Constanza's future father, the young Prince Juan, sought refuge in Gascony.[2] A reconciliation between the opposing sides in the civil war was effected when the usurper King Enrique II's line and the legitimate King Pedro I's line were united through the marriage of their grandchildren. In 1388, the bastard King Enrique II's grandson, Prince Enrique, Trastámara heir to the throne of Castile, married Catherine of Lancaster, granddaughter of the assassinated King Pedro I.[3] Constanza's future father, Prince Juan, was returned to Castile and handed over to King Enrique II's son, King Juan I, as part of the marriage agreement.[4] Prince Juan was imprisoned in Soria, where he eventually died. While in prison, however, Prince Juan had married Elvira de Falces, the daughter of his jailor, and had fathered two children, Pedro and Constanza.[5]

The children's legitimate royal blood placed them in grave danger, for it constituted a threat to the illegitimate Trastámara dynasty: Prince Pedro might assert his rights as lawful heir to the crown of Castile; some adventurer husband might use an alliance with Constanza to lay claim to the throne. So Catherine of Lancaster, a legitimate granddaughter of the murdered King Pedro I and now queen of Castile by virtue of her marriage to the usurper's grandson, sought to protect King Pedro's other legitimate relatives. She contrived to have her husband, King Enrique III, pardon Constanza's brother Prince Pedro and allow him to become a priest. Likewise, Queen Catherine placed Princess Constanza in the Dominican convent of Santo Domingo el Real in Madrid. Thus, the better part was chosen for Constanza and, if she was never to reign in the secular world, within the convent walls during her half century as prioress she would preside over the most prosperous and brilliant years of Santo Domingo el Real. The chronicler Gracia Dei specifies that, in order to secure Pedro's entry into the priesthood, Queen Catherine took advantage of the king's joy at the birth of an heir, the future Juan II, in 1406. It is logical to conclude that it was likewise around 1406 that Constanza entered the convent.[6]

Constanza was raised among powerful female role models, with Queen Catherine as the focus of that group of strong and capable women. When King Enrique III died in 1406, he left behind his widow Catherine, several daughters, and their infant son and heir, Prince Juan. Catherine, in conjunction with the deceased king's brother, Fernando de Antequera, would reign as co-regent until her death in 1418.[7] Queen Catherine's rule was characterized by what one might anachronistically call a sense of sisterhood, for her closest advisers were women, most notably Leonor López de Córdoba[8] and then Inés de Torres. Contemporary chroniclers took note of the unusual nature of the bond between the queen and her confidantes. The chronicler Alvar García de Santa María wrote that Catherine did nothing without seeking Leonor's advice.[9] Clara Estow concludes that Leonor and Catherine "enjoyed a relationship that defied accepted limits of convention (and possibly propriety)" and that "this situation was intolerable. Never, in the history of Castile had there been a queen who so relied on the political advice and savvy of another woman and who received encouragement throughout their association to fulfill her responsibilities as a monarch and resist attempts to have her position undermined."[10] Catherine's co-regent, Fernando de Antequera, was duly alarmed by Leonor's power,[11] and in 1408 or 1409 he managed to have her banished from the court.[12] The queen nonetheless continued to treat Leonor with great affection.[13]

In the charged political climate of Catherine's co-regency, even sisterhood had its limits. Inés de Torres, whom Leonor López de Córdoba had introduced at court, turned against Leonor and replaced her as the queen's favorite.[14] Inés de Torres was Catherine's confidante from 1414 to 1416.[15] As in the case of her predecessor, contemporary chroniclers noted that all matters had first to pass through the hands of the queen's favorite.[16] The nobility resented Inés's influence over the queen and managed to have her exiled, accusing her of having had an affair (*ayuntamiento*) with Juan Alvarez de Osorio.[17]

Thus, Queen Catherine governed with the help and advice of female confidantes, first Leonor López de Córdoba, then Inés de Torres. The queen also maintained close relations with two Dominican nuns, her cousin Princess Constanza and Teresa de Ayala, the prioress of another important convent, Santo Domingo el Real in Toledo.[18] Teresa had been the mistress of King Pedro I and had given birth to a daughter, María, in 1367.[19] Teresa had become prioress of Santo Domingo by 1394,[20] but her religious status did not prevent her from maintaining close contact with her royal relatives, among them King Enrique III and his wife Catherine of Lancaster.[21] After she was widowed and was ruling as co-regent, Queen Catherine collaborated with Teresa and María in helping the children of yet another of King Pedro's mistresses, Lady Isabel.[22]

Constanza, now Sor Constanza, grew up in the context of this female bonding. In a sense King Pedro I's mistress Teresa, her daughter María, and Constanza had parallel trajectories. All three were related to or associated with King Pedro I: Teresa as the monarch's mistress, María as their illegitimate daughter, and Constanza as legitimate granddaughter of the king. All three sought refuge in Dominican convents. All three maintained affectionate and even intimate relations with their royal relatives, and, in particular, with Queen Catherine. These women were bound to the queen by ties of consanguinity: Teresa's daughter María and Queen Catherine were aunt and niece; Catherine and Constanza were cousins. Catherine, Constanza, and Teresa occupied powerful positions and gave aid to their less fortunate relatives.[23] Queen Catherine might have been expected to guard zealously the rights of her own children as legitimate heirs of the legitimate King Pedro I, viewing as potentially rival lines Pedro's illegitimate offspring by Teresa de Ayala and Lady Isabel. Instead, dynastic considerations, that is, a sense of the clan as a whole, prevailed over a sense of the nuclear family unit and created a sense of sisterhood among the women. King Pedro's offspring and his mistresses bonded together to protect their children, especially the males of the family.

A letter of 1416 in which Queen Catherine refers to Constanza as "Mi parienta" ("my relative") reveals that Constanza was already prioress of Santo Domingo el Real.[24] The princess was thus quite young when she became the head of the community,[25] and that youth invites speculation that her election may have been due to the influence of her cousin, Queen Catherine.[26] Constanza was obviously proud of her royal birth, and those she dealt with as prioress were acutely aware of her high social standing. In a document from 1417 the signers mention her first as royal princess and second as prioress: "Lady Constanza, daughter of Lord Juan and grand-daughter of King Pedro, . . . Prioress of the Convent of Santo Domingo in Madrid."[27] Constanza's royal blood gave her great influence at court and helped to gain royal favor for her convent. King Juan II (Constanza's first cousin once removed) bestowed many privileges and immunities on Santo Domingo el Real.[28] Moreover, Constanza was able to secure from King Juan II permission to transfer the mortal remains of her father Prince Juan (in 1442) and her grandfather King Pedro I (in 1446) to her convent, where she had the appropriate funeral monuments erected for them.[29] Documents from 1451 and 1465 indicate that Juan II's son, Enrique IV, and his wife Juana of Portugal favored the convent of Santo Domingo el Real with their economic support. In such documents the monarchs refer affectionately to Constanza as their "aunt."[30]

Constanza presided over the era of her convent's greatest material splendor. Under her supervision a building program resulted in the completion in 1444 of the community's main chapel, whose construction had begun under King Alfonso XI (1310–1350). It was here that the body of her grandfather King Pedro I was buried. Constanza was also responsible for the construction of the convent church and, with the financial help of her brother, who had risen in the Church hierarchy to become bishop of Osma, she had a refectory constructed.[31] Constanza governed Santo Domingo el Real as prioress for some fifty years, stepping down in 1465, probably because of her advanced age.[32] She died in 1478.[33]

Manuscript 7495 of the Biblioteca Nacional (Madrid) is a collection of prayers, devotional treatises, and liturgical offices. Its author is a Dominican nun who calls herself Constanza. As Ana María Huélamo San José has argued, internal evidence permits us to identify that nun as Constanza de Castilla, prioress of the convent of Santo Domingo el Real in Madrid.[34] Among other information, Constanza reveals that she exercises authority over the other nuns in her convent.[35] Later, she prays for the souls of her parents and for the souls of King Pedro, Queen Catherine, and Lady

María (fol. 26^r). Huélamo San José (140) identifies these personages as Constanza's grandfather, Pedro I; her cousin, Catherine of Lancaster; and most likely, Queen María, the wife of her first cousin once removed King Juan II.[36] Folio 27^v mentions a King Enrique who is still alive; Huélamo San José (140) identifies this monarch as Enrique IV. This piece of evidence leads to the conclusion that the work in question was written or copied during Enrique IV's reign, 1454–1474. Perhaps Constanza copied out the manuscript, or had it copied in its present form, after her retirement as prioress in 1465.

Huélamo San José (144–147) discusses the question of whether Constanza is to be considered the author of the works contained in Manuscript 7495 or whether she is merely compiling an anthology of preexisting materials. In some cases the rubrics indicate that Constanza is copying out a well-known prayer (fol. 93^v)[37] or translating texts written by an Apostolic Father, Saint Ignatius of Antioch (fols. 94^r–97^r). One rubric identifies her as the person who "conpuso" a lengthy *Prayer* (fol. 1^r). Other rubrics specify that she "ordenó" the Latin version of the *Hours of the Nails* (fol. 44^r), the *Fifteen Joys* (fol. 75^v), and the *Seven Sorrows* (fol. 78^v). Obviously, the verb *componer* refers to the act of literary creation, while *ordenar* means to put in order or to compile.[38] Nonetheless, folio 82^v contains a sort of bibliography in which Constanza explicitly identifies herself as the author of many of the works copied in the manuscript, naming specifically the initial *Prayer*, the *Hours of the Nails*, the *Fifteen Joys*, the *Seven Sorrows*, and the *Litany of Our Lady*. Thus, *componer* and *ordenar* seem to be used as synonyms. Or, perhaps *ordenar* refers to the compiling in this manuscript of works written previously and circulated separately for "in-house" use.

Folio 82^v also contains passages in which Constanza pauses to reflect on her works and on herself as author. She views her compositions as a means of praising and serving God.[39] As Huélamo San José observes (147), Constanza uses the topos of false modesty, emphasizing her ignorance and her status as a sinner. Great is her simplemindedness (*sinpleza*) and considerable is her stupidity (*grosería*). "Creo mis obras ser defectuosas," she says ("I believe my works to be faulty"). While medieval women writers often relate such formulas of humility to their female gender,[40] Constanza chooses not to do this, adopting instead the more generic and thereby not gender-specific status of sinner. She asks the Lord's pardon for any ill-conceived expression or any ill-chosen word and, calling herself a faithful Catholic, she renounces any such word or phrase and submits herself to the eventual correction of the Church. The same formulas of submission to the authority of the Church occur at the end of the *Fifteen Joys* (fol. 78ᵛ) and the end of the *Hours of the Nails* (fol. 75ʳ). In the latter case, Constanza renounces any passage that may be contrary to the teachings of the Church, attributing such lapses to her weakness or frailty (*flaqueza*) and to the evil influence of Satan. Frailty and susceptibility to diabolical temptation were negative attributes commonly ascribed to women in the Middle Ages.[41] It is once again significant that Constanza fails to associate her shortcomings with her female gender. She may have wished to portray herself as humble, but she chose not to view her gender as contributing to her self-abasement. It is tempting to relate Constanza's positive sense of herself as a woman to her status as royal princess and her experience of such strong and decisive women as Queen Catherine.

Constanza's works are largely prayers and translations originally conceived for "in-house" consumption. The prioress seemed to consider her writings as a volume of private devotions or a prayer book to be used by both her and the other nuns under her supervision. Constanza herself was, of course, literate. Despite the unfortunate circumstances of her birth, she doubtlessly received an education suitable for a royal princess. As was customary in the Middle Ages, Constanza's works could also have been "performed," that is to say, read aloud to the other nuns in the convent. Nonetheless, Constanza's companions were probably also literate and thus able to read her writings for themselves. Three documents from Santo Domingo el Real dated 1420 include among their witnesses a *maestra de escuela*,[42] that is, a nun who was in charge of teaching the novices to read.[43] Constanza herself was sufficiently proficient in Latin as to be able to compose liturgical offices in that language and to translate her own writings and the writings of others from Latin into Castilian. The very fact that she chose to translate such texts suggests that at least some of her companions did not know Latin.[44] Indeed, the practice of translating liturgical offices was not new at Santo Domingo el Real, for a fourteenth-century manuscript from the convent contains, among other texts, a translation of the office of Saint Thomas Aquinas.[45]

Constanza was more than merely literate in Castilian and Latin; she also engaged in erudite activities, composing prayers and devotional works. These endeavors were not just a pastime, for prayer and the singing of the Divine Offices occupied the greater part of the day for the community. The Dominicans were the Order of Preachers, but preaching was an activity reserved for the friars of the First Order, for males alone were permitted to exercise that public function.[46] The nuns of the Second Order remained cloistered and derived their identity above all from their life of prayer. Thus, the prayers and liturgical offices that make up Constanza's manuscript represent a crucial aspect of the community's daily existence and are central to the prioress's self-image and to that of her companions as Dominican nuns.

Constanza's prayers make extensive use of the first person. On several occasions she identifies herself explicitly as the female voice of her meditations: "Yo Costanza."[47] Medieval authors were often reticent to identify themselves, as is evinced by those cases in which the writer's name is revealed in an acrostic.[48] Moreover, to judge by the number of anonymous works in the Middle Ages, the practice of self-naming appears to be relatively infrequent, or at least sporadic, in vernacular texts, with the exception of chronicles, where it becomes a formulaic feature of the prologue.[49] Such authorial reticence notwithstanding, the beginning or end of a work was a traditional place for the author to affix his or her literary signature. In what is taken to be the general prologue to his collected works, Don Juan Manuel refers to himself in the third person.[50] However, in the specific prologue to *El conde Lucanor* (1335), he identifies himself as "I, Lord Juan, son of Prince Manuel."[51] Gonzalo de Berceo ends his *Vida de San Millán* (ca. 1230?) with the following strophe:

Gonzalvo fue so nomne qui fizo est tractado,
en Sant Millán de Suso fue de ninnez crïado,
natural de Verceo, ond sant Millán fue nado.
Dios guarde la su alma del poder del Peccado.[52]

(Gonzalo was the name of he who wrote this work;
he was raised from childhood in San Millán de Suso,
a native of Berceo, where Saint Emilian was born.
May God preserve his soul from the Devil's power.)

Legal documents were another accepted context for self-naming. The memoirs of Leonor López de Córdoba begin with a formula commonly found in notarial documents, a formula that includes self-naming:

Por ende, sepan quantos esta Escriptura vieren, como yo Doña Leonor López de Córdoba, fija de mi Señor el Maestre Don Martín López de Córdoba, e Doña Sancha Carrillo . . .[53]

(Therefore, know all who see this document, how I, Doña Leonor López de Córdoba, daughter of my Lord Grand Master Don Martín López de Córdoba and Doña Sancha Carrillo . . .[54])

Like Don Juan Manuel, but unlike Berceo, Leonor's identity as a member of the nobility links her name to her lineage.

As in the case of Berceo, Constanza's self-naming occurs within one of the traditional contexts for that practice, her prayers. Two such instances can be found in her extensive *Prayer*. In the chapter devoted to the moment in the Passion when Christ said, "Into thy hands I commend my spirit," Constanza interpolates fragments of the Dominican liturgy for Good Friday and then a long *Suplicación*. At the beginning of this prayer-within-a-prayer, she refers to herself as "I, Constanza, your unworthy servant," and goes on to offer God her praise and to beg him to put her life in order. She compares herself to a blind and sick sheep that wanders lost, asking that God pardon her sins and extend to her the hand of his mercy (fol. 20$^\text{v}$). This worm[55] prostrates itself at his feet, as did the Magdalen, begging for pardon and mercy (fol. 21$^\text{r}$). Her human nature is prone to sin, she says, but since Christ was also a man, he understands the weakness of human flesh. Therefore, let Christ pardon her, as he did Mary Magdalene (fols. 21$^\text{v}$–22$^\text{r}$). Later, at the very end of the *Prayer*, after evoking Pentecost and incorporating extensive quotations from the Divine Offices for that day, she names herself ("Yo Costança") and confesses to being a great sinner and unworthy of any grace. Therefore, she asks all the saints mentioned "en esta oración" ("in this prayer") to offer their sufferings and death to our Lord so that he will hear her petitions and do as he will with her (fol. 31).

Two further instances of self-naming occur in symmetrical positions at the end of two other prayers, the *Fifteen Joys* and the *Seven Sorrows*. In the first case, "yo Costança," unworthy slave of the Virgin Mary, prays these fifteen joys, asking for the Virgin's mercy and begging that she be present at the hour of her death (fol. 78$^\text{r}$). In the second case, "yo Costança," Mary's unworthy slave, who prays these great sorrows of hers with devotion, asks for the Virgin's mercy, that she hear her prayers, and that she preserve her from the spiritual and corporal dangers of this life (fol. 79$^\text{v}$). In both cases self-naming occurs in a formulaic context and forms part of the actual saying of the prayer. A fifth instance of self-naming is found in the "bibliography" in which Constanza lists her works and reflects on her shortcomings as an author (fol. 82$^\text{v}$). A final case occurs in the *Suplicación: In die mortis*, which is found in the last folios of the manuscript. Here, Constanza quite literally signs off, the end of the manuscript coinciding with a short meditation in which she expresses her consciousness of her approaching death (fol. 101$^\text{r}$).

While self-naming may or may not have been an unusual practice, in Constanza's case it occurs within an authorized context, namely, her prayers and their epilogues. At first glance, it seems noteworthy that her Christian name appears devoid of any rank. Don Juan Manuel identified himself as the son of a prince; Leonor López de Córdoba grounded her identity in the names of her noble parents. Although of royal birth, Constanza asserts her identity as a humble nun and uses only her Christian name. This is a rhetorical pose dictated by the generic conventions of prayer, for in official documents Constanza projects a more public self and does not hesitate to identify herself as Lady Constanza, granddaughter of King Pedro, prioress of Santo Domingo el Real.[56]

Because female proper names are gender markers, these six instances of self-naming identify Constanza unequivocally as a woman. On other occasions it is the feminine form of the noun or adjective that identifies the speaker as a woman: *pecadora* (fol. 4[v]), *aquella* (fol. 9[r]), *digna* (fol. 16[r]), *sierva* (fol. 92[r]), and so forth. This female voice could be easily taken over by the other nuns and by other female readers as well. It is evident that Constanza envisions others reciting her prayers, for she twice asks to share in the merits of the persons who will recite them.[57]

Another indication that Constanza is writing for a female audience and, specifically, for an audience of nuns can be found on folios 97–99, which contain a series of questions that are to be addressed to those on their deathbed. The work is a translation of part of the ritual for visiting the sick, the *Ordo ad visitandum infirmum*.[58] Its rubric, *Capítulo de las preguntas que deven fazer al omne desque está en punto de muerte* ("Chapter concerning the questions that should be posed to one who is at the point of death") is technically ambiguous because *al omne* could mean either "to the man" or the more neutral "to one" in medieval Spanish. Constanza begins the work proper by referring to the *enfermo o enferma* ("sick man or sick woman"). Thus, in rewriting a source characterized by its exclusively masculine referent, she tries to address a wider audience of both men and women.[59] Nonetheless, the adjectives that follow (*dispuesta* and *informada*) are in the feminine, and Constanza goes on to refer to the dying person as *hermana* ("sister"), that is, she tailors her translation for use in the case of a dying nun: Does the sister realize that she has not served God as well as she might have? Will she change her life if she should recover? Does she believe that Christ suffered the Passion for her? and so forth.

Constanza, then, either identifies herself explicitly as the feminine voice of her prayers or is identified as female by the feminine form of the noun she uses. The question that logically follows is whether, aside from these feminine gender markers, there are any other indications that the manuscript was composed by a woman. Constanza's translation of the letters of Saint Ignatius of Antioch may suggest some answers. In the Middle Ages the collection of Latin letters associated with Ignatius consisted of seventeen letters, the seven now recognized as canonical and some ten others that are now considered spurious.[60] Interestingly, Constanza translates four of the apocryphal epistles: Saint Ignatius's letter to the Blessed Virgin, Mary's response to Ignatius, Saint Ignatius's letter to Saint John, and the latter's response to Ignatius.

Constanza's choice of the noncanonical, apocryphal epistles would, at first glance, appear to reveal an element of subversion. Tempting as this hypothesis may be, however, the four letters that she translates were not recognized as apocryphal during the Middle Ages. The appeal of these apocryphal letters must be sought elsewhere, then. One might more licitly observe that Constanza rejects the more doctrine-oriented canonical letters, preferring the more homey and intimate tone of the apocryphal letters. The seven canonical epistles were written while Ignatius was a prisoner being taken to Rome to die a martyr in the arena; they arise largely out of his ecclesiastical role as bishop of Antioch. While Ignatius does express his personal longing for martyrdom, his authentic correspondence, addressed to a broad audience, is highly doctrinal in content and dwells mostly on issues of authority: the need for unity, the need to combat heresy, and the need to obey the church hierarchy. With the exception of a letter directed to Polycarp, bishop of Smyrna, the seven canonical letters are addressed to collective bodies: the church at Ephesus, the church at Magnesia, and so on.

On the other hand, the letters that Constanza transcribes in Latin and then translates into Castilian are addressed to individuals and emphasize a more personal experience of Christ and his teachings. In Ignatius's letter to the Virgin Mary, the future martyr praises Mary for her role as companion and eyewitness to Christ's life and miracles.[61] The bishop refers to a previous letter or letters—no longer extant or perhaps fictitious—in which he had questioned the Virgin about such secrets.[62] Mary responds, certifying that what Ignatius has heard concerning Christ is true and promising to go with the apostle John to visit the bishop and his disciples. Meanwhile, the Virgin continues, Ignatius should act in a manly fashion (*virilmente*) and not be shaken by the threat of persecution.

Ignatius's letter to Saint John expresses the desire that John hasten to visit Ignatius and his disciples. The holy women with Ignatius are similarly anxious to see the Virgin Mary and to touch her body, specifically, the breasts that nursed Christ; the women further wish Mary to reveal her secret knowledge to them. Ignatius goes on to observe that Mary has shown herself to be a model of cheerfulness and forbearance in the face of persecution and adversity. Saint John's response echoes Ignatius's praise of the Virgin, for who would not delight in seeing and speaking with her who gave birth to Christ? Likewise, continues John, all will rejoice to see the venerable Jacob, who is so like Christ in both physical appearance and comportment.[63]

J. B. Lightfoot observes that the apocryphal Latin correspondence with Saint John and the Virgin was very popular and was often copied out separately; sometimes, Ignatius was known only through it.[64] For that reason, we should not exclude the possibility that the Latin manuscript from which Constanza copied the correspondence contained only the four apocryphal letters. Her choice of texts would thereby have been determined not by personal criteria but by the fact that those letters were the only Ignatian correspondence with which she was acquainted. In any case, what is important is that Constanza chose to copy and to translate those texts and not the words of another Apostolic Father. It is therefore useful to speculate as to the appeal Ignatius's apocryphal correspondence may have had for a community of nuns.

Ignatius highlights Mary's privileged role as mother and companion to Christ. In so doing, his letters attribute to the Virgin both female and male roles. On the one hand, Ignatius calls attention to Mary's biological role as mother of Christ. That physicality is emphasized in the passage that portrays the other holy women as desirous of touching with their own hands the breasts that nourished Jesus. In I Timothy 2:12 the Bible forbids women to teach; the biblical injunction notwithstanding, Ignatius also accords the Virgin the masculine role of teacher. As someone privy to the most intimate details of Christ's life, the Virgin is valued as a source of privileged information that she can pass on to those who were not so fortunate. Moreover, Ignatius praises the Virgin for her cheerful forbearance in the face of persecution and adversities. The Virgin, for her part, encourages Ignatius to act manfully (*virilmente*). Thus, the standard for measuring courage remains masculine; nonetheless, it is the Mother of God who most cogently incarnates that standard, while Ignatius, who is to be inspired by the Virgin's assumption of a male role, has yet to act fully like a man.

Saint John's letter to Ignatius highlights the notion of resemblance: the venerable Jacob is so similar to Christ in physical aspect and mode of living that he might be considered Christ's identical twin (fols. 96ᵛ–97ʳ). As readers of a text that foregrounds the notion of imitation, nuns might be encouraged not only to imitate Christ but also to emulate the Virgin's patient suffering of tribulations as recounted in Ignatius's letter to John. If their vocation does not permit the sisters of Santo Domingo el Real to imitate Mary's biological role as mother, by their very vows they imitate her role as virgin. In addition, the apocryphal letters authorize the nuns, and specifically, Constanza herself, to adopt the Virgin's role as teacher. Just as the epistles encourage Mary to share her privileged knowledge with the disciples gathered around Ignatius, so it could be argued that such texts encourage Constanza to emulate the Virgin by sharing her knowledge with her disciples, that is, with the other nuns in her convent. In a sense Constanza is even authorized to write down her teachings and prayers, for the fact that the Virgin Mary committed her thoughts to paper in the form of a letter provides an important precedent for other women to take up the pen. Moreover, for medieval Christians, the Virgin Mary was a poet; specifically, she was the author of a prayer, the Magnificat.[65] Thus, the Virgin is a significant model that empowers Constanza and other holy women in turn to compose prayers. Finally, to the extent that the Virgin Mary set a standard for courage, Constanza is able to appropriate this masculine quality for herself and to encourage the other nuns to do likewise. Perhaps the act of self-expression—as manifested in the masculine spheres of teaching and composing prayers—melds here with the quality of courage; certainly, as a manly quality to be emulated, it justifies Constanza's adoption of the male prerogative of teaching and writing.

Constanza's manuscript contains several prayers to the Virgin: the *Fifteen Joys*, the *Seven Sorrows*, and a litany, all of which attest to her devotion to Mary. To be sure, the Virgin was a powerful model for women in general and nuns in particular, but it is useful to recall Caroline Walker Bynum's observation that Mary "is not really as important as one might expect in women's spirituality."[66] Women were far more likely to identify with Christ, and, specifically, with his suffering humanity, than with his mother.[67] Although an exacerbated devotion to Christ's Passion was especially widespread at the end of the Middle Ages, devotion to the Passion was particularly relevant to women. To the extent that it was Christ's humanity that suffered the Passion, women identified with that humanity. This identification with Christ's feminine side empowered women like Constanza as no other identification could make possible. For her part, Constanza signaled this identification with Christ via her concern with those moments in the Virgin's life that are most intimately related to her son's humanity: the Nativity and the Passion. The Virgin Mary thus acquired a particular importance for Constanza's spirituality—perhaps an even greater importance than for many other late medieval holy women—to the extent that Constanza extols Mary's maternity and celebrates the female flesh that Christ received from his mother.

A key point of intersection between the Blessed Virgin and Christ's suffering can be seen in the *Hours of the Nails*,[68] the liturgical office that Constanza composed in commemoration of the nails of Christ's Passion. This composition celebrates Christ's blood, an essentially human substance, that poured from the wounds made by the nails, as the price of humankind's redemption (fol. 59^v). Christ put on the mantle of our human and mortal flesh, undergoing the Passion so that his precious blood could wash away the stains of the sins of humankind (fol. 61^r). As Constanza later remarks, Jesus received the mantle of his human flesh from his mother. Another significant point of intersection between the Blessed Virgin and Christ's suffering humanity is the *compassio*, namely, the notion that Mary, in contemplating the sufferings of her son, underwent a passion parallel to his. The theme is already implicit in Constanza's prayer of the *Seven Sorrows* of the Virgin, which includes the Passion, the Crucifixion, the Pietà, and the entombment (fol. 79). However, Mary's *compassio* occupies a truly prominent role in the Passion-centered *Hours of the Nails*.

In Constanza's liturgical office, the first lesson for matins recapitulates the events of the Passion, the second lesson focuses on the nails themselves, while the third lesson highlights Mary's *compassio*. The third lesson dwells on the pain that the Virgin suffered when she witnessed her son's Passion, especially when Christ's blood dripped onto her head as she stood at the foot of the cross. The Virgin's heart was wounded along with Christ's hands and feet. Specifically, the three nails that pierced Christ's flesh also pierced the Virgin's heart, for the flesh that suffered the Passion was the human flesh that he had received from his mother:

> Creemos verdaderamente sin dubda que aquellos tres clavos que en la cruz al tu fijo traspasaron a ti non perdonaron, mas propiamente dentro en tu coraçón fueron fincados con aquellos mesmos dolores, los cuales el fijo tuyo en la tu propia carne padesçía, la cual de ti verdaderamente avía tomado. (fol. 66^r)

> (We truly believe without any doubt that those three nails that pierced your son on the cross did not spare you, but sank right into your heart with the same pain that your son suffered in your own flesh, which he truly had taken from you.)

The lesson then expresses wonder that the Virgin did not spend that day confined in her house.[69] Since it was not Mary's wont to attend public executions, why did not that fear which is normally attributed to women prevent her from going out to witness such acts of cruelty?

> Queremos saber por qué aquel día qu'el fijo tuyo padescía, recibiendo tan cruel muerte, non estoviste en casa ence[r]rada, mas saliste a la çibdat toda escandalizada e turbada e fueste [a] aquel espantable lugar, Monte de Calvarie. En como la costunbre tuya non fuesse de ver los omnes muertos crucificados nin aforcados, ¿por qué'l temor que a las mugeres retraen a ti non detovo aquel día de ver tan grandes crueldades, señaladamente en el fijo tuyo? ¿Por qué, Señora, la tu linpia virginidat non te detuvo? (fol. 66[rv])

> (We want to know why on that day when your son was suffering, accepting such a cruel death, you were not shut up at home but [instead] went out into the city all shocked and upset and went to that fearful place, Mount Calvary. Since it was not your wont to see men crucified or hanged, why did not that fear which is attributed to women prevent you on that day from seeing such great cruelties, especially [those inflicted] on your own son? Why, Lady, did not your very virginity hold you back?)

The answer is that out of the natural love that Mary bore her son, on that day customs and innate character traits were changed, and the Virgin was obliged to leave her house so that she could be present at the Crucifixion and suffer martyrdom:

> Sentimos, Señora, e piadosamente creemos aquel día las costunbres e condiciones ser mudadas por amor natural del tu fijo e el tu coraçón ser agenado de ti, puesto totalmente en medio de tantos oprobrios, denuestos, tormentos e dolores intensos, los cuales tú, Señora, en spíritu conosciste el tu fijo padescedero. E por ende tú fueste constrenida a salir de tu casa e ser presente a tantos dolores por que la tu absencia non acrecentase penas e dolores al tu fijo mucho amado e aun por que a ti non fallesciese martirio. (fols. 66[v]–67[r])

> (We feel, Lady, and piously believe that on that day customs and natures were changed by the natural love for your son and that your heart was alienated from you, put entirely in the midst of so many insults, affronts, torments and intense pains, which you, Lady, knew in spirit that your son was about to suffer. And therefore you were forced to leave your house and to witness so much pain, so that your absence would not increase the pains and travails of your most beloved son and even so that you would not fail to suffer martyrdom.)

Normally, the Virgin's compassion is associated with Mary's martyr-like sufferings that paralleled those of Christ as he suffered the Passion. However, in the light of Constanza's appropriation of the medieval common-place that Christ received his human flesh from Mary, the Virgin's compassion can also be construed to refer to her vicarious participation in the Passion by virtue of the identification between Christ's suffering humanity and the human flesh that he received from his mother. Compassion thus becomes a quintessentially female quality that Constanza, her nuns, and all women share with the Virgin via their identification with her. Thus, to the extent that Constanza identifies with Mary—as Mary identifies with Christ—Constanza is empowered to suffer the Passion vicariously when, in her prayers and meditations on that event, she meditates on the sufferings of the Blessed Virgin. Instead of identifying directly with Christ's sufferings, Constanza and her sisters are to imitate the Virgin's reaction to the Passion, her *compassio*. Thus, Mary becomes the agent of Constanza's experience of the Passion, an experience rendered much more intense via the *compassio*.

Constanza's third lesson in her *Hours of the Nails* differs remarkably from those found in similar liturgical offices. Liturgical lessons normally consist of scriptural verses, narratives of a saint's life, or excerpts from the writings of the Church Fathers. In her lesson, Constanza creates a pseudo-dialogue between the *we* of the nuns who are praying and the *you* of their addressee, the Blessed Virgin. I call the text pseudo-dialogic because Constanza both poses and answers the questions in the first person plural. Now, a liturgical lesson is an unconventional occasion for putting words into the Virgin's mouth. A more conventional setting for recording the words of the Virgin is the revelation, which a visionary claims to have received and then written down as a message from a sacred personage such as the Virgin. In such a case it is the supernatural context that authorizes the content of the revelation, guaranteeing that it represents the very words of Mary or another sacred figure. Constanza's imagined dialogue is also different from the novelization of the Scriptures one finds in such works as the *Meditationes vitae Christi*, which are reader-centered, constantly exhorting the reader to participate imaginatively in the events of Christ's life. While the *Meditationes* often puts dialogue in the mouths of the sacred characters, only very rarely does the narrator address those characters directly.[70] For her part, Constanza adopts a strategy—the pseudo-dialogue—that gives her absolute control over the content of her prayer-like lesson. Creating such a dialogue permits the prioress to create her own authority, for she composes both the questions and the answers. As a result, the Virgin herself is made to explain her unorthodox behavior, and thereby she ends up empowering Constanza to engage in another unconventional task for a woman, the composition of a liturgical office.

The passage in question contrasts an expected pattern of female behavior and its transgression. Women, and especially that paradigm of womanhood, the Blessed Virgin, are expected to remain enclosed within the feminine space of the home. While accepting the notion of female enclosure as natural, the lesson does allow that rule to be broken under unusual circumstances. The text attempts to account for individual situations and for extraordinary cases; it does not say that such transgressions are licit or even desirable for all women. It is tempting to read into this passage an allegory of Constanza's attitude toward her works in the context of a patriarchal society's hostility toward writing women. It must be observed, however, that in general Constanza voices little anxiety over the question of authority. As has been already observed, her use of humility formulas is not linked to her status as a female. Nonetheless, it is possible that in the case of the third lesson from the *Hours of the Nails*, Constanza voices an implicit awareness of the problematic relation between writing and the female gender. Surely, the composition of a liturgical office in no way lay within the bounds prescribed for female comportment in the late Middle Ages. To be sure, Constanza appends to the end of the Castilian translation of the office a profession of orthodoxy and avows her submission to the correction of the Church. Nonetheless, similar disclaimers appear after considerably less daring works (the *Fifteen Joys*, for example). It is possible to conclude that just as the Virgin Mary broke with tradition by leaving the prescribed female space of her house and entering the public space of an execution in order to undergo the *compassio*, so Constanza is metaphorically empowered to leave the protected female space of the cloister in order to enter the more public masculine space of written discourse, penning a liturgical composition to be copied and possibly made public through the medium of manuscript transmission. For both the Virgin Mary and Constanza, entering a masculine space is not an end in itself, but a means to an end. The Virgin Mary leaves the feminine space of her house in order to enter the masculine space of a public execution where, through her *compassio*, she undergoes the "meta-feminine" experience of the Passion through her identification with Christ's suffering female flesh. Constanza metaphorically leaves the enclosed space of the cloister in order to enter the "masculine" space of writing. However, that space turns out to be "meta-feminine" in its own right because, ultimately, Constanza is engaging in the female activity of nurturing and mothering her companions through her writing.

While Constanza is identified explicitly as the author of the Latin text of the *Hours of the Nails* ("Estas horas que se siguen ordenó la dicha soror de la Orden de Sancto Domingo de los Predicadores" [fol. 44ʳ]), the rubric of the Castilian translation does not identify her as the translator ("El romançe de las mesmas oras de los clavos" [fol. 58ᵛ]). Nonetheless, it is logical to assume that Constanza did indeed translate that text and that, in so doing, she took on multiple roles, all of them uncharacteristic for women. First, it is her knowledge of Latin that enables her to perform the task of composing liturgical texts in that language. As Walter Ong argued, Latin learning was a sort of masculine rite of passage and, as such, a monopoly of the male gender.[71] Thus, the very fact that Constanza knew Latin sets her apart and constitutes an appropriation of a male role. Second, by playing a creative role in the writing of a Latin text and, concretely, of a text designed for liturgical use, Constanza performs a task that was the monopoly of the male clerical establishment.[72] Third, as the translator of that text, Constanza participates in the process of transmission of knowledge that was likewise a monopoly of the male gender.

It is nonetheless possible that an activity that we perceive as daring may not have been so in Constanza's time. Moreover, practical necessity and breaking the rules are not mutually exclusive. Perhaps the composition of liturgical works for in-house use was an acceptable form of erudite activity for nuns. Apropos of the liturgical songs of Hildegard of Bingen (1098–1179), for example, Sabina Flanagan observes that "her compositions arose directly from the needs of the monastic life and, unlike the writing of a theological treatise, required little apology or justification."[73] Indeed, Hildegard's contemporaries did not criticize her; rather, they praised the beauty and strangeness of her musical compositions.[74] Although what may have been acceptable in the twelfth century may not necessarily have been acceptable in the fifteenth, it does appear that the embellishment of the liturgy was an area in which nuns were allowed to participate. Nonetheless, writing was one thing, performance another, for it appears that such new offices could only be celebrated with the permission of the Church hierarchy.[75]

With the exception of the Ignatian correspondence and the various liturgical offices, Constanza's manuscript consists largely of prayers for private devotion. How did the late Middle Ages view prayer? In his *Oracional* of about 1454, Alonso de Cartagena defines prayer as a humble plea to God for eternal life and for those spiritual and temporal riches that will help us to achieve life everlasting.[76] Later, quoting Saint Augustine, Cartagena says that prayer is a petition in which we ask God for things that are suitable for us to have.[77] Thus, prayer was essentially a request for a specific spiritual reward, and it was generally believed that prayers said in the appropriate devotional state would be answered. Indeed, popular preaching manuals like the *Libro de los exenplos por a.b.c.* disseminated exemplary tales that extolled the power of prayer. In illustration of the mnemonic device "La oración de negro faze blanco, / e de obscuro faze claro" ("Prayer makes black white, / and darkness light"), the manual tells how the abbot Paul saw a man all black and dark enter a church accompanied by the devil. After the man humbly prayed that God forgive him his sins, he left all white and bright, accompanied by his guardian angel.[78] Thus, for the late Middle Ages prayer was anything but a disinterested activity. Folio 93^v of Constanza's manuscript contains a prayer in Latin[79] headed with the following rubric:

> El papa Bonifacio Sexto, a petición de Felipo, rey de França, otorgó dos mill años de perdón a cualquier que dixere esta oración yuso escripta, depués que fuere alçado el cuerpo de Dios fasta el tercero agnus Dei.

> (Pope Boniface the Sixth, at the request of Philip, the king of France, granted an indulgence of two thousand years to anyone who says the prayer written below between the Elevation of the Host and the third Agnus Dei.)

Constanza does not translate the prayer that follows, a clear indication that, to gain the indulgence, the mechanical repetition of the words, albeit in Latin, is more important than any devotional mind-set.[80]

Time and time again Constanza requests divine favors in exchange for the recitation of her prayers. For example, Constanza's version of the Joys of the Virgin are of the type Margherita Morreale calls "devotional," that is to say, the Joys are the pretext for a series of petitions asking for the Virgin's intercession.[81] This is made explicit in the rubric of the work, *E ordenólos la dicha soror por aver la Virgen por abogada* ("And said sister composed them [the Joys] in order to have the Virgin as her advocate"), and then again in the first Joy:

> Señora Santa María, madre de Dios, reina de los ángeles, abogada de los pecadores, misericordia te demando por el muy grant gozo que tú reçebiste cuando el Verbo de Dios desçendió del cielo e se ençer[r]ó en tus santas entrañas e d'ellas tomó vestidura de omne en su propia virtud por salvar a nós. Señora mía, por este primero gozo te suplico que tú le ruegues que por tu amor Él ordene mi vida, mis obras e mi fin a servicio suyo e a salvación mía. (fol. 75^v)

> (Holy Lady Mary, mother of God, queen of angels, advocate of sinners, I beseech your mercy by virtue of the very great joy you received when the Word

of God descended from heaven and was enclosed in your holy womb and put on the garment of humanity by his own power to save us. My lady, by virtue of this first joy I beg you to ask him that for your love he dispose my life, my works, and my end for his service and for my salvation.)

Then, in the *Suplicación* and the *Protestación* that follow the *Fifteen Joys*, Constanza, the Virgin's unworthy slave, asks for Mary's mercy, and begs her to intercede for her at the moment of her death (78ʳ). Finally, it appears that the daily recitation of the Joys of the Virgin was granted an indulgence by Pope John XXII.[82]

In the Middle Ages, the Joys were commonly fixed at five or seven, but could include as many as twenty-five.[83] Constanza's version has fifteen, a number justified in the work's rubric as reflecting the fifteen steps that the Blessed Virgin climbed when she was presented in the temple: "Estos quinze gozos de la gloriosa virgen Santa María son por el número de las quinze gradas que Nuestra Señora subió en el tenplo, que sinificaron los mesmos gozos" (fol. 75).[84] The Presentation of the Virgin had a special meaning for nuns because, according to tradition, Mary remained in the temple with the other virgins, where she lived a cloistered life *avant la lettre*. The *Golden Legend* says:

> Around the Temple there were fifteen steps, corresponding to the fifteen Gradual Psalms, and because the Temple was built on a hill, there was no way to go to the altar of holocaust, which stood in the open, except by climbing the steps. The virgin child was set down at the lowest step and mounted to the top without help from anyone, as if she were already fully grown up. Having made their offering, Joachim and Anna left their daughter in the Temple with the other virgins and went home. Mary advanced steadily in all holiness. Angels visited her every day, and she enjoyed the vision of God daily. In a letter to Chromatius and Heliodorus, Jerome says that the Blessed Virgin had made a rule for herself: the time from dawn to the third hour she devoted to prayer, from the third to the ninth hour she worked at weaving, and from the ninth hour on she prayed without stopping until an angel appeared and brought her food.[85]

Constanza includes the more or less traditional seven Joys: the Incarnation, the Nativity, Epiphany, the Resurrection, the Ascension, Pentecost, and the Assumption. Eight additional Joys give Constanza's version its particular orientation by emphasizing and extolling the Virgin's maternity. Thus, Constanza beseeches the Virgin's intercession by virtue of the joy with which she carried Christ for nine months in the tabernacle (*sagrario*) of her belly, the joy and sweetness with which she gave birth to the

Son of God, the joy of being the mother of God, the joy of the milk of her breasts, and the joy she experienced while diapering, nursing, cradling, and kissing Christ. One must assume that the particular thrust given to Constanza's version of the Fifteen Joys is purposeful, for other long versions of the Joys amplify the traditional seven differently. For example, the French text preserved in the hours of René of Anjou (first half of the fifteenth century) adds the Visitation, the Adoration of the Shepherds, the Presentation, the Finding of Jesus in the Temple, the Wedding at Cana, the Feeding of the Five Thousand, and Mary's Compassion. Aside from the evocation of the Virgin's joy when the babe first moved within her womb, only the brief introduction to that French version of the Joys calls attention to the Virgin's maternity, mentioning the loins that carried Christ for nine months and the breasts that nursed him.[86] In a Castilian poem by the Marqués de Santillana (d. 1458) there are twelve Joys: the traditional seven, plus the Visitation, the Presentation, the Return from Egypt, the Finding of Jesus in the Temple, and the Wedding at Cana.[87] To the extent that other long versions of the Joys amplify them with rather different events, we must therefore conclude that Constanza's insistence on the Virgin's experience of motherhood is a conscious choice on her part. Constanza thus creates a poetic world without adult men in which she celebrates the physicality of female bodily functions—nursing—and such maternal activities as diapering and cradling. Constanza's audience is entirely female, and to the extent that she is recreating the Joys of the Virgin, Constanza is also celebrating the joys of femaledom.

The emphasis given to the Virgin's maternity in her version of the Fifteen Joys can perhaps be related to one of the realia associated with Constanza that the Dominican community to which she belonged conserved for centuries. The object in question is a doll or statuette of the Child Jesus, which is said to have been a gift to Constanza from her grandfather King Pedro I.[88] The doll is dressed as a prince sitting on a chair with his head resting on his hand and his eyes closed as if in meditation. A ribbon hanging from the doll's neck contains the insignia of the Passion.[89] An iconographic reading of the doll reveals the affinities between the iconic text and a doctrinal point reiterated in Constanza's verbal texts: the Child Jesus who bears the emblems of the Passion foregrounds the motif of Christ's humanity, for it is the human flesh that Christ took from Mary at his birth that will later suffer the Passion.

In Renaissance Italy, such dolls were given to young girls upon their marriage as well as to nuns, who were encouraged to identify imaginatively with the Blessed Virgin. Christiane Klapisch-Zuber cites a seventeenth-century case in which a confraternity was founded "to care for, wash, swaddle, and cradle the newborn Christ. Here the effigy was not only inter-preted and adored, but handled, coddled, and taken for walks through the convent, purifying the entire community by its gaze and its presence."[90] Such practices were already thriving at the end of the fifteenth century. Nuns were never to know an adult "husband," but Klapisch-Zuber ob-serves that playing with dolls of the infant Jesus "allowed the recluse her primary social function—the maternal function—and put her desire and frustrations within limits that her male confessors recognized and could accept. The child-husband allowed these women an experience that their secluded life condemned them never to know" (327). Whether or not one can establish a relation between the emphasis given to the Blessed Virgin's maternity in Constanza's prayer of the Fifteen Joys and the playing out of a maternal function by means of dolls similar to the one that is said to have belonged to Constanza, it is evident that renouncing physiological mater-nity did not mean that nuns lacked the opportunity to extol the biological functions of their sex and even to experience them vicariously. While only the Blessed Virgin was able to fulfill the dual role of virgin and mother, nuns, by the very nature of their vocation, were able to imitate Mary's vir-ginity. Furthermore, by celebrating the motherhood of the Virgin Mary in their devotions and by using dolls to play at appropriating Mary's mater-nal role, nuns were able to participate imaginatively in the Blessed Virgin's maternity, that is, in a gender role otherwise denied to them.

Constanza's most ambitious work, her *Oración* (*Prayer*), is an extended meditation on the life of Christ, divided into forty-four chapters. The text's rubric provides information on the work's genre, function, and audience.[91] The prayer is to be recited before Communion: "Dévese dezir esta oración ante de la comunión." The phrase "ante de la comunión" is ambiguous, because it can mean either before receiving Communion or as preparation for the Communion of the Mass.[92] Although the text is marked with two specific first-person references to Constanza, who calls herself by name, the rubric indicates that she envisions her work as being read by other persons as well, most likely the other nuns in her convent. That is to say, the *I* of the prayer becomes a sort of universal sinner who directs her (or perhaps even his) supplications to the invariable *You*, who is God. Such other users of the text are asked to remember Constanza as they pray so that she can re-ceive part of the benefits that Christ will give them for reciting it. This means that it is not the composition of the prayer that its author regards as particularly meritorious for her salvation; rather, the writing of the prayer is an effort that will eventually be rewarded through its recitation by other pious readers.

Each chapter centers on a specific incident in Jesus' life (the Nativity, the Agony in the Garden, and so on) and begins with one of two pious ejaculations in Latin: *Ihesu, miserere mei* or *Ihesu, parce michi*. These phrases not only articulate the formal divisions of the text, but also underscore its generic identity, for such formulaic repetitions are antinarrative and characteristic of prayer, litanies being the most extreme example. Despite its organization around concrete events in the life of Christ, the work is not a novelesque re-creation of that life[93] but a prayer that uses those events as a pretext for begging God's mercy. The episodes chosen evoke Christ's entire earthly existence, beginning with the Incarnation and ending with Pentecost. In general, such events are evoked in a few deft strokes, often with just one or two sentences. Nonetheless, the work gives special attention to the Passion, Death, and Resurrection, thus establishing a strong connection with the Eucharistic sacrifice that is the heart of the Mass and at the same time evidencing the special affinity that medieval holy women felt for Christ's sufferings. To this end, the work passes rapidly through the Incarnation, Nativity, Circumcision, Presentation, Flight into Egypt, Baptism, and Temptation in the Wilderness, and then slows down to evoke in greater detail such episodes of Christ's Passion as the Arrest, the Mocking, and the Crucifixion itself.

As mentioned above, in general, Constanza cannot be said to be interested in novelizing the Scriptures. Nonetheless, occasionally, and even self-consciously, such novelization occurs, especially when it is a question of the Blessed Virgin's participation in her son's Passion. For example, in the evocation of Christ's meeting with his sorrowful mother while he is bearing the cross, Christ is so disfigured by his torments that Mary does not recognize him. The Blessed Virgin asks the Jews who the condemned man is, and they answer that it is her son Jesus. Mary then asks to approach her son, but the Jews do not permit her to do so. Constanza indicates her awareness of the noncanonical nature of this episode by introducing the Virgin's words with *pudo preguntar* ("she could have asked") and *pudo dezir* ("she could have said"). The Virgin is similarly present in another of the more elaborate episodes, namely, the moment when the crucified Christ asks his mother to receive Saint John as a son and then asks John to receive the Virgin as his mother. Here, the text calls particular attention to the Virgin's *compassio*, that is to say, the parallel passion she suffered along with her son's. Mary's heart became an *ovillo de dolores* ("ball or knot of pain") and was pierced with a sharp sword. Her soul was so bloodied that she received a martyrdom of pain (fol. 17[rv]). *Posumus credere* ("We can believe"), Constanza goes on to say, that Saint John's pain was so great that he probably became faint, tore out his hair, and beat his face and chest.[94] Constanza never asserts that these things did happen, only that they could have happened, much as in the same episode she conjectures that the holy women tore out their hair and scored their faces.[95]

In each chapter, after briefly evoking a significant incident of Christ's life, Constanza observes that he accomplished such and such a deed for her benefit and, in the process, illustrated some particularly desirable virtue. For that reason she humbly begs Christ to grant her that virtue and to free her from the yoke of the corresponding vice. Sometimes there is a logical relationship between narrative episode and petition. Thus, Constanza exhorts Christ by virtue of his holy baptism to wash the many stains from her soul and to grant her the virtue of cleanliness (fol. 3[v]). By virtue of Christ's humility in consenting to so humble himself as to take on mortal flesh, Constanza exhorts him to free her of the sin of pride and to grant her the virtue of humility (fol. 1[rv]). The episode known as "Christ Stripped of His Garments" serves as a pretext to ask for the ability to disdain unnecessary wealth and to cast off vainglorious clothing and adornments. In other cases, there is a more tenuous relation between event and petition, as when the evocation of Christ's five wounds becomes a pretext for asking for five virtues (devotion, acknowledgment of her sins, perfect contrition, true confession, and full satisfaction) that, however desirable, have no explicit relation with Christ's wounds (fol. 15[rv]).

As mentioned above, Constanza evokes the episodes of the Passion in greater detail than she does other events of Christ's life. Instead of treating the scene of the Agony in the Garden in a single chapter, Constanza subdivides the episode into four sections (chapters 11–14). However, this slowing down of the narrative tempo is but one reason why those chapters call attention to themselves. These sections are also unique because they superimpose upon the expected petitions for specific virtues a special request for succor at the moment of death. Thus, Christ's preparation for his death is taken as a model to help the individual sinner, and concretely, Constanza, to prepare for her own death. Christ's words to the Father, "Pater, si posible est, transeat a me calix iste" ("Father, if it be possible, let this chalice pass from me"), elicit a request for the virtue of fortitude (*esfuerço*) in the face of the demoniac temptations that will harass the spirit of the dying (fol. 5ᵛ). The scene in which Christ sweated drops of blood furnishes a pretext to ask for consolation when at her death Constanza's sins and her enemies will cry out for judgment against her (fol. 6ʳ). Christ's solitude when he was abandoned by his sleeping disciples prompts a request that he visit her at the moment of death (fol. 6ᵛ). The episode of the angel that came to console Christ when he expressed his obedience to the will of his Father elicits a parallel request for angelic consolation in the sinner's last hour (fol. 7ᵛ).

More than half of the chapters end with an allusion to Christ's endowing a certain saint with the virtue that Constanza is requesting. Thus, the evocation of the Nativity prompts a petition for the virtue of charity as in the case of the founder of the Dominican order, Saint Dominic himself (fols. 1ᵛ–2ʳ). The Flight into Egypt is a pretext for seeking the virtue of obedience. Specifically, Constanza asks for the strength to comply with God's commandments and to obey the rules of her order, as when Saint Peter, heeding Christ's example, returned to Rome to be crucified (fol. 3ʳ). In a few cases the chapter ends with Constanza appropriating a scriptural quotation, usually a verse from the Book of Psalms. Thus, the Incarnation is a pretext for seeking the virtue of humility so that Constanza can recognize her own baseness as did David: "Quia ego sum pulvis, cinis, vermis et non homo, opprobrium hominum et abieccio plebbis" (fol. 1ᵛ).[96]

Beginning with the chapter that deals with the Death of Christ on the cross, the narrative part of the text incorporates extensive quotations in Latin from the corresponding Divine Offices. From then on, that procedure furnishes an alternative way to end a given chapter. Thus, the chapter devoted to the episode in which the Roman soldier Longinus pierced Christ's side with a lance ends with a lengthy quotation from the Improperia sung on Good Friday (fol. 22ᵛ). Even more extensive is the liturgical material that constitutes the entire second half of the chapter devoted to how the Virgin Mary kept the faith during the three days that Christ's body was in the sepulcher. These liturgical texts include the Good Friday hymns "O crux fidelis" and "Vexilla regis prodeunt," as well as the antiphon "Super omnia ligna cedrorum" (fol. 25ᵛ). Ascension and Pentecost, the final two chapters of the prayer, have a similarly disproportionate amount of liturgical material. This means that, if a tension between the narration of events and supplication characterizes the text as a whole, as it incorporates ever longer quotations from liturgical hymns, the work becomes ever more true to its generic identity as a prayer as well as more self-conscious of its function as a text to be prayed during the celebration of the liturgy.

The extensive quotations in Latin that characterize the latter part of the prayer are not the only occasions when Constanza uses Latin, for previous narrative passages intersperse short biblical quotations in that language. In general, these Latin phrases correspond either to Christ's words ("Tristis est anima mea usque ad mortem" [fol. 5ʳ]) or to other instances of direct discourse from the Scriptures (Simeon's words when he took the infant Christ into his arms: "Nunc dimictis servum tuum, Domine, secundum verbum tuum in pace" [fol. 2ᵛ]) or to epithets applied to Christ (*fons pietatis* [fol. 15ʳ]). Although Constanza was literate in Latin, none of the quotations in that language are translated into Castilian. The fact that she chose not to translate the Latin quotations in her prayer suggests either that other nuns were familiar with Latin or that such phrases were so well known that Constanza's companions could be expected to know what they meant without actually being literate in Latin.

The *Prayer* is Constanza's most extensive work. It is also her most original in the sense that it is neither a translation of a preexisting text nor is it a reelaboration of a traditional prayer as, for example, is the *Fifteen Joys*. The *Prayer* can be viewed as a sort of summa that brings together Constanza's major preoccupations. Prayer and the singing of the Divine Offices constituted the primary activity of Dominican sisters and thus formed an essential part of their identity as nuns. It is therefore significant that Constanza's *Prayer* was intended to be said during the liturgy, where the private *I* of individual supplication is incorporated into the communal celebration of the Mass. The prayer for personal salvation and intercession at the hour of death is both Constanza's personal request and that of her companions who pray from her book. Theologically, the *Prayer* concentrates on the Passion and thereby on the suffering humanity of Christ, but also calls attention to the Virgin Mary's *compassio*. Constanza's identity as both princess and prioress is also in evidence. Ever conscious of her family ties, she prays for the souls of her departed relatives, all of whom are of royal blood. The private and the public are conjoined here, for those departed souls are both members of her family and public figures. In her capacity as prioress, Constanza asks God to bless the nuns in her charge,[97] and the very composition of the work is directly related to her role as leader and teacher of the community. Thus, the *Prayer* is a place where the public and the private, the princess and the worm, the individual and the communal, the prioress and her sisters intersect.

Constanza never got to be a real princess. The chaos created by fourteenth-century Castilian politics saw to that and assured that the convent was the only place where she could be safe. That chaos was created by men—her grandfather King Pedro I and his bastard brother King Enrique II. Constanza was raised in a world in which, in sharp contrast to the destructive forces unleashed by males, it was the women who kept civilization going. Queen Catherine and her female confidants created new life through procreation and then protected their offspring, providing models of strong and creative female leadership. In her writings, Constanza creates a world in which men—with the exception of a "feminized" Christ—are all but absent. She writes for a female audience, her sisters at Santo Domingo el Real, celebrating the maternity and the *compassio* of the Virgin Mary and that which is feminine in Christ. In the self-sufficient female world of the cloister women bond together and celebrate the things that matter, ranging from Mary's maternity to how to die well, and all the other positive acts that lie in between. It is a quintessentially human—and humane—world because it celebrates what it takes to be a human being, compassion. Constanza may have been proud of her lineage, but in her spiritual writings she rejects the masculine world of her male ancestors' fratricidal wars. What matters to her is that which is essentially female—mothering, for example, and all the acts that follow compassion. What she does draw from the world of men—building chapels and writing, for example—she feminizes. By this I mean that she drew from traditionally male realms of endeavor for an essentially female purpose, that is, the preservation of her ancestors' memory, the survival of the legitimate royal blood, and, most importantly, the cultivation of the spirit, not because of the desire for power—she already had that—but out of compassion. Such a program grew out of concrete and very traumatic historical circumstances and sought to create a world that was deliberately female, not only by design (that is, as a rejection of male values) but that deliberately celebrated and rejoiced in uniquely female virtues—even when these virtues were "feminized" male virtues. In a word, it was a productive, anti-war world of women, acutely aware of the pain that can be inflicted on the flesh—whether Christ's or King Pedro's—and acutely aware of the joys that living and learning according to compassion can bring.

Although she suffered the results of a history created by males, Constanza turns out to be anything but just another victim of a patriarchal society. The prioress had no need to subvert a male authority because, for her, writing was less an appropriation of a masculine activity than a naturally female activity, as legitimate—innately so—as breastfeeding. If Mary suckled Christ with the milk of her female breast, Constanza gives her charges the spiritual milk of her writings. To the extent that Constanza's work was *imitatio* of Mary's work—both having the ultimate goal of *compassio*—then Constanza could bypass male authority altogether and claim the realm of compassion as her own and as that of all women. This sort of self-confidence, ironically, could only have come about in a princess. As prioress of Santo Domingo el Real, Constanza managed to be queen in a realm of women and did precisely what Queen Catherine did when, as co-regent, she decided to raise her son herself. In many ways, Constanza's proto-feminism is quite radical. In the female utopia that she sought to create, she is "mother" of her convent, as well as builder, writer, and teacher. In short, she is a nurturer, for teaching and praying become a natural extension of nurturing.

*   *   *

Constanza's sarcophagus is decorated with allegorical figures representing Prudence, Temperance, Hope, and Faith, the last dressed like a nun. The effigy of Constanza herself is likewise dressed in a nun's habit, the hands crossed on the breast and a prayer book between them.[98] However unlikely, one would like to believe that the volume represents the book of devotions that Constanza herself wrote.[99]

3. María de Ajofrín:
The Scourge of Toledo

María de Ajofrín (d. 1489) was a holy woman closely associated with the Hieronymite order. In the later years of her life she had a series of visions that had a direct relevance to the social and religious situation of late fifteenth-century Toledo. By short-circuiting the traditional system of mediation with the divine afforded by the ecclesiastical hierarchy, María provided the inhabitants of Toledo with a more personal experience of God and a more direct way of contacting the supernatural.

The principal source for the life and visions of María de Ajofrín is the biography written by her confessor Juan de Corrales.[1] Embedded in this hagiographic text is a series of mystical visions and revelations. Corrales's narrative was in turn incorporated, with some additions and suppressions, into José de Sigüenza's late sixteenth-century chronicle of the Hieronymite order.[2] María's confessor privileges his role as eyewitness to many events of María's life and as earwitness to the mystic's oral account of her visions. In an effort to authorize the veracity of his biography, Corrales quotes documents, interjects himself into the narrative with expressions like "según que ella me dixo" ("as she told me"), and mentions such icons as the cloths soaked in the blood from María's wounds that are still in his possession (Corrales, 198[r] and 202[v]). The phenomenon of confessor-as-biographer, though commonplace,[3] poses the question of the accuracy of the narration of the penitent's visions, less in their general outline than in detail. In other words, to what extent was the confessor-biographer a kind of faithful stenographer and to what extent was he an editor of the words of his penitent?[4] Were there another primary narrative source for María's life, it would be possible to gauge the degree of editorial activity on the part of Corrales, but since that is lacking, we must assume his probity as a trustworthy recorder of María's visions.

María de Ajofrín was the daughter of Pero Martín Maestro and Marina García, fairly well-off commoners from the town of Ajofrín near Toledo

(Corrales, 193ᵛ). María exhibited signs of unusual piety from an early age (Sigüenza, 358).⁵ She had many suitors and her relatives made plans to marry her off, but when María got wind of their intentions, at the age of thirteen she made a vow of chastity and determined to enter a religious order. According to Corrales (194ʳ), María resisted *baronilmente* (virilely) the attempts to marry her off. That is to say, her strength in resisting marriage was so great that the highest compliment her biographer could pay her is that she acted with the strength of a man.⁶ María so pestered her parents and siblings with her requests to enter the religious life that all began to detest her.⁷ Finally, at the age of fifteen, María convinced her father to take her to Toledo. Entering the cathedral, María was divinely inspired to join the Hieronymite convent of San Pablo, where she distinguished herself as a model of humility and sanctity (Corrales, 194ʳ).

Technically speaking, María lived in the place that would later become the convent of San Pablo, for at that time it was known as merely the "casa de María García" after its foundress. This means that it was a lay residence (*beaterio*) and that the women who lived there were not nuns but *beatas*. A *beata* was usually "a woman who had made a simple (that is, private) vow of chastity, wore a habit, and observed a religious rule of some kind, whether temporarily or permanently, cloistered or in society, or alone or in company of others."⁸ As Sigüenza explains (383), the *beatas* of the "casa de María García" were subject to the prior of the Hieronymite monastery of La Sisla, and it was not until 1506 that the residence was formally incorporated into the Hieronymite order.⁹

After more than ten years in the convent, María underwent a sort of conversion experience and resolved to make a general confession of her sins. As she prostrated herself before a painting of the Madonna and Child, a strange light illuminated the image, and the Child extended his hand toward her in a gesture of absolution. Although frightened by what she saw, María nonetheless managed to make her confession, and when she left the confessional, the same mysterious light illuminated the image of the Infant Christ, which once again made a sign of absolution (Corrales, 194ᵛ). This time María was not afraid and truly believed that her sins had been forgiven by the Lord himself (Sigüenza, 359). It was only much later that María revealed this vision to her biographer and second confessor, Juan de Corrales (Corrales, 194ᵛ). Such miraculous phenomena continued until the visionary's death in 1489.

In the first part of this chapter I will concentrate on the series of visions that served to establish María's credibility as a bearer of messages

from the other world. Eight days after Easter in 1484, María had a vision
in which an old man wearing a red cape appeared and told her to come
with him, for the queen had summoned her: "Ven, que te llama la reina"
(Corrales, 195ᵛ). In the vision, the old man takes her to a church outside
Toledo where she sees the Virgin Mary with the Infant Christ in her arms.
As María kneels before the Virgin, the old man places a silken cloth in her
hands and then the Virgin herself places the Child on the cloth. Ordering
the old man and a somewhat younger man to accompany María, the Virgin
commands her to take the Child and to follow the two men, who are to act
as guides in their search for lodging in Toledo. They knock on door after
door, saying: "Open up, for the Lord is coming to lodge in your house."[10]
No one gives them shelter: some shut the door in their faces; others offer
excuses.[11] Finally, two women accompanied by two clergymen, who are in
too much of a hurry to take them in, advise them to take shelter in a nearby
stable.

When María returns to the church where she first saw the Virgin,
Mary prophesies:

> Venido es el tienpo en el cual tan gran deshonra es venida al Hijo de Dios,
> mas ya tienpo es que enbíe el Señor su ángel e con azotes fiera a unos[12] y a
> otros con espada e a otros con pena de fuego. (Corrales, 196ʳ)

> (The time has come when the Son of God is so greatly dishonored, but
> it is now [also] time for the Lord to send his angel and strike some with
> the scourge and others with the sword and still others with the punishment
> of fire.)

Pedro de la Vega's version (fol. 95ᵛ) adds to the Virgin's words a particular
warning to ecclesiastics, whom the Lord made the shepherds of his flock,
but who, although dressed like sheep and lambs, are really rabid wolves
who seek only to drink the blood of their charges. If such prelates strive
for earthly honors and privileges, it is not to serve better their Lord but to
gratify their own desires. Corrales does not mention whether María told
this vision to her confessor at that time or at a later date. However, he
does observe that the Virgin's prophecies were fulfilled after María's death
(1489) and after that of Cardinal Mendoza of Toledo (1495):

> Y se cunplió lo que dixo María de Ajofrín en la revelatión cuando le puso
> Nuestra Señora el Niño en las manos sobre un paño de seda y le dijo que ver-
> nía gran mortandad en todos estos reinos. Y aquí se cunplió lo que dijo que
> feriría el ángel a unos con açote y a [o]tros con espada y los otros con pena de

fuego. A los que firió el ángel con azotes cunplióse que se entiende las hanbres que ovo en todos estos reinos. A los que feriría el ángel con espada cunplióse que uvo en todos estos reinos muy gran mortandad. A los que firió el ángel con pena de fuego, cunplióse porque vinieron muchas bubas sobre muchos honbres y mugeres, las cuales no podían ser sanas por los físicos. (Corrales, 229^{v}–230^{r})

(And that came to pass which María de Ajofrín said in the revelation in which Our Lady placed the Child on a silken cloth in her hands and told her that a great loss of life was coming to all these realms. And here was fulfilled what she said, that the angel would strike some with the scourge and others with the sword and still others with the punishment of fire. That the angel struck some persons with the scourge was fulfilled in the sense that there was famine in all these realms. That the angel would strike some with the sword came to pass, for there was a deadly plague in all these realms. That the angel would strike some with the punishment of fire came true because a great outbreak of venereal disease befell many men and women, which disease the doctors could not cure.)

On Ascension Day in the year 1484 María received a vision in which she saw a marvelously decorated cloister with five crystalline doors on which was sculpted the Annunciation. A solemn procession of priests emerged from each door and filed to another building, where the clergymen prostrated themselves before an altar singing the Gloria. On the altar was the Virgin Mary holding the Child Jesus, and Our Lady addressed the crowd in a plaintive voice, saying:

He aquí el fruto de mi vientre. Tomaldo e comeldo, que en çinco maneras es cada día cruçificado en las manos de los malos sacerdotes: la una es por la mengua de la fe; la otra es por cobdiçia; la otra por luxuria; la cuarta, por ignorantia de sinp[l]es y necios sacerdotes que no saben discerner *inter lepran et lepran*;[13] lo quinto, por la poca reverentia que façen al Señor despúes que le an reçebido. . . . Más sin reverentia es comida la carne de mi Hijo de los indignos sacerdotes que el pan que es dado a los perros. (Corrales, 197^{r})

(Behold the fruit of my womb. Take it and eat of it, for he is crucified every day in five ways at the hands of immoral priests: first, out of lack of faith; second, out of avarice; third, on account of lust; fourth, out of the ignorance of simpleminded and stupid priests who do not know how to distinguish between leprosy and leprosy; fifth, because of the little veneration they show their God after they have received him. . . . My Son's flesh is consumed with less reverence by unworthy priests than the bread that is thrown to the dogs.)

Then there appeared a particularly venerable priest who put on his vestments for Mass, and at the moment of the Consecration, Our Lady placed the Child in the priest's hands, whereupon the Infant changed into a host. When the priest raised the host on high, it was like a sunbeam and rose to heaven, where the Heavenly Father received it, saying "This is my beloved Son."[14] Then another priest, the recently deceased chaplain of the convent where María lived, came up to her and explained that what she has seen refers to those who receive only the form of the Eucharist but do not participate in its fruits.[15] The vision ends as the priest orders her to reveal all that she has seen to her confessor so that he may in turn reveal it to the dean and the *capellán mayor* of the Cathedral of Toledo.[16]

María was confused, for she feared that the vision was inspired by the devil. Nonetheless, she had an inner certainty that such was not the case. When she revealed the vision to her confessor, Juan de Velma, he was incredulous and expressed his contempt toward her. Nonetheless, María's biographer explains that Velma merely pretended not to understand lest he believe too easily *fantasías de mujeres* ("female fantasies") and in the hope that in time he might be more convinced (Corrales, 198[r]).

At the end of September of that same year, María had another vision in which she was borne toward the same cloister as in the previous revelation. In this vision, when the devil tries to approach her, the Virgin Mary pushes him away with her own hand. Then the Virgin recalls the mandate to reveal what María had witnessed in that place and orders her once again to tell all that she has seen and heard to her confessor, who, in turn, should report it to the dean and the *capellán mayor* of the cathedral of Toledo, who in turn should reveal it to the archbishop and then to the entire Church (Corrales, 199[r]).[17] When María told her confessor about the second vision, he was more conciliatory toward her. He reminded María that the three Marys had not been believed and that the Jews had demanded signs from Christ before they would believe. Velma therefore suggested that, although he himself was now willing to believe her, were she to receive some sort of divine sign, the venerable members of the Church hierarchy might be more inclined to accept his testimony.

María was much grieved and decided to respond by letter to her confessor. She found a piece of paper and then shut herself up in a basement room. Although she did not know how to write, a mysterious light illuminated the paper and suddenly, her hand, moved by unknown forces, wrote two letters, one to her confessor and the other to the dean and the *capellán mayor* of Toledo. Although her confessor realized that she could not have written the letters herself, he was nonetheless afraid to tell anyone about them, hesitating "like Saint Thomas." María, "strong like a lion," berated her confessor for his harshness and incredulity, insisting that she herself had written the letters with the help of an angel.[18] She prayed to the Lord that he give her confessor a sign or that he punish him until he believed her.

And so it was, according to her biographer, that on All Saints' Day in 1484 the Lord decided to have María share in the torments of his Passion. As she received Communion, she felt intense pain and cried out as a blade wound appeared on her forehead. After Communion, María had a vision of Christ enthroned and holding a double-edged sword in his mouth. She was told that the sword represented his anger at the clergy, and she was ordered to reveal this to the prelates already indicated to her. In particular, she was to tell the archbishop of Toledo to eradicate those five sins by which immoral clergymen were daily crucifying Christ: lack of faith, greed, lust, ignorance, and lack of reverence for sacred things. Furthermore, the archbishop should extirpate the heresies that abounded in Toledo and forbid the saying of Mass in private homes. Finally, as a sign so that María would be believed, the sword that Christ held would pierce her heart and the blood that flowed from it would be a living testimony for all:

> Y esta señal del cielo te doy por que seas creída en estas cosas que as visto y en las pasadas. Y este cuchillo que ves en la boca de Dios poderoso traspasará tu coraçón y hará en él llaga y saldrá sangre biba que será verdadero testimonio a todos. Y tú serás remediadora y parcionera en la Passión del Hijo de Dios. (Corrales, 202ᵛ)

> (And I give you this heavenly sign so that you will be believed concerning these and past things that you have seen. And this sword that you see in the mouth of powerful God will pierce your heart and wound it and living blood will issue from it that will be true evidence for everyone. And you will be a helper and a sharer in the Passion of the Son of God.)

Just as Christ had promised, after the vision María experienced unspeakable pain as blood flowed forth from an open wound in her heart, a wound so large, specifies Corrales, that a man's thumb could fit into it.[19] When María's confessor found out about the wound, he ordered the other *beatas* to keep silent about it, fearing that it might be a simulation. But when he saw the wound, he believed, and summoned the dean, the *capellán mayor*, and other witnesses, as well as a notary public, to attest to the phenomenon. The confessor ordered a notarial document drawn up (which Corrales later transcribes [230ᵛ–231ᵛ]), stating how he and the other witnesses saw the wound on María's body (Corrales, 203ʳ).

Although the wound in María's side was the most significant sign she bore of Christ's Passion, it was not the only one. While she was still lying in bed suffering from the pain of the wound in her side, she heard the sound of the bells that signaled the moment of the Elevation of the Host during Mass. María arose from her bed and knelt before a painted image of a crucifix. She experienced great pain in her hands and feet, as if they were being pierced with large nails (Corrales, 203[rv]). Then, María felt as if nails of fire were being driven into her head, forming a circle of drops of blood. Corrales's chapter heading explicitly identifies this torment with Christ's Passion, and concretely with the crown of thorns: "Concerning the crown of thorns that she felt on her head in memory of Our Lord's crown."[20]

In a vision María received on the Feast of the Circumcision in 1485, she is once again admonished to reveal what she has seen and heard in the previous revelations. She answers that she is unworthy of such a task, but the following night in another vision she is brought before a judge who rebukes her and orders an angel to whip her (Corrales, 204[r]). At this point, the narrative recalls another vision that she received when she was given the wound in her heart: An angel brings her to purgatory where she sees a priest, who was still alive at the time, undergo severe torments. A two-headed serpent is coiled around his body, one head gnawing at his spine, the other at his belly. Nearby is a frightful dragon with a basket on its back which contains a small child who demands justice, for it is the priest's fault that he is never to see God. When María asks the angel to explain, he reveals that, due to the priest's neglect of his duties, the child died unbaptized (Corrales, 205[rv]).

A week after having had these visions, María was present as the priest was saying Mass, and after the Consecration, she had a vision in which a three-headed serpent is tormenting the priest by gnawing at his heart, tongue, and back, while the child cries out as before. Several days later, María told the priest what she had seen, and he was amazed that the visionary knew of his secret sins (Corrales, 205[v]). In the light of this and the other marvelous signs, María's confessor finally believed in the divine origin of her visions and wrote a letter to the archbishop of Toledo, Cardinal Pedro González de Mendoza.[21] It is evident that by this time María's confessor was Corrales himself.[22] Corrales's letter to the archbishop either accompanied or incorporated a copy of his written record of María's experiences, for González de Mendoza's response refers to reading a *letura* (lesson) divided into chapters (Corrales, 230[r]) and then to the *cuaderno* (notebook) he is returning (Corrales, 230[v]).[23] In his response to Corrales, the archbishop acknowledges his initial skepticism of María's holiness, but admits to believing it when he saw the testimony of the papal notary and of so many other witnesses.[24] He also expresses his admiration for María's humility in refusing to reveal what she had seen and heard, even if that meant disobeying God's divine command (Corrales, 230ʳᵛ).

The archbishop's belief in the authenticity of María's extraordinary experiences meant that those experiences had been validated by the highest ecclesiastical authority in Spain. From then on, she could be reasonably assured that her messages would be considered to be of divine origin and that attention would be paid to them. In succeeding visions, María continued to convey God's wrath at clerical immorality and at the presence of heretics in Toledo. But before discussing these later revelations, I would like to pause to comment on the series of visions that led to the establishment of her credibility.

First of all, it seems likely that the first confessor's suspicion of his penitent and his reluctance to believe her arose from his concern for his own reputation, for should María have turned out to be a fraud, then, presumably, he would have been implicated in that deception. Thus, it was the confessor who suggested that María should ask for a divine sign, for as William Christian has noted in his study of Marian apparitions in late medieval and Renaissance Spain, the need for a visible sign before the visionary is believed is a standard feature of such manifestations of the divine.[25] To judge from the ordering of the visions in Corrales's narrative, it appears that it was both the physical sign of the wound in María's heart and the oral testimony of a priest (the one who had failed to baptize the child) that succeeded in convincing María's confessor of the genuineness of her visionary experiences. With corroboration from male ecclesiastics, the physical sign was authenticated; despite the proven immorality of the neglectful priest, his status as a priest and his male gender gave him a credibility that María herself lacked.

The sign, that is, the wound on María's breast, was not just any sign. Rather, as a replication of the Passion, it was a crucial element in the construction of María's holiness. The physical imitation of Christ's suffering was frequently experienced by women in the late Middle Ages and, as such, the corporal manifestations of that imitation were eminently readable by their contemporaries, who were accustomed to interpret them as a sign of sanctity. The corporal sign was crucial in persuading the archbishop of María's holiness, not because he himself had seen it, but because of the existence of the written notarial testimony, which her confessor had had drawn up. As a woman and an illiterate,[26] María was excluded from written culture, for writing was a monopoly of the ecclesiastical and civic establishment, that is, of the male gender. Although María herself was at one point miraculously empowered to write, her letters were not read as documents, that is, as linguistic signs, for her biographer does not even bother to quote them. Rather, they were, first, signs of divine intervention that could be acknowledged or ignored and, second, a sort of talisman that would later effect miraculous cures (Sigüenza, 362). Although Christ writes the sign of his Passion on María's body, it is not the physical sign itself that ultimately convinces the archbishop, but the notarial document, that is to say, the wound's inscription in patriarchal discourse. Thus, the sign inscribed on the female body is insufficient evidence until it is validated by the male written word. The experience of the Passion, even if translated into the language of María's body, cannot be duly read by the clerical establishment until it is retranslated into written discourse.

The preliminary vision in which María de Ajofrín and the Child Jesus seek shelter in Toledo introduces several important themes. The scene is an obvious calque of the apocryphal episode of the Holy Family's search for lodging in Bethlehem. Both male and female mystics had visions in which the Blessed Virgin handed them the Child Jesus to hold and caress.[27] Gertrud the Great of Helfta (1256–1302) had a Christmas vision in which she said to Christ: "I took you from the lap of your virgin mother in the shape of a most tender and delicate little child."[28] In a Candlemas vision, it is the Virgin who hands Gertrud the Child: "with her spotless hands your spotless mother proffered me you, the child of her virginity, a loveable baby struggling with all his might to be embraced by me" (141). Henry Suso (ca. 1300–1366) had a Candlemas vision in which, after spiritually accompanying the Virgin and the Child to the temple, he "asked her to show him the Child and also to let him kiss it. And when she kindly offered it to him, he spread out his arms to the ends of the earth, took the beloved Child, and embraced it countless times. He looked at its pretty little eyes, gazed at its tiny hands, and kissed its tender little mouth."[29] The Feast of the Purification seems to have been a traditional moment for this sort of vision,[30] for it was also on that day that Angela of Foligno (ca. 1248–1309) had a vision in which the Virgin handed her the Child, and Angela held it in her arms, experiencing an indescribable love when she gazed into his eyes.[31]

What is notable in the case of María de Ajofrín is that, despite the fact that she plays the Blessed Virgin's maternal role in the vision, her participation in sacred history is decidedly lacking in motherly affection. There is no caressing, no tenderness; holding the Child does not produce a moment of mystical union. In María's case, what matters is the anecdote, the role: she reenacts the sacred narrative, casting herself in the part of the Virgin Mother of Christ. Thus, not only does the visionary appropriate a leading role in the revelation, but that appropriation foregrounds the equivalence between the two Marys, the Virgin Mary and María de Ajofrín. That equivalence also calls attention to the underlying tension between María's pride and her humility. Although María does not hesitate to equate herself to the Virgin Mary within the private world of her visions, when it is a question of projecting a public self, the desire to cultivate the virtue of humility leads her to refuse to communicate her revelations. While the traditional justification for female silence is the notion that Eve's words led Adam to sin, the Virgin Mary was also a model for cultivating the virtue of silence. In the case of the vision in question, it is possible that María seeks to imitate the Virgin Mary who, after witnessing and participating in the marvels of the Nativity, "kept all these words, pondering them in her heart" (Luke 2:19).

Significantly, in joining biblical past and historical present, it is the inhabitants of Toledo, not those of Bethlehem, who refuse to give shelter to this restructured "Holy Family." Thus, not only is María able to censure the lack of charity among the citizens of Toledo, but in attributing the root of the problem to the failings of the ecclesiastical hierarchy, she introduces the important theme of clerical immorality.

The question of clerical immorality reappears in the Ascension Day vision and, significantly, in that vision it is not Christ himself but a woman, his mother, who is the spokesperson for the divine will. The Virgin's first utterance, "Take it and eat of it," is an appropriation of both her son's words at the Last Supper and the celebrant's words at the Consecration of the Mass. While in María's vision it is ultimately the priest figure who performs the Consecration, it is nonetheless the Virgin Mary, strategically placed on the altar, who hands the priest the Child who will become the host.[32] The scene thus highlights two important points. First, when the Virgin hands the Child to the priest, she calls attention to Christ's humanity, to the human flesh that he received from her that would later suffer the Passion that the Eucharist commemorates.[33] Second, Mary's gesture also suggests her participation in a priestly function.[34]

Mary's priesthood was not an entirely recondite motif in the Middle Ages. When the Pseudo-Albert the Great's *Mariale* asks whether the Virgin received the sacrament of Holy Orders, the answer is affirmative.[35] Jean Gerson argued that although Mary was not invested with the priestly office and therefore did not possess the power to consecrate, she was anointed into the royal priesthood and was thus able to offer her son as victim on the altar of her heart.[36] María's considerably younger contemporary, Mother Juana de la Cruz, had a vision on the Feast of the Purification in which Our Lady distributed her son in the form of hosts to the blessed souls in the celestial kingdom who wished to receive him. Juana's vision refers explicitly to Mary as a priest.[37] Bynum argues that representations of Mary as priest in the visual arts "have nothing to do with claiming sacerdotal functions for ordinary women. Mary is priest because it is she who offers to ordinary mortals the saving flesh of God, which comes most regularly and predictably in the mass."[38] Nonetheless, representations of Mary as priest must have been powerful polysemous images. In addition to calling attention to the human flesh that Christ received from his mother, could not that image at least suggest the possibility of women appropriating the sacerdotal roles abdicated or profaned by unworthy males?

Although the vision targets the question of immoral priests, it does not attack the principle of clerical authority, for it is still a priest who pronounces the words of the Consecration. While common medieval belief disassociated the validity of the sacrament from the unworthiness of the celebrant, the vision nonetheless suggests that women are untainted by the stigma of immorality and are thus authorized to participate in priestly functions—in the case of the Blessed Virgin—and in such female alternatives to the priesthood as the visionary experience—in the case of María.[39] Thus, the Virgin Mary's preeminent role in the vision serves to empower her namesake, María de Ajofrín, to function as a worthy vehicle for God's revelation.

It is therefore no accident that the sign that María finally receives is both a calque of the Passion of Christ and a calque of the *compassio* of the Virgin Mary,[40] for in preparing María de Ajofrín for her role as prophetess and message-bearer, Christ establishes her authority by assimilating her to both himself and his mother. Christ's explicit intention when he appears to María with a sword in his mouth is to make her a participant in his Passion. Concretely, María's *imitatio Christi* involves her suffering a passion analogous to that of Christ when her body receives a wound like the lance wound in Christ's side.[41] However, the image of the blade piercing María's heart also recalls Simeon's prophecy in Luke 2:35 that the soul of Christ's mother would be pierced with a sword, a prophecy fulfilled when the Virgin suffered the Passion along with her son. Thus, if in the previous revelation María appropriated the Virgin's role in the Nativity, here the visionary assumes the Virgin's role in the Passion: María's *imitatio Christi* is an *imitatio* of both the *Passio* of Christ and the *compassio* of Our Lady. Moreover, not only is María de Ajofrín assimilated to her namesake through their mutual participation in the Passion of Christ, but both will perform a mediating function. Just as the Virgin is the prime advocate for sinners before her son, so likewise will María de Ajofrín function as an intermediary between the inhabitants of Toledo and the divine.

Finally, María's prophetic role is highlighted through the biblical reminiscences suggested by the vision. Christ's manifestation with a double-edged sword in his mouth appears to be an amplification of Revelation 1:16 ("And from his mouth came out a sharp two-edged sword") and Revelation 19:15 ("And out of his mouth proceedeth a sharp two-edged sword, that with it he may strike the nations"). Thus, when Christ speaks through María, prophesying the punishments that are to befall the immoral clergy of Toledo, the visionary is called upon to play an apocalyptic role analogous to that of Saint John in his Book of Revelation. Likewise, the words that come out of María's mouth can be viewed as equivalent to the sword in Christ's mouth.[42] Although she cannot take up the phallic sword to punish sinners, her phallic tongue becomes the symbolic equivalent of the Lord's sword. In this way female speech acquires the authority of divine speech.

It is difficult to assess the effectiveness of María de Ajofrín's mediumistic role, first, because her biographers are primarily interested in the miraculous favors she enjoyed and not in their tangible results, and second, because her task was merely to bear such messages, not to carry them out. It is probably no accident that Cardinal Mendoza, the archbishop of Toledo, was singled out as the primary receiver of the messages intended to convey God's anger at clerical immorality, for the cardinal himself seemed more interested in furthering the political and economic interests of the powerful Mendoza clan, which included two of his own illegitimate children, than in reforming the clergy of Toledo.[43] Indeed, the cardinal spent relatively little time in residence in Toledo, and if we are to judge his attempts at reform by the number of diocesan synods that were convoked, then Mendoza had a dismal record, for he called none.[44]

Most of María de Ajofrín's other visions are likewise linked to the Toledo of her time. In a vision she received in July of 1488, the flagellated Christ instructed her to encourage the Inquisition to pursue heretics with greater vigor. She told Corrales that

Nuestro Señor le avía aparecido en forma humanal como cuando estava atado a la coluna y que avía hablado con ella por espacio de hora y media y que le avía mostrado las espaldas como que corrían sangre y que le dijo: "Hija, mira cuál me ponen los herejes cada día y di esto al Deán de Toledo y al Prior de La Sisla, que están en la Inquisitión." (Corrales, fol. 223ᵛ)

(Our Lord Jesus Christ had appeared to her in human form as when he was bound to the column and that he had spoken to her for an hour and a half and that he had shown her his shoulders dripping blood and that he said: "Daughter, see what the heretics do to me every day. And tell this to the Dean of the Cathedral of Toledo and the Prior of the monastery of La Sisla, who are involved with the Inquisition.")

This mandate had particular relevance in the context of late fifteenth-century Toledo. Because the city had a large and important Jewish population since Visigothic times, the mass conversions of the late fourteenth century led to the creation of a particularly large and important population of converted Jews or New Christians. While many New Christians were sincere in their new faith, others were Judaizers, that is, they reverted in secret to their Jewish practices.

Particularly scandalous was the discovery of Judaizers in the very heart of the Hieronymite order and in the very same city of Toledo. Inquisitorial documents from the years 1486–1488 reveal that some of the monks from the Hieronymite monastery of La Sisla had engaged in especially outrageous Judaizing practices. For example, several monks had managed to observe the major Jewish feasts, and a former prior of the monastery was accused of saying to the host "sus periquete, que te mira la gente" ("Up with you now; everyone's looking at you") at the moment of the Consecration.[45] Since María herself was associated with the Hieronymite order and her confessor, Corrales, was a monk at La Sisla, it is likely that she felt a moral obligation to encourage the eradication of even the slightest tinge of heresy both within and without her order. In fact, according to Sigüenza (375–376), María was a witness during the trial of one of the Judaizing monks. Although the accused were tried privately before the order's own in-house inquisitorial court, those condemned were turned over to the secular authorities for execution. Thus, Juan de Madrid, a Judaizing monk from La Sisla, was handed over to Gómez Manrique, corregidor of Toledo, for burning, presumably in a public spectacle.[46] According to Haim Beinart, Juan de Madrid was tried in 1487–1488,[47] which would in all probability place his execution in 1488.[48] María de Ajofrín might have been led to believe that her vision influenced the tribunal's decision to mete out so exemplary a punishment to a heretic.

There is evidence of hostility toward the implantation of the Inquisition in Toledo and further evidence that Cardinal Mendoza himself may have been personally opposed to its establishment.[49] It appears that previously, when he was archbishop of Seville, Mendoza was rather lukewarm in dealing with Judaizers and did not always go out of his way to help the Inquisition to do its work smoothly.[50] Archbishop Carrillo, Mendoza's predecessor, had blocked the establishment of the Inquisition in Toledo, and so it began to function in Ciudad Real.[51] In 1485, under Mendoza, the tribunal was transferred to Toledo itself, and the first *auto de fe* took place in 1486.[52] María de Ajofrín's role in the establishment and operation of the Inquisition in Toledo is not clear, but she did manage to convey to the Church hierarchy God's divine approval of the tribunal's rigorous extirpation of heresy.

Although María received the Inquisition vision after her credibility had been established, the timing of such a vision in the political climate of Toledo may have served to validate even further her authority as a visionary. Particularly evident in this case is the coincidence between the private world of the visionary and the public sphere of ecclesiastical politics, an intersection of interests that was mutually beneficial, for the visionary seemed to gain credibility while the Church hierarchy saw its political aims validated by a divine message. Mutual opportunism worked to serve all those concerned: María's vision was of use to the Church so that it could further its own political agenda; María's usefulness was in turn rewarded with authentication from the ecclesiastical hierarchy, which empowered her as a female.

Although María's vision presents the need for harsh measures against heretics as a strictly religious concern, it must also be remembered that as the daughter of peasants, no matter how well-to-do they may have been, she was presumably of Old Christian stock, that is, she had no trace of Jewish or Moorish blood. Thus, María probably shared the sociological prejudices of her class and could therefore be expected to be hostile to the rich and powerful New Christians. For that reason, it is likely that she was personally gratified by the fact that, as a result of the scandal of the Judaizing monks, in 1486 the Hieronymites adopted a statute of blood purity that excluded Christians of Jewish origin from the order.[53] Opposition to the statute from both within and without the order led to considerable debate. Cardinal Mendoza, Queen Isabella, and King Ferdinand opposed the statute, while, among others, María's confessor and biographer Juan de Corrales was in favor.[54] While the statute was not confirmed by the pope until 1495,[55] that is, after María's death, it could be argued that María received her Inquisition vision at a critical moment, for 1488 corresponded to the period of intense debate over the statute of blood purity adopted by the Hieronymite order. The visionary may have viewed the struggle to impose the statute as an attempt to carry out the will of God as expressed in her vision of Christ tormented by the sins of the heretics.

If María was a mediating figure between Toledo and the divine, her confessor appears to have acted as the mediatrix's mediator. Corrales was anything but disinterested in matters pertaining to heresy, for as he himself observes in his biography of María de Ajofrín, he also played a role in the Toledo Inquisition. Indeed, his references to his inquisitorial activities occur in the same chapter in which he records his penitent's Inquisition vision[56] and in which he recalls a conversation during which María exhorted him to be strong in the Lord's battles.[57] Moreover, it is likely that he was involved in the in-house investigations of Judaizing monks in the Hieronymites and, as noted above, he was actively engaged in the movement to adopt a statute that would exclude converts from Judaism and their descendants from the order. Perhaps María's vision influenced her confessor's decision to support the measure. Or, perhaps Corrales perceived her vision as confirmation of the righteousness of his position.

Cases like that of the former prior of La Sisla who uttered blasphemous words at the moment of the Consecration shed light on María's earlier visions, for already in 1484 she was issuing warnings against unworthy priests. While such visions seemed aimed at clerical immorality in general, it is also possible that in the charged atmosphere of the first years of inquisitorial activity in Toledo, María's admonitions were interpreted as referring to Judaizing clergymen. Indeed, several priests were numbered among the tribunal's initial victims. On August 17, 1486, two clergymen, a cathedral chaplain and a parish priest, were burned at the stake for Judaizing.[58] On May 7, 1487, a cathedral canon, found guilty of abominable Judaizing acts, was likewise burned at the stake. Like the former prior of La Sisla, the canon was accused of saying "Sus, periquete, que os mira la gente" instead of the words of the Consecration.[59] Although María's primary concern in the period of 1484–1485 was the validation of her supernatural experiences, the denunciation of bad priests in the sociopolitical context of the establishment of the Inquisition in Toledo could hardly have gotten her into trouble. Indeed, her warnings of divine anger directed at unworthy priests could have enhanced her status as a visionary to the extent that her personal agenda of official recognition was perceived by the Church to coincide with its own desire to cleanse a reputation tarnished by the scandalous behavior of the heretical priests it had harbored in its very bosom.

Sigüenza (376) juxtaposes to the Inquisition vision (1488) a Eucharistic miracle that Corrales (206ʳ) recounts at an earlier point, namely, after the vision (1485) of the serpent tormenting the priest in purgatory. In the Eucharistic vision María sees a group of clergymen bringing the Blessed Sacrament to a sick man. A young man riding a white horse and dressed all in white approaches María and bids her to run and tell the priests to return to the cathedral, for the sick man is a heretic. When María hastens to tell one of the priests what she has heard, he refuses to believe her. The celestial apparition tells her not to fear and that, as a sign that what he has told her is the truth, she will see the host bleed during Mass. Those bearing the host return to the cathedral and, sure enough, at the moment of the Elevation, María sees the host bleed. Now, as Caroline Walker Bynum has indicated, such Eucharistic visions are a common feature of medieval female spirituality, and the bleeding host as a miraculous sign of profanation by Jews is commonplace.[60] However, since the priests would not be knowingly carrying the host to a Jew, it is evident that in this context "heretic" refers to an insincere convert from Judaism. Thus, María's involvement in questions of heresy appears to antedate the vision of the flagellated Christ that served to support and encourage the activities of the Inquisition. In any case, it is her visionary experiences that authorize her intervention in ecclesiastical affairs.

The visionary's mediumistic role is even more evident when she is called on to mediate between the living and the dead. It was assumed in the late Middle Ages that only near saints would go directly to heaven upon their death. Everyone else, except the damned, of course, could be expected to spend at least some time in purgatory, a time that could be shortened through the efforts of the deceased himself during his earthly life or after his death by members of his family. In fact, the Church had already instituted a system of suffrages by which the living could perform good works and pious devotions for the benefit of the dead. But how were the living to know if their relatives in purgatory needed more suffrages or some other task performed in order to ascend to paradise? Preaching manuals popularized stories of souls in torment that appeared to the living to exhort them to perform certain good works or to carry out the instructions of their last will and testament. The *Libro de los exenplos por a.b.c.* tells of the apparition to a bishop of a soul made to suffer in a block of ice until thirty masses be said over a period of thirty days.[61] In another case a man was condemned to hell for not distributing the alms as requested in a relative's will.[62] It is in a similar capacity that visionaries like María de Ajofrín could play a useful role, bearing messages from the souls in purgatory to their still living friends and relatives. In 1486, the spirit of Juan de Velma, María's first confessor, appeared to her and begged her forgiveness for not immediately believing in her divine favors. This rather self-serving message is made more credible when he further requests that certain people he had offended pardon him, that a sum of money he owes the convent be forgiven, that fifty masses be said for his soul, and that María herself pray for him, all so that he can be released from his sufferings (Corrales, 215ᵛ–216ᵛ). On another occasion, María prays to the Virgin Mary, inquiring after the state of the soul of her deceased brother. In response, the brother appears to her, explains that he is in purgatory, and reveals to his sister certain obligations that he had incurred (Corrales, 220ʳ).

María de Ajofrín was doubly distanced from the civic and ecclesiastical establishment by her humble birth and her gender, but once her visionary experiences were validated, she enjoyed a status and an authority that would otherwise have been denied to her. Functioning as both a locus of spiritual power and a channel of divine grace, the visionary became a sort of direct pipeline between late medieval Toledo and the eternal. Indeed, her visions empowered her to reproach the sinfulness of the clergy and, more concretely, to sermonize none other than Cardinal Mendoza, the highest ecclesiastical authority in Spain. Once her experiences were validated, she became a sort of collaborator with the Church hierarchy and may have even played a role in the establishment of the Inquisition in Toledo. Her status as woman and as visionary was enhanced by that official support, while her visions were put to political use by the ecclesiastical establishment in order to enhance its own agenda of rigorous extirpation of heresy.

4. The New Magdalen: María de Santo Domingo

The life of María de Santo Domingo is relatively well documented for two rather different reasons. First, criticism of María's unorthodox behavior and of her involvement in the reform of the Dominican order occasioned a series of investigations, the last of which left a written record. Second, while the words of many other holy women are preserved only in manuscript form, an anthology of María's utterances and writings was not only published during her lifetime,[1] but was prefaced with an editor's introduction that gives some details of her life and mystical experiences.

María de Santo Domingo was born of lowly farmers around 1486 in Aldeanueva, a village in the bishopric of Avila, and she died in about 1524.[2] Around 1502 she received the habit of the Third Order of Saint Dominic at the monastery of Santo Domingo in Piedrahita, whence the name by which she is often referred to, the Beata de Piedrahita. As a *beata*, María chose to live a religious life associated with the Dominican order, but without actually taking formal vows as a nun. After receiving the habit, María resided in Avila in the *beaterio* or residence for lay sisters of Santa Catalina, but had to leave in 1507 because of disagreements with the other *beatas*. María and her supporters claimed that she left because she was the object of persecution. In any case, at Santa Catalina she was already attracting a certain notoriety for her mystical raptures.[3]

María moved to the male Dominican monastery of Santo Tomás in Avila, and then, in about October of 1507, she and some companions were allowed to go to Toledo to help with the reform of the order and to promote the union of *claustrales* (unreformed friars) and *observantes* (reformed friars). María's supporters and detractors put forth several reasons for her departure from Toledo. She was said to have slandered certain *conversos* (converts from Judaism or their descendants), who complained to King Ferdinand and to Cardinal Cisneros. According to other witnesses, while in a trance she threatened the provincial for not being more zealous in promoting the reform of the order. In any case, the result was an order (November 26, 1507) from the king asking the Dominican officials to have María return to the monastery in Avila. Ferdinand also summoned the provincial and María's confessor, Diego de Vitoria, to Burgos, where the resulting conversations concerning María and her supernatural experiences led the king to ask her to come to the royal court. She spent the winter of 1507–1508 there, astounding witnesses with her raptures and revelations.[4]

The archbishop of Toledo, Cardinal Francisco Jiménez de Cisneros, hearing of María's ecstasies, asked her to come to Santa María de Nieva, where he was impressed by the authenticity of her extraordinary experiences. He ordered María's confessor, Diego de Vitoria, to write down her revelations and to send them to him for his spiritual edification. María's favorable reception led her and her followers to make plans for founding a convent in Aldeanueva. The duke of Alba, under whose jurisdiction the town was located, offered to fund the project.[5]

Nonetheless, not everyone approved of the conduct of María and her followers, and she was ordered to appear before the chapter meeting in Zamora in February of 1508. The chapter objected to the extremes to which the reformers under her aegis had gone. Specifically, its ordinances sought to mitigate the more severe forms of asceticism instituted by the reformers, which went considerably beyond the practices stipulated by the constitutions of the order. For example, the chapter authorized the use of wool mattresses, instead of the wooden board that María herself slept on and recommended to the others. The chapter also prohibited the reformers, under pain of excommunication, from seeking support from those outside the Dominican order. Finally, the chapter expressed its concern over what it deemed to be María's scandalous behavior, specifically, her excessive familiarity with certain male clerics ("ex nimia communicatione et familiaritate quorumdam religiosorum"). It was therefore stipulated that no friar could visit her without written permission from the provincial. In an effort to subvert these ordinances, María's powerful protectors, King Ferdinand and Cardinal Cisneros, appealed to the master general of the order, Thomas Cajetan, who ordered an official investigation of María.[6]

It is important to keep in mind that the controversy surrounding María had a personal dimension involving her behavior as well as a "political" dimension involving the reform of the Dominican order. María's participation in a dissident reform movement that sought, in Jodi Bilinkoff's words, "a life of more intense personal prayer and more austere penitential practices,"[7] threatened friars satisfied with the status quo and raised the specter of a schism within the order. The reforming friars saw in María's ecstasies the validation of their movement; in turn, María, to the extent that she shared the same reforming zeal, found in the reformers' support the validation of her own experiences. For that reason, the conventual Dominicans who sought to subvert the reform movement probably saw María herself as the weak spot where they might mount an attack, for female revelations were suspect by their very nature and the propriety of María's life-style was at best ambiguous. By discrediting María, opponents could discredit the whole movement. The investigations thus hinged around the issue of the authenticity of María's experiences and the decorum of her life-style. As Bilinkoff, echoing the words of María's contemporaries, phrases it: "Was María de Santo Domingo a holy mystic and prophetess or an elaborate fake and seductress?"[8]

The controversy surrounding María and the danger of a schism within the order led to not just one, but four investigations. None other than María's confessor, Diego de Vitoria, was put in charge of the first. Continued complaints against María and the reformers resulted in a second commission convoked by the Dominican hierarchy in Rome, a commission that was never able to perform its duty, for it was superseded by a panel of apostolic judges appointed by Pope Julius II. María's supporters convinced the pope of the bias of that third commission, with the resultant naming of a panel more favorable to María and her followers, for the panel included King Ferdinand's Dominican confessor, Juan de Enguera. This fourth trial took place in Valladolid in October and early December of 1509, and it is the proceedings of this inquiry, the only ones preserved, that give us a picture of María and her life-style.[9]

Beltrán de Heredia calls this trial a "parody," for there was not even a prosecuting attorney (99). Moreover, the witnesses were for the most part favorable to María, and she continued to enjoy the protection of Cardinal Cisneros, King Ferdinand, and the duke of Alba. It is thus no surprise that María was officially exonerated in the sentence made public on March 26, 1510. The investigation reveals a number of details of her life, many of which are hagiographic commonplaces: precocious sanctity, extreme asceticism, and numerous good works. María frequently went into religious ecstasy, during which time her body became rigid and she was able to answer questions concerning theology and the Scriptures. On Holy Thursday of 1509 a wound in her side opened and blood flowed forth, leaving a visible scar.[10] What María's accusers saw as unorthodox or even scandalous behavior, her defenders saw as examples of extreme holiness. Although she sometimes wore silk garments, coral jewelry, and fancy hats, it was not out of frivolity but at the request of devotees who treated those objects as relics in the hope that they had become imbued with some of her sanctity.[11] If she danced or played chess, it was to better raise her spirit to higher things, with the result that those pastimes often led to a mystical trance.[12] The men who frequented her cell to witness her raptures and hear her words were of irreproachable virtue. If this practice meant that sometimes friars spent the night in her cell, *solus cum sola*, it was to protect her against the torments caused by the devil and by bodily infirmities.[13]

Despite the favorable outcome of all four investigations, María's detractors continued their campaign against her. Cajetan, the master general of the order in Rome, had meanwhile ordered (September 15, 1509) that no friar be allowed to visit her without the prior permission of the provincial,[14] but once again María's supporters managed to subvert those orders. On July 17, 1510, Cajetan renewed his previous orders that María not be allowed to leave her convent except to visit the new one under construction in Aldeanueva, that no one except her confessor have contact with her without written permission, and that her prophecies and revelations be communicated only to the highest officials of the order.[15] In time, María's extreme reform movement, centered in the monasteries of Piedrahita and Aldeanueva, renounced its secessionist tendencies, resulting in the return of those centers to the jurisdiction of the province.[16]

The *Libro de la oración* [*Book of Prayer*], an anthology of María's revelations, was published around 1518.[17] The editor's prologue and brief biography provide a reading of María's life and mystical phenomena in the aftermath of her examinations. The prologue begins by calling attention to the intimate connection between María and the Passion, for Christ caused the wound in her side to open every Good Friday. It is noteworthy that the *Libro*'s editor, who is supposedly introducing an anthology of María's writings, mentions the wound first, that is to say, he appears to consider Christ's inscription of his lance wound in her side more significant than anything she herself may have written about the Passion (or about any other subject, for that matter). María's defender goes on to remark that such "words of sublime and beneficial teaching" ("palabras de doctrina tan alta y tan provechosa") uttered by an unlettered peasant woman ("siendo mujer sin letras y aldeana")[18] are a source of great consternation to men, especially to learned men. Appropriating a passage from Saint Augustine, he says: "The unlettered rise up and grasp Heaven while we with our learning sink into Hell" (124).[19] He then contrasts two kinds of knowledge, the infused wis-

dom ("la sciencia infusa") that God has given to María and the book learning of men ("sciencia acquisita"). Finally, he underscores the orthodoxy
of María's doctrine and recommends highly its reading to the prologue's
dedicatee, Adrian of Utrecht[20] and, by extension, to the general reader.

The brief summary of María's life that follows includes a "reply to
the maligning defamers and gossipers without reply" ("respuesta a los de-
tractores maldizientes y murmuradores sin respuesta"). That is to say, even
after the positive outcome of four examinations, María still had critics and
needed to be defended by her supporters, and for that reason, it is significant that the space devoted to recounting the biographical details of her
life is considerably less than the space devoted to shielding her against her
detractors. María's biographer observes that her doctrine is "very holy and
beneficial," but the authenticity of her visions and her life-style have been
a source of criticism on the part of her diabolically inspired persecutors.
The fact that her raptures most often occur soon before or after receiving
Communion is a sign of their authenticity, for God would never permit
so great an offense to himself nor, were such visions diabolically inspired,
would he permit the devil to approach the Holy Eucharist (130–131). After
a thumbnail sketch of María's precocious holiness, extreme asceticism, and
severe illnesses, the biographer observes that the persecutions she has suffered at the hands of her detractors have served to fortify her devotion and
that of her followers.

María's biographer then replies to a number of specific criticisms that
have been leveled against her. First, María's detractors doubt that she lives
without eating and suggest that, even if that were the case, since Christ ate,
the servant should not be greater than his or her lord and teacher. Christ
himself fasted, answers María's defender, but chose to eat to prove his most
sacred humanity. María does not need to prove her humanity, therefore
"it proves nothing to argue that since Christ ate she also must eat" (133).
Citing examples of extreme fasting that range from the Old Testament to
contemporary times, the biographer observes that in any case it is charity,
and not fasting, that determines greater or lesser holiness (134–135).

Regarding the wound in María's side, her champion observes that such
a phenomenon is not entirely new—Saint Francis and Saint Catherine of
Siena were blessed with similar wounds. Nonetheless, the cause of such a
phenomenon must be left to the inscrutable designs of God (136–137).

Finally, María's biographer recalls that she was accused of three things
in the course of the investigations: "that she eats when she has gone for
a long time without eating; that she puts on and wears clothes of worldly

taste; that she rides a mule and amuses herself with worldly but decent pleasure and pastimes" (138). María's defender answers that since she vomits
what she eats, eating becomes a source of charity (because it causes suffering), as well as of humility (because it leads her critics to persecute her).
Wearing fine clothes is similarly a sign of humility, for it causes people to
think less of her. Moreover, she demonstrates charity toward those who
give her the clothes, for the clothing serves to remind her to remember
them in her prayers. Trivial pastimes become a source of suffering, for
they cause her to abandon the sublime spiritual sphere. Moreover, the
fact that such pastimes often lead to mystical raptures demonstrates that
her thoughts are not on worldly pleasure but on the pleasure of God.
Therefore, those who are scandalized by María's behavior should not be
so shocked and should consider instead the sufferings she has endured
(138–139).

María's champion goes on to observe that her success in converting
sinners and her persecution by the devil are signs that she is favored by
God, for Satan more often than not treats sinners well in this life (139–
140). It is not María but her critics who are deceived by the devil, for they
do not recognize the hand of God at work. If her enemies cite the case of
a certain woman once believed to be very holy but later discovered to be a
fraud, that constitutes falacious reasoning. Indeed, many women who have
enjoyed experiences similar to those of María are considered saints by the
Church (141). María's success in overseeing the large convent at Aldeanueva
where so much good is being done is a further indication of divine favor
(142). Although María has been accused of many things, she has been examined by a panel of apostolic judges and her life, doctrine, and works have
been declared holy and beneficial. Alas, men do not believe unless they see
miracles wrought. Therefore, let no one resemble the Pharisees and seek a
greater miracle than María's holy life and teachings (143). Finally, María's
champion asks the readers of the *Libro de la oración* to pay attention to the
content of her message and not to the vehicle, that is, to María herself. If
doctrine is good, it is good no matter who utters it. Furthermore, if someone says good but does evil, then we should take from the good that that
person says and leave the bad that he or she does (144). María's champion
thus ends his prologue on this surprisingly ambiguous note, as if he too
shared in some of the reservations expressed by her critics.

A brief prefatory section titled "Division of the Work" states that the
Libro de la oración is intended to give representative examples of "the four
ways she speaks and teaches doctrine" (127). These four ways are: when en-

raptured upon receiving the Eucharist; when considering some aspect of God's creation; when enraptured and questions are posed to her; and when she writes letters of elegant and fruitful style. Since so many of María's words have been recorded, asserts the prologuist, it would be difficult to print all of them. Therefore, what follows is but an anthology of María's utterances.

This chapter will concentrate on the first of the revelations preserved in the *Libro de la oración*.[21] Although the vision is primarily a novelesque re-creation of Christ's appearances after the Resurrection and a meditation on the spiritual meaning of those events, it also bears an implicit relevance to María and to her situation as a woman whose critics questioned her credibility. Specifically, María emphasizes certain aspects of Christ's appearances to his mother and to Mary Magdalene in such a way that the two Marys become emblems for their namesake, María de Santo Domingo.

The rubric that María's editor added to the Easter revelation explains that what follows is but a partial record ("algo de lo que se pudo cojer") of her words and refers to the vision as an "oración y contemplación," which is to say, "prayer and contemplation" (147). The rubric then explains the circumstances of the reception of the vision: María had just received Communion in the convent of Santa Cruz de la Magdalena in Aldeanueva. This means that the revelation was received some time after the installation of the community in the convent in 1512.[22] In an effort to guarantee the veracity of the vision, the editor cites as witnesses those who were present: a few friars, a knight from Talavera, a learned judge from the royal chancery in Valladolid, canons from Zaragoza and Segovia, and other religious and laypersons.

As mentioned above, the vision's point of departure is Christ's appearances after the Resurrection to his mother, Mary Magdalene, and the apostles, but María fleshes out the biblical episode in the Franciscan manner with noncanonical dialogue.[23] However, as its rubric suggests, the vision is also a gigantic prayer in which the eternal present of the expectation of Christ's manifestation is made relevant to the individual soul, in this case, María, who acts as a spokesperson for all humankind. To that extent, María herself is the center of the vision, not as protagonist, but as a sort of *metteur en scène*, addressing now the cast of sacred characters, now the audience assembled at Aldeanueva to witness her ecstasies.

Mary Magdalene occupies a privileged position in the revelation from the very beginning. The vision opens with a series of three prayer-like vocatives addressed to God, the Blessed Virgin, and the Magdalen. María first asks God that she be resuscitated in his love and fear,[24] then she begs the Virgin Mary to remember her on such a joyous day. Finally, she asks that through the intercession of the Magdalen she may be received by Christ. Specifically, she asks the Magdalen to receive her in her arms so that her soul can find peace and joy in Christ.[25] Curiously, in this passage the Magdalen has usurped the Virgin Mary's traditional role of intercessor,[26] for it is Mary Magdalene's mother-like embrace that will enable María to approach Christ and in turn be received in his arms (147).

In the passage that follows, María expresses the desire to rest in Christ's arms and laments that her sins have brought about his crucifixion. She asks to be punished now so that later on Judgment Day she will not have to render a final account and begs Christ to grant her the love and fervor that he gave to the pious Magdalen so that she too will cry a stream of tears. When, asks María, will she be able to leave the darkness and, accompanied by Mary Magdalene, go out into the light? Continuing with the darkness/ light motif, María contrasts the bright morning of Christ's Resurrection with the dark night of sin, sleep, and death (148–149).

At this point in the text an editorial voice enters with a sort of stage direction to indicate that María repeated Psalm 50:6[27] three times, received Communion, and then spoke in her own voice what follows.[28] In the ensuing prayer, María addresses the Blessed Virgin, emphasizing her role, not only as mother of Christ, but also as mother of all sinners (150). Thereupon, María re-creates imaginatively the noncanonical scene of Christ's appearance to his mother.[29] The Virgin Mary is seen weeping in her house and reading a passage from the Scriptures that prophesies the Resurrection. María asks the Virgin: "And why are you looking at this little verse so much? *Exurge gloria mea exurgam diluculo.*[30] [Rise up, my glory, I will rise up at dawn.] You are looking at what you seek. You find it and now you are sad" (151).[31] Although the motif of the Virgin interpreting the Scriptures is authorized by pious tradition[32] and perhaps by iconographical convention,[33] it is nonetheless certain that the episode presents Mary engaging in an activity expressly forbidden to women—scriptural exegesis.[34] Since María herself engaged in that very activity,[35] it is tempting to see in her re-creation of the appearance of Christ to his mother a defense of the right of at least some exceptional women—herself among them—to interpret the Scriptures.

In a gesture at once verisimilar and symbolic, the Virgin goes to the window to see if the dawn, that is, Christ, has come. She then looks at her garments, stained with blood when she embraced her son as he carried the cross. Christ finally appears, accompanied by Saint Joseph, David, and other Old Testament patriarchs and prophets.[36] The Virgin asks:

> Desseado mío, ¿quién puso estas rosas tan graciosas en estas manos sagradas? ¿Quién açucenas tan olorosas puso en tan hermosos lugares? Tomásteslas vós porque érades delectable, hermoso, blanco y colorado para los pecadores y por mostraros a ellos suave, aunque para mí lastimado. (sig. b 6ʳ)

> (My beloved, who put these lovely roses in your sacred hands? Who put such fragrant lilies in such beautiful places? You took them for you were delectable, beautiful, white and red to sinners to whom you showed yourself gentle, though injured to me [152].)

The red wounds on Christ's white body have become a garden of red roses and white lilies, perhaps reflecting "My beloved is white and ruddy, chosen out of thousands" (Song of Songs 5:10). In any case, the comparison of Christ's wounds to roses is traditional[37] and accords well with both the spring/morning motif associated with the Resurrection and the garden motif that will come to the fore in the evocation of Christ's encounter with Mary Magdalene.

The Virgin tells Christ of the grief of the Magdalen and of the apostles, especially Peter and John. In the two long speeches that follow, first Christ and then María, echoing his words, note that Christ was abandoned by all with the exception of his mother. Only the Virgin Mary kept faith, believing firmly that he would rise again.[38] As Christ took human flesh and was enclosed in the Virgin's bosom so she was the ark that enclosed the last remnant of faith on earth. It is therefore necessary for all to take off the old garment of sin and to put on the new garment (154–156).

After an ecstatic prayer of praise to the Blessed Virgin, María turns to address Mary Magdalene, evoking her search for Christ after the angels told her he was not in the tomb. Thereupon María re-creates John 20:14–17, novelizing the episode in which the Magdalen takes Christ for a gardener. Speaking to Mary Magdalene, María develops an allegory of Christ's arrival with the hoe of penance in his hand. Sinners must take up the hoe of penance in order to uproot the weeds from the garden of the good conscience. Then, the garden must be watered with the jet of the fountain of conformity to God's will so that the beloved can rest in it:

> ¿Quién pues no se holgará de tener en sí un jardín fresco y hermoso adó su amado le recrehe y descanse con él? . . . Ay de nosotros que, porque no miramos esto, están secos nuestros vergeles y nacen las malas yervas en ellos. ¿Por

qué, pues, no consideraremos que tenemos por una hora la vida y que si dexa-
mos en nosotros las malas yervas para que hagan raízes y hábitos de mala
castumbre [*sic*], no las podremos después arrancar? Devríamos en est̃ mucho
mirar y que cuando las raízes son grandes, aunque algunas vezes se arranquen,
todavía queda algo d'ellas para bolver a caer y muy pocas vezes se arrancan de
todo. Y que tanbién las malas yervas no se secan ni se carcomescen tan presto
como las buenas. Esto, pues, nos espante y tanbién que cuando el Señor entra
en su jardín y coje para traer en su mano las hermosas rosas y flores, cuando
vee la mala yerva, córtala y échala fuera y no se le da nada que se pierda. (sig.
c 1ᵛ)

(Who, then, would not rejoice to have within a fresh, beautiful garden where
his Beloved could relax and rest with him? . . . Woe to us if we do not realize
that our gardens are dry and overgrown with weeds! Why, then, do we not
realize that we have but a single hour of life and if we leave untended the
weeds within, they will sink their roots and habits of bad behavior so deeply
we will not be able to pull them out later? We ought to ponder this carefully,
for when our roots are deep, even if they are pulled out at times, there always
remains a bit of them to take root again and they are very seldom completely
eradicated. Moreover, weeds do not wither nor are they eaten by insects as
quickly as good plants are. Let this observation shock us as well as the fact
that if the Lord sees a weed when He enters His garden to gather and carry
beautiful roses and flowers, He cuts it, throws it away, and does not care that
it is lost [159].)

Here, María re-creates a series of traditional images, one of which is
the notion of the soul as a garden. Mary Giles (88) connects this image
with a passage from *The Dialogue* of Catherine of Siena:

Each of you has your own vineyard, your soul, in which your free will is the
appointed worker during this life. Once the time of your life has passed, your
will can work neither for good nor for evil; but while you live it can till the
vineyard of your soul where I have placed it. This tiller of your soul has been
given such power that neither the devil nor any other creature can steal it
without the will's consent, for in holy baptism the will was armed with a knife
that is love of virtue and hatred of sin.[39]

Even closer to María's version of the allegory is a passage from one of
Catherine of Siena's letters in which sinners are to prune vice from the soul
with the knife of penitence that Christ gives them in confession.[40]

The allegorical garden was an exegetical commonplace in the interpretation of John 20:14–17. Saint Augustine's *Homilies on the Gospel of St.
John* remark of the Magdalen that "Jesus was giving a lesson in faith to the
woman, who had recognized Him as her Master, and called Him so in her

reply; and this gardener was sowing in her heart, as in His own garden, the grain of mustard seed."[41] Gregory the Great asks: "Was he not spiritually a gardener for her, when he planted the fruitful seeds of virtue in her heart by the force of his love?"[42] In Odo of Cluny's sermon for the Feast of Mary Magdalene, just as it is the gardener's task to pull out the weeds in order that the desirable plants can thrive, so Christ seeks to eradicate the vices from the garden of the Church in order for the virtues to flourish.[43] In a sermon informed by floral symbolism, Guerric of Igny connects the Magdalen with the image of Christ as the true gardener who cultivates the garden of the world.[44] María was obviously fond of the garden allegory, for variants of it reappear frequently in her manuscript *Revelations*.[45] Although the image is traditional, perhaps María's peasant origins and her ministry in rural Spain made it a particularly appropriate image.[46]

In the concluding section of María's re-creation of Christ's appearance to Mary Magdalene, the image of ridding the garden of weeds leads to that of cleansing the soul of all dross and rot. Just as Christ did not want the Magdalen to touch him, but nonetheless approached her, so the creature alone does not have sufficient strength to reject what separates it from Christ; it must of necessity require the help of its Creator. When the soul feels disconsolate, it should wait for its Savior to come to it, and if it feels itself growing cool and separated from Christ, it should run in its heart to search for him as did his two beloved disciples (161–162). At this point, the spiritual interpretation of Christ's appearances after the Resurrection gives way once again to novelistic re-creation, this time of the episode of John and Peter vying with one another to arrive first at the sepulcher (John 20:2–4). John arrives first, but waits to allow Peter to enter before him, since Peter is his elder.[47] When Christ appears to them, they fall at his feet, not daring to look him in the eye. John laments that, although Christ entrusted his mother to his care, he "fell asleep in the dream of death" (163). In a lengthy speech Peter expresses his guilt at having denied his Lord, but Christ forgives both apostles and raises them up.

María then addresses Mary Magdalene again to console her because her testimony regarding the Resurrection was not believed. Thereupon, the vision closes with an extended exhortation that sums up the main spiritual themes it has presented. Sinners are urged to repent and to embrace the crucified Christ, making certain that their garden is well kept and that the jet of the fountain of their will conforms to his will. The vision ends, as it began, with a prayer. María switches to the first person and asks the Father to grant her "that wisdom and those tears you bestowed on your precious Magdalen" (168). Finally, she asks the Virgin Mary to be a mother to sinners as she was a mother to Christ.

Despite this seemingly positive ending that calls upon God and the Blessed Virgin to shed their divine favor upon humankind, for women in general and María in particular the latter part of the revelation is clouded by certain disturbing considerations on the question of feminine credibility. Specifically, María raises the issue of credibility when she evokes the fact that the apostles did not believe the Magdalen's testimony regarding the Resurrection. The point of departure for such considerations is, of course, the Bible. In Mark 16 the Marys are too afraid to obey the angel's order to spread the news of the Resurrection, but when Christ appears in person to Mary Magdalene, she goes to tell the news to the apostles. However, they do not believe her, nor do they believe the testimony of the two disciples who are walking in the country; the eleven apostles believe only when Christ himself appears to them, upbraiding them for their incredulity. In Luke 24 the holy women are similarly not believed when they announce the Resurrection to the disciples.[48] John 20 foregrounds Christ's appearance to Mary Magdalene, but makes no mention of the disciples not believing her. Although María's re-creation of Christ's appearance to Mary of Magdala relies heavily on John 20 with its gardener episode, she conflates that gospel with the others, at least as far as the motif of male incredulity is concerned.

The revelation first evokes the apostles' refusal to believe the Magdalen when, during María's re-creation of the events of Easter, Peter and John race to the Holy Sepulcher only to find it empty, and the holy women tell them that Christ is risen. Nonetheless, the disciples' joy is tempered by doubts that they will not be believed:

> ¿Cómo certificaremos a los de dura cerviz que El es ya fuera de sus manos? ¿Cómo, siendo ellos tan duros, seremos nosotros creídos, diziéndoles que lo sabemos (porque unas mujeres nos lo dixeron), si no tenemos para esto firmeza mayor de certificárgeles? (sig. c 3^{rv})

> (How will we assure the hard-headed ones that He is out of their hands? Since they are so obstinate, how will we be believed when we tell them that we are sure of it (because some women told us) unless we have firm proof? [163])

This means that the testimony of women, even of eyewitnesses, is considered of little value when it is a question of convincing the incredulous, and more specifically, the Jews ("los de dura cerviz"),[49] of the Resurrection. The issue of the value of feminine testimony is sidestepped, at least for the moment, when Christ appears to the two apostles (163), thus bolstering their credibility as males by making them in turn eyewitnesses to his Resurrection.

The same issue is raised soon afterward when María addresses Mary Magdalene, consoling her because her testimony was not believed:

¡O hermana! Y tú, ¿por qué te entristeces entre ellos, pues están todos alegres? ¿Entristéceste porque no te creyeron? Mira pues que aunque le vieron, no han de quedar con aquel crédito ellos. Tú te gozas de tu consolación con su vista (no te acordando del testimonio que es menester de cómo fue levantado) y ellos alégranse con El y con el amor que le tienen. Dessean mostrar y satisfazer a los otros cómo es Hijo de Dios y que por esso es levantado. No te entristezcas, pues que alguno de los suyos no te creerá ni aun creerá a los otros. Y conviene por esso que sea palpado y coma con ellos y por que los malignos no puedan dezir a los suyos: "Parecióos a vosotros que le vistes y no era El sino alguna fantasma." Por esso conviene ser d'ellos palpado y que coma con ellos y trate, porque comer y tener huessos todo junto no es cosa que pueda caber en fantasma. (sig. c 4^v)

(Oh sister, why do you become sad among them since they are all rejoicing? Are you sad because they did not believe you? Consider, then, that even though they saw Him, they are not going to be believed. You rejoice in the consolation of what you saw (not remembering the proof that is necessary of how He was raised from the dead), and they rejoice with Him and the love they bear Him. They long to prove to the others and satisfy them that He is the Son of God, and for that reason He is risen from the dead. Do not be sad, for one of His own will not believe you nor will he believe even the others.[50] Thus it is necessary for Him to eat with them and to be touched by them so that evil people cannot tell the others that He appeared only to you who saw Him and that it was but an apparition. That is why He must be touched by them and why He must eat with them and deal with them, because eating and also having flesh is not proper for a ghost [165–166].)

María admits that while men and women are equal with regard to their souls, man is nonetheless physically stronger, bodily strength being considered a sign of greater authority ("mayor testimonio"). Moreover, it is man's greater physical strength that, according to María, will enable the apostles to die as martyrs for Christ:

¿Y qué testimonio fuera para con estos endurecidos dezir "Levantado es," e diziendo ellos "¿Cómo lo sabéis?", ¿qué les respondieran? "Sabémoslo porque unas mujeres nos lo dixeron." Y aunque en los spíritus sean iguales la mujer y el varón, en lo natural es más fuerte el varón a la vista de los naturales. Y por esso para lo certificar a los otros y para osar morir ellos sobre ello, mayor testimonio era menester que verle levantado solamente mujeres. (sig. c 4ᵛ)

(What proof would it be for these obstinate ones to say "He is risen"? And if they asked "How do you know?" what would they [the apostles] say to them? "We know because some women told us." Even though men and women are equal in spirit, in the eyes of humans man is stronger in the sense of nature. Therefore, in order to prove this to others and for them to dare die for it, stronger proof was needed than the statement of women that they had seen Him risen [166].)

Insofar as "martyr" comes from the Greek word for "witness," the apostles' ultimate testimony will be manifested when their stronger bodies endure the torments of martyrdom as public witnesses for Christ. While María demonstrates here an awareness of the problematic nature of female testimony, she nonetheless once again sidesteps the issue in two ways. First, she fails to bring up the question of female martyrdom, presumably because, according to her own criterion, women are excluded from the glory of martyrdom by virtue of their inferior physical strength. Perhaps this silence is actually a strategic ploy intended to call into play her readers' presumed familiarity with cases of female martyrdom, which, in turn, will lead them to call into question the presumed inferiority of women as witnesses in all senses. Second, María observes that in the near future Christ's public and dramatic Ascension will resolve the problem of incredulity independently of the question of the gender of its witnesses:

Y aun tanbién cuando huviere de subir a su reino, no irá por esto secretamente ni a vista de pocos. Porque es tanta la malignidad y dureza de la corrupción del pecado y desobediencia que dirían: "Por aí se quedó entre los hombres como cosa de poca fuerça y muy tierna para con ellos." Irá por ende para entonces con gran seguridad de muy gran espacio a vista y en presencia de todos, viéndolo El e mirándolo todos ellos. No te entristezcas pues que tus hermanos no miran a solo su plazer como tú, mas junto con su plazer miran a ser certificados del secreto de la verdad para lo poder osadamente afirmar por el provecho de todos y para mayor confusión y vergüença de los de la dura cerviz. Y es menester para los confundir muy averiguada probança en cosa que es tan contra sus voluntades y tan gran daño d'ellos. (sigs. c 4ᵛ–c 5ʳ)

(Also, even when He is to ascend to His kingdom, He will not go secretly or in the sight of only a few people, for wickedness and hardness of the corruption of sin and disobedience are so enormous that they would say He remained there among men as something of little matter and because He was very tender toward them. Therefore, He will leave this earth with all certainty and very slowly in the sight and presence of all, with His witnessing it and all of them watching Him. So do not be sad that your brothers consider only their pleasure, as do you, but together with their pleasure they also think about being proven right concerning the secret of the truth so that they can affirm it boldly for the benefit of all and the greater shame and confusion of those who are stubborn. In order to confuse them, it is necessary to have well-certified proof in this matter that goes against their will and works so much to their harm [166].)

It is tempting to read into María's sympathy toward the Magdalen and her cautious treatment of the problematic nature of female testimony a certain awareness of the parallels between the biblical figure and herself. Indeed, the Magdalen seems to have had a special meaning in María's life: the parish church in Aldeanueva was dedicated to Mary of Magdala, the convent founded for María was called Santa Cruz de la Magdalena, and all the *beatas* who lived there took the name Mary in honor of the Magdalen.[51] Mary Magdalene was, a course, a female figure with a rich exegetical and iconographical tradition behind her, as well as a saint of considerable popular appeal. In an effort to accentuate the dramatic nature of her repentance, pious tradition—with no scriptural precedent—made Mary Magdalene a prostitute before her conversion. Pious tradition also identified her with the unnamed sinful woman in Luke 7:37–39 who washes Christ's feet with her tears, dries them with her hair, and anoints them with precious ointment. Iconographically, the Magdalen was depicted with flowing red hair and exaggerated gestures. Margaret R. Miles sees the Magdalen as a sort of extravagant counterpart to the Blessed Virgin. Her "uninhibited and histrionic gestures provided both the perfect foil for the dignified restraint of the Virgin and a model with whom most people could readily identify." Since the Virgin "could not represent shame and sorrow over sinfulness," nor "was she capable of the extreme gratitude of the forgiven sinner," the Magdalen's "emotional repertoire was much broader than the Virgin's." She was thus a more accessible model with which to identify:

> Mary Magdalene, the sinful woman, the sexual woman, is singularly loved by Christ, and so every sinner can hope for a similar forgiveness and acceptance. Moreover, her conversion does not require a change of personality. Mary Magdalene is quite as flamboyant, uninhibited, and sensual—though not sexual—as a great saint as she had been as a great sinner.[52]

"Flamboyant" and "histrionic" are adjectives that could be applied as well to María de Santo Domingo, for it was those very qualities that both antagonized her critics and assimilated her to Mary Magdalene. As prophetess, Mary of Magdala prophesied the Ascension;[53] María de Santo Domingo's celebrity was due, in part, to her prophecies.[54] Simon the Pharisee criticized the familiarity of Christ and the Magdalen (Luke 7:39); María was criticized for her excessive familiarity with male clerics. Mary Magdalene ultimately performed a male role, first as "apostle to the apostles"[55] (when she announced the news of the Resurrection), and then, as a missionary (when she preached in Marseilles).[56] Similarly, María was accused of performing priestly tasks unsuitable to her female status. Specifically, she was said to have heard confessions—albeit not *sacramentaliter*—and to have preached.[57] In addition, María's involvement in the reform of the order was highly irregular, especially because of her female gender.[58] As Bilinkoff observes:

> In general the opponents of María de Santo Domingo objected to the unrestrained, indecorous and highly public nature of her behavior. Her dramatic, some would say, theatrical raptures and strange prophecies created controversy and dissention. Many saw this young woman who let her hair grow long, wore jewelry and danced in churches as an exhibitionist. Her nights alone with her confessor and public sermons seemed to challenge the accepted role of religious women as humble, discreet and obedient.[59]

Mary Magdalene was not believed when she sought to disseminate the good news of the Resurrection. For her part, María claimed to have seen Christ, to have spoken to him, and to have received messages from him. Yet, some refused to believe her and sought to discredit her testimony. If the efforts to undermine her credibility were not overtly directed at her female status, that was the case indirectly when her critics attacked her lifestyle by impugning her sexual purity. As Bilinkoff observes: "Even her supporters admitted that María frequently kept the company of friars, without female escort. She maintained a particularly close, some felt, unhealthy, relationship with her confessor Diego de Vitoria."[60] The accusation that she wore fine clothing went beyond the question of donning the appropriate religious habit to evoke patristic injunctions against female finery and its concomitant enhancement of woman's powers of seduction. María wore her hair in long tresses, which, as Bilinkoff observes, were regarded "as a sign of women's beauty and seductive power in the Christian tradition since St. Paul composed his letters."[61] In short, the criticisms of María's life-style both invoked misogynist commonplaces and called attention to the parallel with the Magdalen.

Obviously, neither the Bible nor María denies the authenticity of Mary

Magdalene's testimony; when María raises the problem of credibility, she is more likely than not reflecting her own issues. The Magdalen was not believed until her testimony was corroborated by men, who then became the vehicle of its dissemination. Similarly, María was not believed until the authenticity of her experiences was investigated and sanctioned by male clerics. Moreover, the public dissemination of María's messages was the work of males: her confessor wrote down her revelations and the *Libro de la oración* was compiled and edited by a man.

Nonetheless, the parallel with Mary of Magdala is ultimately made to serve María's cause. By casting her detractors in the role of the incredulous Jews, not unlike those who refused to acknowledge the Resurrection, María in a sense blackmails her critics into abandoning their incredulity in order to avoid that unflattering characterization. In the context of early sixteenth-century Spain, the casting of a detractor in the role of an unbelieving Jew took on very specific connotations. The presence of large numbers of converted Jews (*conversos*) and their descendants and the concomitant social tension between such New Christians, as they were called, and the Old Christian majority made the Jewish label a particularly strong social stigma. In this, María shares the prejudices of her social class, for as the daughter of peasants, she could be sure of her own Old Christian status, with no taint of Jewish (or Moorish) blood. She had already acted as a spokesperson for that Old Christian majority when, according to some witnesses, she had to leave Toledo for slandering certain *conversos*. Her Old Christian ancestry might also be a factor in her choice of images based on peasant life, for only Old Christians tilled the soil. The anti-Jewish, that is, anti-*converso* strategy has a significant link with Mary Magdalene, for medieval commentators interpreted the Magdalen as a figure of the gentiles or of the Church, that is, of true believers.[62] In a Spanish context, Mary of Magdala was at once a figure of the gentiles and a sort of figure of their alleged descendants, the Old Christians.

This sociological dimension did not go unnoticed by María's editor, who appropriates it in turn to defend her. In his prologue, the editor suggests that the wound in her side is the result of her detractors' "scorn and neglect of the shedding of the Creator's blood" and thus a sign of their "lack of zealousness" of faith (124). In addition to associating María's critics with Christ's persecutors, that is, with the Jews, the editor also suggests that María has suffered an unjust persecution not unlike her Savior's. The editor reiterates this notion later in his biography and defense of María, when he compares her persecutors to those of Christ, even to the extent that as Christ suffered at the hands of the Jews, so María was persecuted by those "of the lineage of Our Lord," that is to say, by Christians descended from converted Jews, as well as by those of scant prudence and reason (131–132). Thus, both the *Libro de la oración*'s prefatory materials and its first vision exploit the social tensions of early sixteenth-century Spain in order to control the reception of the book and, concretely, to assure a favorable acceptance by readers loathe to be associated with the Jews/*conversos*.

The sociological blackmail of the reader is not the only way in which the liminal vision of the *Libro de la oración* is used to shield María's revelations against her critics. Biblical commentators stress that Mary Magdalene was the first person to whom Christ appeared after the Resurrection, a privilege admitted even by authors who, in contradiction, include the alleged first appearance to his mother.[63] Scriptural exegesis interpreted Christ's initial revelation to women after his Resurrection as an instance of his privileging of the female sex.[64] Moreover, in the Resurrection episode in the Scriptures, Mary of Magdala replaces the Virgin Mary as a foil to Eve, that is, she becomes the female figure that in some way repairs the damage done by the first woman.[65] For example, Gregory the Great writes:

> In paradise a woman was the cause of death for a man; coming from the sepulchre a woman proclaimed life to men. Mary related the words of the one who restored her to life; Eve had related the words of the serpent who brought death.[66]

Odo of Cluny repeats the same notion,[67] and then adds that Mary Magdalene removed the opprobrium that Eve had brought upon the female sex.[68] The Bible points out—and commentators call attention to the fact—that Christ was abandoned by his disciples, while the holy women stood watch at the cross and then came to anoint his body with precious spices.[69] As Bilinkoff observes, in the face of masculine incredulity and feminine faith, it is no surprise "that God would choose women, his unwavering and unquestioning servants, to serve as his messengers."[70] Thus, Christ's appearance to Mary Magdalene can be interpreted as the validation of woman as the medium of divine messages.[71] In his appearances to the holy women after the Resurrection, Christ repairs the damage done by Eve, redeeming woman in her role as messenger.[72] This has important consequences for María's re-creation of Mary Magdalene's role in the events of the Resurrection: in evoking the biblical episode, María validates her own role as messenger.

The editor has chosen to begin the *Libro de la oración* with a strategic text, namely, a divine message about the reception and dissemination of divine messages. The liminal revelation thus seeks to control the readers' reception of the book by incorporating the re-creation of a biblical story that foregrounds the question of belief and credibility. Thus, María's initial message is a self-conscious text to the extent that it contains instructions on how to read and receive her messages. María's readers must not behave like the incredulous apostles whose disbelief was ultimately reprimanded by Christ, nor must they behave like the incredulous Jews who refused to believe, lest they be taken for New Christians who betray their Jewish ancestry by doubting the authenticity of María's messages. Rather, as Christ redeemed womankind in Mary Magdalene by making her the vehicle of the reception and dissemination of the good news of his Resurrection, so he has chosen María de Santo Domingo to be the vehicle of the reception and dissemination of his latter-day messages.

5. Juana de la Cruz and the Secret Garden

Juana de la Cruz was born in 1481 to Catalina Gutiérrez and Juan Vázquez, farmers of modest means who lived in the small town of Azaña in
the archbishopric of Toledo. She began to have visions even in her cradle,
and those extraordinary religious experiences continued for the rest of her
life. Juana was precocious in her holiness and asceticism, and resolved at an
early age to become a nun. Nonetheless, her relatives were opposed to the
idea, for they had plans to marry her off. At the age of fifteen, Juana dis-
guised herself in male clothing, secretly left home, and made her way to the
convent of regular Franciscan tertiaries of Santa María de la Cruz in Cubas.
The abbess received her, and when Juana's relatives arrived, Juana asked
for their pardon, and they and the nuns negotiated the dowry necessary for
her entry into the order.[1]

As a nun, Juana distinguished herself for her harsh asceticism and her
mystical raptures. In 1509 she was elected abbess. Important personages
came to visit her, above all to hear the sermons she pronounced during her
mystical trances. So great was her renown that in 1512, a certain Franciscan
visionary, convinced that he was predestined to engender a sort of Messiah, wrote to Mother Juana, inviting her to be the mother of the future
prophet. A dutiful daughter of the Church, Juana refused to be swayed
by such a scandalous proposal and denounced the unfortunate friar to the
ecclesiastical authorities.[2]

Meanwhile, the archbishop of Toledo, Cardinal Cisneros, sought to
assure the economic well-being of the convent by permitting the parish
church of Cubas to be annexed to the convent. In orders written in March
and December of 1510, Cisneros determined that the nuns would acquire
the profits from the parish's property, and he empowered them to name
a chaplain to attend to the spiritual needs of the parishioners. The abbess
of Santa María de la Cruz, that is, a woman, thereby acquired the right to
exercise a spiritual jurisdiction.[3] Not everyone agreed with that arrange-

ment. After Cisneros's death in 1517, certain ecclesiastics tried to take the benefice of Cubas away from the convent, alleging that it was improper for women to hold such a position of authority. Ever concerned for the well-being of her convent, Mother Juana consulted other ecclesiastics, who advised her to secure a papal bull that would confirm the community's privileges. This she did, but then her enemy, the vicaress of the convent, denounced her to the superiors of the order for acting without their permission and for spending too much money to obtain the bull. As a result, Juana was removed as abbess, probably in 1527. In time, she was vindicated, for the vicaress fell gravely ill and confessed that she had accused Juana falsely. Juana was reinstated as abbess, occupying that post until her death in 1534.

Beginning in 1505, when Juana had mystical raptures, it was believed that the Holy Spirit spoke through her mouth in the person of Christ. This phenomenon lasted for thirteen years. Her sermons, as such locutions were called, would last as long as five or six hours, and those corresponding to the liturgical year 1508–1509 were written down by one of Juana's companions. The resulting volume, *El libro del conorte* [*The Book of Consolation*], is Juana's only extant work.[4]

Like most of the other sermons, the sermon for the Nativity of the Virgin is articulated in two parts. First, Juana presents a novelesque version of some episode of sacred history, here the birth and early childhood of the Virgin Mary. Second, Juana narrates the allegorical pageants that take place in heaven, here those performed in honor of Mary's Nativity. Each part of the sermon is accompanied by glosses, likewise uttered in the person of Christ, that purport to explain its meaning.

The sermon for the Nativity of the Virgin Mary opens with the evocation of that very event. The Lord says that when Mary was born, she went into a trance. Her spirit rose up to heaven where God the Father held it in his arms and the entire Trinity played with it. Meanwhile, Mary's relatives, contemplating her lifeless body, believed her dead and began to mourn. After three days God returned the soul to the body, and the baby began to suckle at her mother's breast.

From then on, angels often raised the newborn Mary in body and soul to heaven. Leaving her swaddling clothes behind in the cradle, the angels would offer the naked baby to the Father, who would take her in his arms and play with her very lovingly. Mary would contemplate the entire universe from the Father's arms and, seeing the seats left empty by the fallen angels, would inquire what had happened. The Father would answer that

those who occupied those places had fallen because of their pride and disobedience, but that thanks to her, the seats would once again be occupied.
The angels would then return Mary to her cradle, where Saint Anne would
find her daughter naked, her eyes raised to heaven in contemplation. As
many times as Saint Anne would swaddle Mary, the angels would uncover
her, saying:

> Descúbrete, niña, e no estés cubierta, que no tienes en todo tu cuerpo cosa
> que ayas menester cubrir, mas toda heres linpia e pura e fermosa e perfeta e
> acabada de ver e de mirar. (fol. 335ᵛ)

> (Show yourself, child, and don't be all covered up, for nowhere on your body
> do you have anything you need to cover; rather, you are all spotless and pure
> and lovely and perfect and consummate to see and to contemplate.)

Seeing how the angels would undress her, as Mary grew older she
acquired the habit of disrobing. Saint Anne was upset by her daughter's
strange behavior and was mortified at what people might think. Once,
Mary even stripped in front of everyone in the temple; Saint Anne covered
her with her own cloak, took her home, and gave her a beating. Even
punishment did not break the Virgin of this habit, which lasted until her
Presentation in the temple,[5] at which time the angel Gabriel appeared to
her and explained that it was the will of God that she no longer undress.
When Mary countered that she only stripped because the angels had un-
dressed her, Gabriel explained that such behavior was acceptable when she
was a child, but now that she was a grown woman, it was no longer right
to do so.[6]

The considerably longer second part of the sermon begins with an
elaborate allegorical pageant. God the Father has all the young girls of
twenty years or younger summoned and also the twelve tribes of Israel.
The maidens assemble, performing dances and playing instruments and
singing. God orders the girls separated into smaller bands, and suddenly
all are transformed into children.

Here begins a sort of beauty pageant. God orders a holy man or a king
from one of the twelve tribes to choose the most beautiful maiden from
one of the bands of girls. Meanwhile, the Father tells the Son to conceal
the Virgin Mary, similarly changed into a child, among the other children
in that band. Needless to say, the messenger chooses the Virgin as the most
beautiful, and brings her to the Father, who congratulates the holy man for
his wise choice. Then the Father chooses another emissary and sends him

to another band, and the same process is repeated with twelve thousand messengers, all of whom are of Our Lady's lineage.

In an interpolated gloss the Lord explains that the episode of the messengers signifies that Our Lady is the most lovely and pure and perfect of all the virgins. The angels and heavenly elect take greater delight in looking upon her than upon anyone else except God himself. Even sinners, hearing of her miracles and her advocacy for humankind, become her devotees and seek to know and serve her.

The holy virgins transformed into children continue to sing and dance before the throne of God, who then orders them to offer him their crowns. The Father receives the crowns, noting how sweet smelling they are and stating that they represent the virgins' good works and virtues and love (fol. 336ᵛ). Speaking to the Son, the Father expresses his desire for the Virgin to dance. The Son answers: "Let her dance!" and the Holy Spirit likewise says: "Let her dance!" Then the entire Trinity commands the Virgin to dance naked as she was born. With great humility Mary answers:

> Señor Padre mío e Dios mío todopoderoso, a mí me plaze de salir no solamente desnuda a bailar delante todos los çelestiales mas aun estoy aparejada a obedesçer si me mandare vuestra magestad ir agora al mundo e andar entre todas las gentes así desnuda como nasçí. Aunque según mi ençerramiento e onestidad e vergüença se me faría algo de pena, pero, Señor Dios mío, heme aquí a mí, vuestra sierva. Cúnplase e sea fecha en mí vuestra santa voluntad. (fols. 336ᵛ–337ʳ)
>
> (My Lord Father and my almighty God, it pleases me to dance naked not only before all the inhabitants of heaven, but I am even disposed to obey if your majesty ordered me to go now to the earth and to walk among all people as naked as I was born. Although in accordance with my reclusion and honor and modesty it would somewhat pain me, nonetheless, my Lord God, behold me, your servant. So be it and may your holy will be accomplished and done to me.[7])

And so the Virgin, transformed into a naked little girl, begins to dance.[8] As she dances, her breasts begin to grow little by little. Struck by Mary's beauty, the Father remarks to the Son that, even though his mother is but a child, she has such pretty white breasts. The Father speaks to Mary, saying: "Climb up here, my beloved daughter, and give me your breasts, for you are lovely and more perfect than all the daughters of Sion and Jerusalem."[9] Extending his little finger, he draws her up to him and encloses her in himself. Mary is immediately richly dressed and adorned.

In the gloss interpolated at this point in the narrative, the Lord explains that Mary's nudity signifies that she was bare of all vices and sins, both mortal and venial, present and original. The early development of her breasts signifies that from the time she was born she had breasts of good desires and great love for her God and Creator.

The narrative resumes with Our Lady in the arms of the Father. She is dressed with more precious garments and adornments than those of any of the other virgins. The Father again orders her to dance and to offer him some special gift. Mary begins to dance, and the Father extols her beauty, praising her physical charms one by one: feet, body, breasts, throat, mouth, teeth, and eyes.

In a gloss God explains that when Our Lady was more richly adorned than the other virgins, it meant that, just as she was more bare of sins than the others, so she is more adorned with virtues and grace.

God then invites Mary to offer him some special gift, but she answers that she has nothing to give him. The Virgin then picks up a palm frond covered with golden leaves and golden apples. Among the leaves are roses and lilies, and there is a consecrated host in each rose. Mary presents this gift and sacrifice to the Father.

In a gloss the Lord explains that the palm branch represents the Church, the golden leaves signify altars and their ornaments, the apples denote the Christian people, and the flowers[10] represent priests (who are closer to the Eucharist than are other people and must therefore be more pure and fragrant with virtues). Our Lady offers this gift not only on the feast of her holy Nativity, but every single day as well.

The Father then asks Mary why she offers him naked hosts instead of the crowns and jewels that the other virgins presented to him. Mary answers that she could find no more suitable gift than his precious Son, who is he himself. Since Christ suffered naked on the cross to redeem humankind, so now she offers God naked hosts in order that he will have mercy on sinners. The Father remarks that, although Mary is but a little girl, she is nonetheless concerned about sinners. However, he tells her to forget about the sinners for the moment, saying: "Give me your breasts, for I wish to play with them."[11] The Virgin answers that it is sinners she wants, for she is constantly concerned about them. She asks God to receive this gift of hosts, the sacrifice she offers him for the salvation of the entire Church Militant and for all its priests and clergy. Then she will give him her breasts. When the Father answers that he wants them right away, Our Lady refuses, for she must not give them to him in public. Let them go to the flowery garden, she suggests, where there are pomegranates and olives; there in secret she will give her breasts to him.

Then the Father takes the consecrated hosts in his hands, and suddenly, they become a single host, signifying that, although the same Lord is consecrated in many hosts in many places, it is still one God that is everywhere. The Father observes that the Son is already in the host; therefore, let the Son be in the Father and the Father in the Son and the Son in the host; let the entire Trinity exist in one divinity and one being and one substance. Suddenly, the host is enclosed in the bosom of the Father, and the Holy Trinity is manifested in one majesty and one God and one power and one wisdom and one substance and one divine essence. And the entire Trinity holds the Virgin Mary in its arms and encloses her in its royal throne, where it crowns and adorns and plays with her as its beloved daughter and revered mother and most pure spouse.

A gloss explains that the Virgin's consenting to give the Father her breasts only in a secret place signifies that when she lived on earth, she publicly performed works of charity and gave a good example, but that the deep contemplations and the burning love that she bore her Lord were manifested only in the secret garden of her heart and soul. This is a model for us that our inner love and devotion should be greater than that which we manifest on the exterior. When we pray or perform some act of charity, we should do so in secret where no one can see us.

As Our Lady is enclosed in the throne of the Holy Trinity, the Father takes off his bejeweled mantle and covers her with it, signifying that when she conceived the Redeemer, the power and fortitude and clarity of the Father and the Son—that is, the Holy Spirit, which proceeds from the Father and the Son—covered and surrounded her. When the Son took human flesh from her virginal belly, hiding his divinity with it, Mary surrounded the entire Trinity with her belly as with a precious mantle. For this reason, the Lord explains, in the kingdom of heaven Mary is called "mantle and covering of God" because her precious humanity covered the powerful divinity of God.

When Our Lady is thus covered with the Father's mantle, the Holy Trinity tells her to go enjoy herself with all her relatives in the heavenly kingdom so that they will know how much the Deity loves her and recognize that she is queen of heaven and earth. And so Our Lady promenades through the kingdom of heaven, and since she is still transformed into a little girl and the mantle is so large, the garment stretches over ten thousand leagues. When the seraphim try to carry her, she refuses. A gloss makes it clear that this is due to her great humility. When the holy virgins offer to carry the skirt of her mantle, she once again refuses, addressing them with a stern countenance. A gloss explains that sometimes Our Lady speaks sternly to her devotees so that they will repent of their sins and serve God.

The vision ends when suddenly a band of thieves appears and tries to steal the Virgin's mantle; others defend Mary against those who seek to despoil her. In a gloss the Lord explains that the thieves represent the heretics, who attempt to rob Our Lady of the mantle of her virginity and purity. Those who defended her are Christians and preachers and learned men, who defend her when they praise her in their sermons and disputations. As the sermon draws to a close, a gloss recalls the episode in Mary's infancy when the angels would undress her, since she had nothing to hide, while Saint Anne and the other relatives would cover her up.

Startling as this vision may appear to modern readers, many of its individual elements are traditional. As in the case of her other sermons, Mother Juana draws on a wide variety of biblical and iconographic motifs, interweaving them as if by free association. The vision inspired by Mary's Nativity rewrites the biblical episode of the Fall, incorporating significant reminiscences of the Song of Songs. It also draws on the Double Intercession and other iconographic motifs.

The sermon for the Nativity of the Virgin concentrates on the notion of Mary as advocate for humankind and on the role that Mary's body plays in that intercession.[12] Indeed, the key episode in the vision is the scene in which the Virgin offers the Father the palm frond. On one hand, to the extent that Mary is the Second Eve, the episode rewrites the core event of the Fall as recounted in Genesis.[13] Eve offered Adam the apple and, in so doing, brought sin into the world. The Second Eve presents apples and flowers to the Father, symbolizing her virginal maternity and her advocacy of sinners: not only does Mary participate in the Redemption by giving birth to the Savior, but she continues to intercede daily for the salvation of sinners.[14] Indeed, the Virgin's mediating role was a source of considerable power. Juana herself, in her sermon for the dedication of a church, goes so far as to say that no one, no matter how virtuous a life he or she may have lived, can enter the kingdom of heaven without the intercession of the Blessed Virgin.[15]

In the scene in which Mary offers hosts to the Father, Juana's sermon establishes a symbolic equivalence between the Virgin's divine maternity and the priest's consecration of the sacred host. While the roses and lilies that contain the hosts are explicitly said to represent priests, the association between the Blessed Virgin and those flowers was so frequent that contemporary audiences could not fail to make the connection.[16] Thus, the roses and lilies that enclose the hosts are also the Blessed Virgin who enclosed Christ in her womb.[17] Although the gloss attached to the scene extols the priest who is closer to the Eucharist than anyone else, the symbolic action that the Virgin performs is for all practical purposes a priestly role, since she offers the hosts as a sacrifice (*sacrificio*) to the Father. The relation between the Virgin's role as Mother of God and the consecrated hosts is traditional, for scriptural commentators connected the Eucharist with the fruit of Mary's womb. Jean Gerson calls the Virgin "Mother of the Eucharist."[18] Richard of Saint Laurent speaks of Mary's glorious fruit, that is, Christ, which we receive in the Eucharist. Moreover, it is the Virgin's flesh we receive in the Blessed Sacrament, for Christ and his mother share a single (human) flesh.[19] Likewise, Rupert of Deutz contrasts the lethal fruit that Adam obtained through Eve with the life-giving fruit (the Eucharist) that humankind obtained through Mary.[20] If on the one hand this sort of commentary served to polarize Eve and the Second Eve, the contrast could also serve to redeem Eve and by extension all women. Thus, Saint Bernard observes that before God redeemed humankind, he deposited the entire price of redemption in Mary so that Eve could be rehabilitated through her daughter. Adam could no longer complain that the woman God had given to him gave him of the tree (Genesis 3:12); rather, he should say that the woman God had given to him fed him with a blessed fruit.[21]

Isaiah 11:1 ("And there shall come forth a rod out of the root of Jesse: and a flower shall rise up out of his root") was traditionally interpreted as referring to Christ's birth from the Virgin Mary. Particular significance was attached to the pun on *virga* ("rod") and *virgo* ("virgin"). Perhaps Juana's vision alludes to Isaiah 11:1 when the Virgin offers the palm branch, a sort of *virga*, that produces the flowers that contain the hosts, that is, Christ. An allusion to that biblical verse would be especially appropriate in the context of a vision that highlights the Virgin's role as advocate, for such medieval commentators as Richard of Saint Laurent relate Isaiah 11:1 to the Virgin's role as intercessor for humankind.[22]

The presence of the palm frond as a symbolic representation of the virginal body that produced the fruit of Christ calls attention to Mary's role in the redemption of humankind. Elsewhere, the vision focuses on a specific part of the Virgin's body, her breasts. While Juana's vision highlights Mary's adolescent breasts, they are nonetheless the same breasts that will later nurse Christ and are therefore the signifiers of a series of highly charged symbolic meanings. First and foremost, the Virgin's breasts were associated with her role as maternal advocate for humankind. According to Richard of Saint Laurent, the Virgin has both *ubera* and *mammae* because she is both virgin and mother,[23] the *ubera* and *mammae* symbolizing her "pietas et misericordia" ("pity and mercy") toward sinners.[24]

Richard of Saint Laurent establishes a connection between the milk of the Virgin's breasts and the blood that Christ shed for sinners: the milk that Christ suckled at the Virgin's breast was transformed into the blood he shed as the price of our Redemption.[25] This equivalence is particularly appropriate because medieval medical treatises viewed a mother's milk as modified menstrual blood.[26] Thus, popular scientific beliefs reinforced the link between the blood of Christ's redeeming humanity and the milk of his human mother, whose divine maternity made the Redemption possible.[27] Later, when Richard of Saint Laurent interprets the Song of Songs 7:8 ("I said: I will go up into the palm tree, and will take hold of the fruit thereof, and thy breasts shall be as the clusters of the vine, and the odor of thy mouth like apples"), the palm tree represents the cross of the Crucifixion, the fruit is the Redemption, and the breasts evoke the milk that Christ suckled at his mother's breast and therefore the human flesh that he received from her.[28] Thus, the scene in which Mary offers the Father the symbolic palm branch appears to be a reworking of the Song of Songs 7:8, for the fruit, the palm, and the breasts are common to both texts. In Juana's vision the Eucharistic hosts (the fruit) are explicitly connected with the naked Christ's death on the cross. However, in that vision it is not Christ who offers himself, but his mother who symbolically offers him in the form of hosts as a sacrifice to the Father. The fact that the Father makes reiterated references to the Virgin's breasts in this episode calls attention to her role as the person from whom Christ received his human flesh that would later shed blood, suffering the Passion that the Eucharist commemorates.

The spiritual implications of the Virgin's breasts inspired a number of iconographic and devotional motifs in the Middle Ages, motifs that highlight the notion of Mary's intercession for humankind. In representations of the Double Intercession, Christ shows his wounds to the Father, while the Blessed Virgin exhorts her son to intercede for sinners, showing him the breast with which she nursed him.[29] In the later Middle Ages the motif is disseminated in such popular works of spirituality as the *Golden Legend* and the *Speculum humanae salvationis*. At the end of the chapter of the *Golden Legend* devoted to the Ascension, Jacobus de Voragine, following Saint Bernard,[30] writes:

O man, you have sure access to God, when the mother stands before the Son and the Son stands before the Father, the mother shows her Son her bosom and her breasts, the Son shows his Father his side and his wounds.[31]

In turn, the *Speculum humanae salvationis*, emphasizing the Virgin's role as mediator, says: "Let us hear how Christ shows his wounds to the Father for us, and Mary shows her son her breast and nipples."[32] Then, the text explains that, since Christ and Mary love one another so much, Christ cannot deny his mother anything: "How could such a son deny anything to such a mother, for they love one another as they love themselves?"[33]

The Double Intercession was also popularized through the pictorial arts. The rationale behind the motif is made explicit in a miniature from the book of hours (ca. 1440) of Catherine of Cleves. A figure representing Catherine herself asks the Virgin to pray for her ("Pray for me, holy Mother of God"). The Virgin, displaying her breast, says to the crucified Christ: "On account of the breasts that suckled you, may you be favorable to her." Christ addresses the Father, saying: "Father, on account of my wounds, spare her," while the Father answers: "Son, your petition is heard."[34] The miniature graphically depicts the chain of advocates that constitutes the motif of the Double Intercession: the sinner does not address the Father directly but instead approaches him through a series of intermediaries. First, the pious soul seeks the aid of the Virgin Mary. Then, Mary, displaying her maternal breast, asks for her son's help. Finally, Christ, showing his wounds, intercedes before the Father, who then grants the petition.[35]

Another work that depicts the Double Intercession is a Florentine painting from the beginning of the fifteenth century. Here, Christ points at the wound in his side, while the Virgin, who kneels beside him, uncovers her breast and begs her son to intercede in favor of eight suppliants whom she presents to him.[36] A curious aspect of this painting can be related to the Mary-Eve connection discussed above. The work depicts the Virgin not merely uncovering her breast but holding it in her hand and extending it as if it were a disembodied object. Now at first glance that object looks strangely like an apple, and the gesture the Virgin executes recalls that of Eve extending the apple to Adam. The apple-breast equivalence is traditional, and in the Christian tradition dates back at least to Isidore of Seville.[37] What is significant here is the theological point that if the Virgin is the New Eve then the similarity of gestures recalls the relation between Eve's offering of the apple, which brought sin into the world, and Mary's offering of her breast, by which she intercedes for sinners and thereby undoes the harm caused by Eve.

Millard Meiss relates the Double Intercession to another iconographic motif, the *Madonna del Latte* or the *Madonna dell'Umiltà*, which portrays the Virgin with one bare breast suckling the Child. For Meiss, representations of the nursing Madonna are intended to convey the message of her power to intercede and protect.[38] While Margaret R. Miles attributes the appeal of that motif partially to sociological factors,[39] she also calls attention to the artistic trend of "portraying scriptural figures as humble people with strong feelings," the bare-breasted Virgin representing "perhaps the furthest extension of homey simplicity and unpretentious accessibility" (202). Miles asks: "If the Virgin gained cosmic power by nursing her son, what was to prevent actual women from recognizing their power, derived from the same source, and irresistible to their adult sons?" This means that women

> must be guided to accept the model of the nursing Virgin without identifying with her power—a power derived from her body, but ultimately a social as well as a physical power. . . . There is, however, little evidence that women identified with the Virgin's power. A delicate message of social control was communicated, apparently effectively, by the creation of a dissonance between verbal messages and visual messages: the latter emphasized the *similarity* of the Virgin and actual women, but it was the *contrast* between actual women and the Virgin that was prominent in the messages conveyed by late medieval and early Renaissance preachers, theologians, and popular devotional texts. (205)

In the light of such comments it is possible to view Juana's sermon as involving a similar interplay of power and control. If on the one hand the vision emphasizes the Virgin's power as an advocate for sinners, a power symbolized by her maternal breast, on the other hand it calls attention to the Virgin's otherness. Indeed, the vision concentrates on Mary's uniqueness, even among virgins. If Mary is greater and more beautiful than any of the other celestial virgins, then surely she is greater than any mortal woman. The Virgin is both similar and different; she is simultaneously accessible and unapproachable.[40] Nonetheless, as we shall see, it appears that Juana herself identifies with Mary's power and uses Mary's uniqueness among women to her own advantage.

If in Juana's vision the Virgin reinforces her role as the Second Eve by offering apples, her nudity is yet another possible connection with Genesis, for surely the *locus classicus* for nudity in the Bible is the episode of the Fall in which Adam and Eve, having sinned, become aware of their own nakedness and cover their bodies with aprons of fig leaves (Genesis 3:7).

Miles, apropos of Ambrose's commentary on Genesis, observes that the clothing of Adam and Eve "marks their existence in a newly sinful condition."[41] Before the Fall, nakedness symbolized Adam and Eve's primal innocence; after the Fall, "Adam and Eve experienced nakedness as shame" (92). Lastly, since Eve's subordination to Adam occurred simultaneously with the first clothing, "clothing symbolizes Eve's subjection to Adam" (93). In Juana's vision the Virgin's nudity is explicitly connected with her innocence and purity, for as the angels explain when they undress her, she quite literally has nothing to hide. If nudity symbolizes independence, then Mary's nudity suggests that she is subject to no man. Moreover, if clothing equals submission, then nakedness equals power. The vision thus links the Virgin's nude body to her powers as an advocate for humankind.

The connection between the first transgression and Adam and Eve's awareness of their nakedness inspired some biblical commentators to interpret the Fall in sexual terms. John A. Phillips observes:

> In this interpretation, the eating of the forbidden fruit becomes a euphemism for sexual congress between Eve and the snake, or between Eve and her husband; or the eating of the forbidden fruit imparts to Eve a sexual consciousness that leads her to seduce her husband.[42]

Saint Augustine establishes an explicit connection between the sexual nature of the Fall and Adam and Eve's perception of their nakedness, for

> sensual desire arose in the disobedient bodies of the first human beings as a result of the sin of disobedience . . . they opened their eyes to their own nakedness, that is, they observed it with anxious curiosity . . . they covered up their shameful parts because an excitement, which resisted voluntary control, made them ashamed.[43]

I do not believe it is an accident that in the first part of Juana's vision Gabriel tells Mary that she can no longer go about naked precisely at the moment of her puberty. The moment of Mary's awakening sexuality, no matter how virginal it may be, nonetheless involves a prohibition that replays, in a new key, Adam and Eve's discovery of their sexuality. If Mary is the New Eve, then even she must cover up her body upon reaching puberty. However, unlike Eve with her fallen sexuality, Mary is perpetually virgin and divinely fruitful. The motif of nakedness thus ends up alluding to the ambiguous sexuality of Mary: she is both virgin and mother, both chaste and fertile.[44]

The topic of nudity poses the question of the interpretation of signs. Mary's nakedness means one thing for Saint Anne and society, another for the angels, another for the Blessed Virgin herself, and still another for the various audiences of the vision. Anne Hollander observes: "Breasts bring pleasure to everyone, and sight of them brings its own visual joy besides; and so images of breasts are always sure conveyers of a complex delight."[45] Iconic representations of the Double Intercession and representations of the Virgin nursing conventionally depict Mary with only one breast uncovered.[46] As Hollander has observed, until the late fifteenth century "single bare breasts were strictly maternal" (187). However, two uncovered breasts "have a slightly different pictorial message" (202). Indeed, severe moralists railed against fashions that left the female breasts exposed. For example, in one of his sermons, Saint Vincent Ferrer (d. 1419) states that women have breasts so that they can function as a *celler* ("wine cellar" or "pantry") for their suckling infants, and he goes on to condemn girls who expose their "lungs" to the birds of the air as if they were prostitutes.[47] Writing in 1477, Hernando de Talavera decried women so dissolute that their low-cut garments revealed not just the breasts, but even the belly.[48]

Although Mary's nursing of the Child Jesus is implicit in the very mention of her breasts, Juana's vision sidesteps that issue by casting the interceding Virgin as a *niña*. Mary is no ordinary little girl, however, for this *niña* has the developing breasts of an adolescent, thus combining the naked innocence of childhood and the sexual awakening of puberty. Indeed, Mary's exposed breasts, the potentially erotic connotations of her naked dance, and her teasing refusals to offer her breasts in order to get what she wants all suggest at the very least a nubile woman and perhaps even a prostitute. The paradox of Mary as little girl, divine mother, and divine prostitute all at once means that sexuality is both asserted and negated. Mary's naked body, that is, her very human sexuality, becomes the source of her power to save souls. This is a dangerous game, however, for it suggests that if Mary uses her powers of seduction to get what she wants, then she is like Eve, whose sinfulness a tradition of misogyny codified. A sexual Mary conforms to negative stereotypes of female behavior; she becomes less unique and more like all other women. Ultimately, the coexistence of purity and sexuality, an impossible combination for an earthly woman, turns out to be possible for that most unique of women, the Virgin Mary.

Juana's complex message of Marian intercession, illustrating just how far the Virgin is willing to go in order to save souls, can be fully communicated only if the vision's eroticism is acknowledged. Nonetheless, this superficial eroticism, perhaps startling to modern readers, does not appear to have been perceived as unusual by readers chronologically closer to Mother Juana. Shortly after Juana's death, a certain Ortiz wrote a series of annotations, mostly approving, in the margins of the Escorial manuscript of *El libro del conorte*. Then, an anonymous inquisitorial censor, apparently a close relative of Mother Juana,[49] examined critically both the sermons and Ortiz's marginal glosses, crossing out the passages he deemed objectionable. Finally, in 1567–1568 Francisco de Torres filled the margins of the Escorial manuscript with annotations intended to defend both Juana's orthodoxy and her status as a female visionary.[50] Although the inquisitorial censor objected to the novelized account of the Virgin's infancy that opens the vision, he did not cross out any of the passages that refer to the Virgin's breasts or to her dancing nude. For his part, Father Torres merely observed that the episode in which the Virgin offers her breasts to the Father is a calque of the Song of Songs, and he gave an approving nod to Mary's wish to accomplish that action in private, rather than in public.[51] He went on to remark that it is surely a manifestation of God's power that an unlettered woman (Juana) should be privy to such truths regarding the Eucharist and the Trinity.[52] Perhaps that should come as no surprise, Torres observes, since the Virgin herself, even as an infant, knew more than the apostles.[53]

Needless to say, the erotically charged atmosphere of Juana's vision, made explicit by the Virgin's exposed adolescent breasts, is at odds with the traditional characterization of the Mother of God. However, one place where the Virgin and a highly allegorized eroticism intersected was interpretations of the Song of Songs that identified the bride with Mary.[54] It is thus no surprise that the Song of Songs is a significant intertext for Juana's vision.[55] I have already commented on the possible relation between the palm frond and Song of Songs 7:8, but that is not the only connection between Juana's vision and that book of the Bible. The motif of a woman offering her breasts in a secluded place is found in Songs of Songs 7:12: "Let us get up early to the vineyards, let us see if the vineyard flourish, if the flowers be ready to bring forth fruits, if the pomegranates flourish; there will I give thee my breasts." In both this passage from the Song of Songs and Juana's vision the secret garden is planted with pomegranates,[56] and in both texts the woman offers her breasts. Richard of Saint Laurent interprets Song of Songs 7:12 as demonstrating the Virgin's concern for the Church.[57] Specifically, "there will I give thee my breasts" is associated with the *interpellationes* ("appeals") that the Virgin offers for the Church, which are in turn connected with the pity and mercy that Richard has previously associated with the Virgin's breasts.[58] Which is to say, the exegesis of Song of Songs 7:12 connected the erotic offering of the breasts with the notion of the Virgin Mary as advocate for sinners.

In Juana's vision, Mary's naked dance, however reluctant, and her eventual consent to having her breasts touched or fondled in exchange for the salvation of souls, all point to the unique nature of the Virgin's sexuality. Mary can be seductive, yet chaste, since as the *Golden Legend* points out, the sight of her body—and presumably even of her naked body—aroused no concupiscence.[59] In any case, the notion of a seductive or coquettish Virgin Mary, while not common in the Middle Ages, was not unknown. Saint Bernardino of Siena, for example, quoting Songs of Songs 4:9 ("Thou hast wounded my heart . . ."), wonders at how a maiden, that is, the Virgin Mary, whether by caresses or cunning or violence, seduced and deceived and, so to speak, wounded and captivated the divine heart and deceived the Wisdom of God.[60] Nonetheless, it could be argued that no matter how praiseworthy the Virgin's intentions may be, no matter how far she is willing to go in order to save souls, she ends up playing a role dangerously close to traditional misogynistic views of female sexuality. As discussed above, sexual interpretations of the Fall cast Eve in the role of seductress. When the Virgin Mary is cast in a similar role, type and antitype are no longer polarized but rather appear to coincide in certain ways. Again, what redeems the Blessed Virgin is the special nature of her seductiveness: she can play a meretricious role for a worthy purpose, while retaining her exemplary chastity. Ironically, this notion of Mary as a sort of divine seductress—even a holy prostitute—redeems all women, for if the Mother of God can exercise her female wiles for a good end, then the possibility suggests itself that ordinary women, too, can exercise their power of seduction for a higher purpose. In this sense, Mary's seductiveness counters the misogynist tradition that would condemn female persuasion in any form.

In Juana's vision both nudity and youth denote innocence.[61] Thus, Mary's nudity symbolizes not only her physical perfection, but also her moral perfection. This means that in one sense the first part of the vision is about growing up and leaving behind the innocent nudity of childhood and entering into the clothed and potentially dangerous—for all but the Virgin Mary—world of sexuality. However, in the pageant part of Juana's vision the Virgin's clothing acquires a special symbolic meaning, for the Father covers her nakedness with his mantle. If Adam and Eve clothed themselves as a sign of their shame, the Virgin, the anti-Eve, is covered to symbolize her glory: the mantle represents the power and fortitude and clarity of the Trinity that surrounded her when she conceived the Son. Juana's sermon goes on to observe that Mary herself became in turn a mantle, her human flesh covering the divinity of God.[62] Just as in the narrative of the Virgin's childhood Mary had to keep herself clothed from the moment of her puberty on, so in the symbolic pageant her donning of the mantle, in a curious reversal, is associated with the assumption of her maternal role as mother of God when Christ donned her human flesh.[63] Mother Juana thus appears to set up a dialogue between the two parts of her vision. If in the novelization of the Virgin's childhood, even Mary's innocent nudity must be covered up at the onset of puberty, in the pageants of the second part of the vision Mary exercises power first through her naked body and then through her clothing.

The motif of the mantle had at least two significant associations in the Middle Ages, one biblical, the other iconographical. In III Kings 19, when God manifests himself to the prophet Elijah, he commands him to anoint Elisha to be prophet in his place. After the divine apparition, Elijah finds Elisha and "cast his mantle upon him" (19:19), a symbolic action that transfers his authority to Elisha. In IV Kings 2:8 Elijah uses his mantle to part the waters; in verses 2:11–14 Elisha takes the mantle that fell from Elijah as he ascended in a fiery chariot and performs the same miracle with it. Again, the transfer of the mantle symbolizes the transfer of power. Likewise, in the episode in which the Father places his mantle on the Virgin, Juana's vision suggests an analogous transfer of divine power that consecrates Mary's role as advocate for humankind.

The iconographic motif of the Madonna of Mercy depicts the Virgin with a voluminous mantle that shelters a multitude of suppliants.[64] According to Emile Mâle, the image expresses "avec une clarté admirable, la confiance de tous les hommes en la puissance auxiliatrice de la Vierge."[65] While Juana's vision does not depict the Virgin's mantle as actually protecting her devotees, the very mention of the Virgin donning a cloak would recall the garment's symbolic associations and, in particular, Mary's role as maternal advocate for humankind. The mantle also highlights the Virgin's authority and influence to the extent that it is a gift from God and symbolizes the transfer of his divine power to Mary. Nonetheless, the scene is ambiguous, for it could be argued that it calls attention to a power that is but borrowed.

Such ambiguities notwithstanding, Juana's vision foregrounds the Virgin's efficacy as a powerful intercessor who achieves salvation for her devotees. The Middle Ages viewed salvation as a kind of business deal: heaven could be gained in exchange for services rendered, such as prayers and good works.[66] The role of the Virgin Mary in this exchange was generally restricted to that of a simple advocate for humankind, but occasionally other possibilities were entertained. Thus, for Saint Bernard, Mary's intercession turned her into a sort of negotiator who would handle the business of our salvation ("salutis nostrae negotia pertractabit") before the Judge.[67] Saint Bonaventure, glossing Proverbs 31:10 ("Who shall find a valiant woman? Far and from the uttermost coasts is the price of her"), used the vocabulary of commerce to emphasize the Virgin's role in salvation. As Eve sells us and expels us from paradise, so Mary buys us and brings us back to paradise.[68] Mary accomplishes this by paying the price, which is accepting the divine will and consenting that her son's life be offered as the price of humankind's redemption (486). In Juana's vision Mary goes even further, playing an almost meretricious role. She must negotiate with the Father so that he will save sinners, and the price of that exchange is her own body.

In representations of the motif of the Double Intercession, the Virgin Mary intercedes for souls by exposing to the Father the breast that nursed the Son, that is, by exposing a part of her female body. Analogously, medieval holy women viewed their suffering female bodies as vehicles for the salvation of souls.[69] Juana herself believed that the many physical infirmities that she endured helped souls to be released from purgatory.[70] As Caroline Walker Bynum notes, it was the identification of their suffering female flesh with Christ's suffering humanity that allowed such women to imagine themselves in a redemptive role.[71] Juana's vision presents a rather different version of the notion that the female body can save souls: Mary intercedes for souls by allowing the Father to touch her adolescent body. More explicitly, it is an unequivocally and specifically feminine part of that body, the breasts, that accomplishes that redemptive role. Juana's vision likewise establishes a symbolic equivalence between female flesh and the Eucharist. Just as the Virgin offers hosts to the Father as a sacrifice for sinners, so she offers her breasts to the Father in order to intercede for the souls in purgatory. This identification with the Eucharist underscores the notion that Christ's body is also female flesh, the humanity he received from his mother. Thus, the female body can redeem souls through an essentially female suffering and a sort of consent that, by virtue of their sex, only women can give. If Juana's own body saves souls through physical suffering, in her vision the Virgin's body saves souls through, as it were, divine foreplay.

Does Mary play the role of a teasing temptress, using her body to achieve the salvation of souls, or is she the victim of the Father's exercise of his power? Technically speaking, the Father does not defile her body, yet the Blessed Virgin pays a price. Mary offers naked hosts as a sacrifice to the Father; she also offers her own naked body to the Father in order to continue to save souls.[72] As Christ suffered the Passion, delivering his naked body into the hands of his human persecutors as a sacrifice for humankind, so Mary must suffer the Father's touch. Christ offered his suffering humanity for the salvation of humankind; the Virgin offers her human sexuality, symbolized by her very human breasts, as a sacrifice and gift for the salvation of souls.

Juana's vision portrays the Virgin as not only naked, but dancing naked. The motif of Mary dancing as a young girl appears in chapter 7 of the apocryphal Protevangelium of James, which recounts that the Blessed Virgin, who was three at the time, danced when she was presented in the temple.[73] The readings for the second nocturn of matins in the Roman Breviary for the Nativity of the Virgin include the following passage taken from a sermon by the Pseudo-Augustine:

> Plaudat nunc organis Maria, et inter veloces articulos tympana puerperae concrepent. Concinant laetantes chori, et alternantibus modulis dulcisona carmina misceantur. Audite igitur quemadmodum tympanistria nostra cantaverit; ait enim: Magnificat anima mea Dominum.

> (Let Mary now play upon her musical instruments, and let the mother's tambourines sound with nimble fingers. Let joyful choirs sing with her and mingle their sweet songs with alternating melodies. Hear then how our tambourine-player sings, saying therefore: My soul doth magnify the Lord.)

This passage reworks the episode of Miriam's song of praise in Exodus 15:20–21:

> So Mary [=Miriam] the prophetess, the sister of Aaron, took a timbrel in her hand; and all the women went forth after her with timbrels and with dances. And she began the song to them, saying: Let us sing to the Lord, for he is gloriously magnified.

Although the Breviary reading does not mention explicitly that Mary dances, dancing is nonetheless suggested by the parallel between Miriam, who leads God's chosen people out of exile amid singing and dancing, and the Virgin Mary, who sings and plays a musical instrument, whose divine maternity made the Redemption possible, and whose intercession for humankind is highlighted throughout the office for her feast day.

Dancing was not unknown in heaven, for it was one of the typical activities of the elect.[74] Nonetheless, the Blessed Virgin's naked dance before the Father is a rather different matter. Although Juana's sermon does not explain exactly why the Virgin dances, except as an act of obedience, to the extent that the episode is related to both the offering of the palm frond and the Father's request to touch Mary's breasts, the text suggests that the dancing is likewise related to the Virgin's role as advocate for humankind.

But Mary's advocacy, in this instance, brings her dangerously close to another less benevolent tradition. The use to which the Virgin is willing to put her naked body for the attainment of a specific goal places her in the company of biblical women who used their bodies for their own treacherous ends. The suggestion that Mary will receive favors in exchange for nude dancing before an old man recalls the episode of Salome's dance before Herod. Erwin Panofsky notes that in the Bible, the real villain is Herodias, not her daughter, for Salome is "a mere tool in the hands of her wicked mother," who cleverly exploits Herod's infatuation with his stepdaughter.[75] Nevertheless, no matter which woman was to blame, the story of the death of John the Baptist became a standard vehicle for misogynist notions.[76] Thus, an Old French poem on the subject places the blame on Herodias[77] and then launches an extended diatribe against such other "evil" women as Eve, Dinah, Potiphar's wife, Delilah, Bathsheba, Solomon's wives, Jezebel, and Athalia (92–102). Although it may seem at first glance hardly flattering to link the Blessed Virgin with Salome's dance and thereby with a traditional example of feminine treachery, Panofsky indicates that at least one "underground version" of the theme sought to rehabilitate Salome.[78] In the early twelfth century, Nivardus of Ghent transformed the death of Saint John into a love story, portraying Salome as passionately in love with the Baptist. She vows to marry no other man, and it is therefore "out of resentment that Herod orders the execution of Saint John and out of amorous despair that Salome requests his head" (45). Although Salome must suffer, haunted by the spirit of Saint John, she is eventually revered as a saint, "perhaps because she . . . had been faithful to a vow of virginity" (45).

Another possible intertext for nude dancing is David's dancing before the ark of the covenant. According to II Kings 6:14, David "was girded with a linen ephod." In this episode the ephod is thought to be a brief loincloth, so that for all practical purposes David dances naked before the ark.[79] The interpretation according to which David dances nearly naked is supported by Michol's sarcastic comment: "How glorious was the king of Israel today, uncovering himself before the handmaids of his servants, and was naked, as if one of the buffoons should be naked" (II Kings 6:20).

Whatever associations the Virgin's dancing may have had for Mother

Juana, it is nevertheless obvious that she has Mary engage in an uncharacteristic activity.[80] Apocryphal legends of the Madonna and novelistic elaborations on them stressed the Virgin's precocious sanctity and the fact that she behaved like a responsible adult even as a child. Frivolity was unknown to her, and she never even laughed.[81] In Juana's vision the Virgin herself admits that nude dancing is against her wont (fol. 336^{v}) and agrees to dance only out of obedience to the Father. As the preacher of what her contemporaries perceived to be sermons, Juana herself is likewise engaged in an activity that many would have considered inappropriate for a nun, indeed, for any woman. Ultimately, Juana's sermon suggests that the Virgin dances naked for a worthy cause, the salvation of souls, and that is perhaps intended to justify her unusual conduct. Similarly, Juana receives visions and reveals them in the form of sermons for the salvation of souls, for Christ explicitly states that he has chosen to manifest himself through her at this time because the need is so great. Specifically, the end of Juana's sermon on the Creation explains that the Lord's speaking through her mouth is a miracle appropriate to times when souls are in such need:

> Que los miraglos e maravillas que El agora quería fazer heran en las ánimas, por quanto ellas heran las que le traían e fazían venir a fablar en esta boz, viendo tan gran muchedunbre de ánimas cómo se le pierden continuamente e se van al infierno. E que se tuviesen por çiertos todos los que miraglos e señales demandavan que no les daría ni les mostraría otras sino la graçia e consolaçión que dava a esta bienaventurada sierva suya que le veía e la fe e gozo muy verdadero que dava en los coraçones e ánimas de todas las personas que le oían e creían. (*Conorte*, fol. 450^{rv})

> (For the miracles and marvels that he wished to work now were in the souls, inasmuch as they were what brought him and made him come to speak in this voice, seeing how so great a multitude of souls is constantly being lost and going to hell. And that all those who desired miracles and signs should rest assured that he would neither give them nor show them signs other than the grace and comfort that he gave to this blessed handmaiden of his who saw him and the faith and true joy that he gave in the hearts and souls of all the persons who heard and believed him.)

The equivalence I have suggested between Juana's preaching and Mary's nudity is very much in line with medieval precepts regarding female comportment. Writing in 1415–1416, Francesco Barbaro borrows the following anecdote from Plutarch:

> When a certain young man saw the noble woman Theano stretch her arm out of her mantle that had been drawn back, he said to his companions: "How

handsome is her arm." To this she replied: "It is not a public one." It is proper, however, that not only arms but indeed also the speech of women never be made public; for the speech of a noble woman can be no less dangerous than the nakedness of her limbs.[82]

In the light of such moral instructions governing female behavior, Juana's detractors might have viewed her preaching sermons as the equivalent of her appearing bare-breasted or dancing nude in public. In order to justify her own unorthodox behavior, Juana shields herself behind the authority of the Blessed Virgin, for in Juana's vision Mary behaves in an unorthodox and unexpected fashion. Through her sermon Juana argues that the end justifies the means. Both she and the Virgin Mary accomplish a worthy end, the salvation of souls, by means deemed inappropriate to their gender.

Such observations are not the only evidence of a more or less conscious parallel between the Virgin Mary and Juana herself. In the initial scene of the vision the newborn Mary has a mystical rapture that lasts for three days. This incident parallels an episode from Juana's official biography, which recounts that even as a baby she experienced mystic raptures, and her mother would find her in ecstasy in her cradle. Once she spent three days in rapture, and her mother, fearing that she was dead, prayed to the Virgin that she resuscitate her baby (*Vida*, fol. 3^r). Juana's vision recounts that from the Father's arms Mary was able to contemplate the entire universe, and her relatives mistook her raptures for death. Later in life, when Juana would have a mystical trance, she might spend as many as forty hours in that state, her body appearing to be lifeless to her companions (*Vida*, fol. 21^v). Meanwhile, an angel carried her spirit to a beautiful place (*Vida*, fol. 23^r). Sometimes, while her spirit was thus transported to heaven, God would permit her to contemplate the entire world (*Vida*, fol. 29^r). These anecdotal analogues between vision and *Vida* create a significant parallel between Juana and the Blessed Virgin: that both experienced mystical raptures established a kinship between the two, a kinship of which Juana must have been keenly aware. Juana's sermon is self-conscious and assertive to the extent that in its liminal episode Mary's childhood raptures replicate Juana's reception of the vision.

Risky as psychological interpretations of centuries' old texts can be, Juana's sermon nevertheless invites speculation from just that perspective. It is possible that early traumas underlie her vision. Juana's mother died when she was seven (*Vida*, fol. 5^r). Her biography does not say how long Juana continued to live with her father, but at some point she went to live with her aunt and uncle, who were relatively well off (*Vida*, fol. 6ᵛ). It is tempting to ask whether Juana felt that her father had abandoned her. Is Juana the little girl who dances to please her father? In the wish fulfillment of dreams, does she grow breasts to attract her father as only her mother could?

Certainly, the episode in which the Father tries to touch Mary's breasts suggests a displaced instance (or several instances) of sexual abuse from Juana's childhood.[83] It is not uncommon for such incidents to be repressed and then revealed much later in the form of dreams or other symbolic representations. Was the abuser her uncle? Was it her father? Is that the explanation for Juana's removal from the parental home?

Perhaps such speculations can be linked to the timing of Juana's acting on her desire to become a nun. At the age of fifteen, in the face of attempts by her relatives to marry her off, Juana escaped from her uncle's house, dressed in male attire, and sought refuge in the convent (*Vida*, fols. 10ᵛ–13ʳ). Her relatives would not have attempted to arrange her marriage had Juana not already undergone puberty.[84] Did her own sexual awakening precipitate her decision to become a nun? While Juana had long desired to take the veil, puberty itself may have signaled that it was time to go. In this respect, her vision may have recast in symbolic form the double trauma of maturing sexuality and departure from home.

Juana's vision thus appears to codify the conflicts and ambiguities inherent in the onset of puberty. With maturing sexuality comes an acute awareness of the power derived from the body. If that body happens to be a girl's, the development of the breasts is an extraordinary event, at once longed-for and startling, immensely pleasing and frightening, for the appearance of breasts signals a girl's entry into the adult world. In her maturing breasts resides the power to attract, to mother, and to nurture. Her literal protrusion into the world is an empowering event. In the context of Juana's vision, the Blessed Virgin's developing breasts symbolize her ability to save souls.

But puberty also has its darker side, for it signifies an end to the safe world of childhood (assuming, of course, that the childhood was free from sexual abuse). For a girl, entry into the adult world also means entry into a place fraught with danger. If her breasts have the power to attract a mate, they can attract predators as well. Breasts may signal the possibility of greater control over one's life as an adult, but as every woman knows, they also make her vulnerable to attack. Her literal protrusion into the world comes at a price: the constant fear of being touched, defiled, raped.

Thus, what she gains in power she loses in freedom. Now her body must be enclosed and protected. By extension, her sphere of influence must be limited to the private space of the home. In the case of the Blessed Virgin, the onset of puberty means that she can no longer go about naked, and that moment coincides with the Presentation and therefore her reclusion in the temple. Juana's vision thus appears to capture the ambiguous essence of the female condition. A woman's sexuality is both empowering and limiting; it is both liberating and imprisoning, a source of both strength from within and vulnerability to assault from without. Medieval iconography captures this dichotomy well: a single exposed breast evokes the power to create and to nurture at its highest; both breasts exposed draw the ire of moralists. If a woman bares one breast, she recalls the Virgin Mary; if she bares both, she recalls Eve. Juana turns this scheme on its head when, in her vision, Mary exposes both breasts.

Whether or not such psychological speculations are valid, it is nonetheless evident that the vision received on the Feast of the Nativity of the Virgin partakes of a rhetorical strategy designed to create or underscore the parallel between Juana de la Cruz and the Virgin Mary. In retrospect, we are able to see such visions as a typical feature of late medieval female spirituality. Nonetheless, male suspicion of the revelations received by holy women meant that the recipients of such visions often felt obligated to defend their authenticity, that is, their divine inspiration. Mother Juana authorizes her reception of visions by shielding herself with the authority of the Blessed Virgin. As the Virgin Mary is seen to perform a priestly function when she offers the hosts to the Father, so Juana is in turn empowered to engage in another priestly function, preaching. If Mary can engage in such extreme activities as nude dancing and erotic behavior for the benefit of souls, then Juana is authorized in turn to preach in order to save souls. As an advocate for humankind, Mary uses her breasts in an act that is at once seduction, sacrifice, and persuasion. Likewise, in preaching, Juana becomes an instrument of the Lord's revelation, using her body, and specifically her speech organs, in an act of seduction—even sacrifice—and persuasion directed toward the worthy cause of saving souls.

Epilogue

Teresa de Cartagena, Constanza de Castilla, María de Ajofrín, María de Santo Domingo, and Juana de la Cruz were Saint Teresa's "mothers" only in the sense that they preceded her in time. They probably did not know about one another, and Teresa never speaks of them. Even if we allow that she may have heard about them—Juana de la Cruz was quite well known—it is unlikely that Teresa ever read their writings.[1] Nonetheless, Saint Teresa's predecessors are important for the study of sixteenth- and seventeenth-century nuns because they codified a set of significant experiential patterns.

Juana de la Cruz and probably Teresa de Cartagena were Franciscans. Constanza de Castilla was a Second Order Dominican, while María de Santo Domingo was a Dominican tertiary. María de Ajofrín was a *beata* closely associated with the Hieronymite order. If affective piety is usually considered a hallmark of the Franciscan order, that characteristic is most cogently demonstrated in the Dominican María de Santo Domingo and the Franciscan Juana de la Cruz, while Teresa de Cartagena, despite her recourse to personal experience, is more intellectualizing than affective in her spirituality. In short, Teresa de Cartagena and Constanza de Castilla determined an intellectual approach to spirituality, while the mystical experiences of María de Ajofrín, Juana de la Cruz, and María de Santo Domingo constituted an affective approach. In this sense Saint Teresa represents the culmination of the options available to her "mothers," for she embodies both patterns, using her own experiences to construct a series of doctrinal treatises that became classic statements of the mystical life.

Inaccessible as their writings were to one another, the utterances of Teresa of Avila's predecessors arose from concrete needs. Teresa de Cartagena wrote a spiritual treatise and then a defense, with a certain autobiographical bent, of her right to do so. Although she claimed after the fact that her devotional treatise was divinely inspired, its writing cannot be considered supernatural in the sense that the revelations received and recorded by visionaries are construed to be otherworldly messages. Constanza de Castilla wrote prayers and liturgical offices for the nuns in her charge. María de Ajofrín, Juana de la Cruz, and María de Santo Domingo were all visionaries, but each offered her own variant of that experience, and each had a different relation with her superiors and/or her public. María de Ajofrín's visions first centered on the problem of their validation by the ecclesiastical establishment and then turned into a series of warnings for the city of Toledo. María de Santo Domingo dictated ecstatic texts that foregrounded such themes as Christ's suffering humanity and the need for penance. Her controversial life-style stirred up a passionate debate between her supporters and her detractors, but in the end she was vindicated thanks to her powerful protectors. Juana de la Cruz's mystical utterances took the form of sermons that included novelesque narrations of gospel episodes, descriptions of celestial pageants, and edifying interpretations of those events. Although she clashed with the Church hierarchy over a question of ecclesiastical jurisdiction, her supernatural experiences, like those of María de Santo Domingo, were validated by Cardinal Cisneros himself.

The visionary experience, it appears, was an option only for later women. To the extent that one can generalize on the basis of five female religious, only the later ones—María de Ajofrín, Juana de la Cruz, and María de Santo Domingo—can be said to be mystics. Writers chronologically closer to them than we are support this observation. Writing in 1599, José de Sigüenza, the noted historian of the Hieronymite order, devotes a section of his chronicle to nuns distinguished for their holiness. He observes that female visionaries were not to be found in the early Church nor were they characteristic of the Church of the martyrs, the confessors, or the desert fathers. However, beginning about two hundred years before his time, it appears that the Lord decided to change his way ("mudar su estilo"); he made an exception to Saint Paul's injunction that women not teach in church and allowed women to write letters and books of revelations and advice, something unaccustomed even among the holy women of the early Church.[2] These observations serve as a prologue to Sigüenza's discussion of religious women in fifteenth-century Castile, and the context makes it clear that in the chronicler's estimation the miraculous experiences those women had were a new phenomenon that had not previously manifested itself in Castile.

Saint Teresa was able to be a model for later religious women not only because of her personal charisma as a writer, but also because her works were published and available to future generations. Among Saint Teresa's predecessors, only María de Santo Domingo saw any of her mystical utterances in print. Thus, Teresa's forerunners worked in isolation; they were probably unfamiliar with the works of one another. They had no female precursors, if by precursors we mean women writers whose works were familiar to them. Instead, they had only "fathers" to look back on: the Bible, the Church Fathers, and the medieval clerical writers that made up the male-dominated bookish culture of the Middle Ages. But these nuns did have "mothers"—strong biblical women—and they believed that Christ himself inspired them directly. The nuns lacked role models for female authors, yet they had paradigms of female strength and authority in the examples of Judith, the Virgin Mary, and Mary Magdalene; their identification with Christ's feminine side, his suffering humanity, validated their religious experiences. In their empathy with strong biblical women, and above all with Christ's female flesh, they acquired a power and authority that no Church Father or contemporary male could bestow.

Cardinal Cisneros died in 1517. María de Santo Domingo probably died in the 1520s. Juana de la Cruz died in 1534. Saint Teresa did not begin to write her major works until 1562. What were the conditions for religious women in the decades between the death of Cardinal Cisneros and the birth of Saint Teresa as a writer? Let us recall that in the period previous to the death of Cisneros, women who had visionary experiences could count on the protection of the highest ecclesiastical and civil authority in Castile. However, the golden age of mysticism that female visionaries enjoyed under Cisneros was followed by a period of repression that limited the participation of women in certain aspects of the religious life and, especially, as mystics and visionaries.

Women played a prominent role in the heretical *alumbrado* movement, whose tenets included *dexamiento* (abandonment of the will to God), opposition to external forms of devotion, and the superiority of mental prayer to vocal prayer. Such heterodox movements allowed women an expanded role in the religious life, for otherwise unlearned women seized the opportunity to explain the Scriptures in the form of informal sermons. María de Cazalla taught the catechism to rural women and preached on the Epistles of Saint Paul.[3] Francisca Hernández taught in public, interpreting key passages of the Scriptures and preaching the doctrine of *dexamiento*.[4] The condemnation of the *alumbrado* movement by the Inquisition in 1525 and the subsequent persecution of its followers led to a general suspicion of increased female participation in the religious life. Although the *alumbrado* movement opposed revelations, raptures, and other charismatic phenomena,[5] the presence of so many women in a movement branded as heretical ended up having a negative effect on their participation as charismatics even in orthodox spiritual movements. The Inquisition became sensitized to such extraordinary phenomena and began to direct its special scrutiny to an area in which women, at least under Cisneros, had been allowed to participate.

As the sixteenth century progressed, the legacy of patristic misogyny and the danger of heresy combined to exacerbate the effort to prevent women from engaging in scriptural exegesis. In his *Excelencias de la fe* (1537), Luis de Maluenda harshly criticized the interpretation of the Scriptures by women, arguing that in matters of the mysteries of the faith, woman should padlock her mouth, for silence is the jewel most becoming to the female sex. Maluenda goes on to say that if the literal meaning of Paul's epistles is complicated for the wise man, it is even more so for the *beata* or the "little woman"—he uses the disdainful diminutive *mujercilla*—who abandons her distaff to presume to interpret Saint Paul.[6] Likewise, in his *Censura* (1558–1559) of Carranza's catechism, Melchor Cano opines that the interpretation of the Scriptures is a task better left to ecclesiastical experts. Lay people need have nothing to do with such an endeavor, and in particular Cano violently opposes women interpreting the Scriptures.[7] Recalling Eve's role in the Fall, Cano states that no matter how great women's appetite for the fruit of the tree of knowledge may be, it must be forbidden and a knife of fire must keep laymen and women away from it.[8]

The discovery in 1558 of Protestant groups in Valladolid and Seville led to what has been called, anachronistically, the Tibetization of Spain, that is, the attempt to seal the country off from nefarious foreign influences.[9] To that end, in 1558 Princess Juana, acting in the name of her brother King Philip II, forbade the importation of foreign books and ordered that no book be published in Spain unless licensed by the Council of Castile.[10] The following year Spanish students were forbidden to study abroad, except in certain "safe" Catholic universities (Bologna, Rome, Naples, and Coimbra).[11] The Inquisitorial Index of 1559 forbade not only vernacular translations of the Bible, but also books that contained excerpts from the New Testament in Castilian translation.[12] In addition, the Index had a decidedly antiaffective and antimystical orientation, prohibiting many spiritual books written in the vernacular.[13] In chapter 26 of her *Vida*, Saint Teresa describes the traumatic effect those prohibitions had on her own spiritual life: "When they forbade the reading of many books in the vernacular, I felt that prohibition very much because reading some of them was an enjoyment for me, and I could no longer do so since only the Latin editions were allowed."[14]

Teresa of Avila's lifetime (1515–1582) spans the change from the Cisneros-sponsored golden age of female spirituality to the crackdown of 1559 and its aftereffects. As the sixteenth century progressed, exterior scrutiny of supernatural experiences was not only maintained, but intensified. Let us recall that some nuns wrote and that their writings are extant only because they were ordered to record their experiences so that the ecclesiastical authorities could examine them for their orthodoxy. If María de Ajofrín saw herself as a collaborator in the work of the Inquisition, and her visions served as a stimulus to extirpate heresy with greater vigor, Teresa of Avila is acutely aware of the possibility that she herself might be brought before that tribunal.[15] Apropos of the vision that led to the founding of her first reformed convent, she writes in chapter 33 of her *Vida*:

> También comenzó aquí el demonio, de una persona en otra, procurar se entendiese que havía yo visto alguna revelación en este negocio y ivan a mí con mucho miedo a decirme que andavan los tiempos recios y que podría ser me levantasen algo y fuesen a los inquisidores. (148)

> (Likewise the devil began striving here through one person and another to make known that I had received some revelation about this work. Some persons came to me with great fear to tell me we were in trouble and that it could happen that others might accuse me of something and report me to the Inquisitors [1:222].)

Teresa's worries about the Holy Office were compounded by many of the same problems her precursors faced. For example, the question of authority, central to medieval and early modern women writers and visionaries, is likewise an important consideration for Saint Teresa. Indeed, to the extent that women continued to lack the male authority of office, it was still necessary for them to seek alternative means to authorize their words. Saint Teresa highlights her awareness of her lack of authority when she writes: "If I were a person who had authority for writing I would willingly and in a very detailed way enlarge upon what I am saying" (1:54),[16] and then: "I should certainly like to have a great deal of authority in this matter so that I might be believed" (1:124).[17] Teresa is particularly aware that she lacks the authority that male clerics derive from their priestly status and their concomitant access to higher education. She writes:

> Havré de aprovecharme de alguna comparación, aunque yo las quisiera escusar por ser mujer, y escrivir simplemente lo que me mandan; mas este lenguaje de espíritu es tan malo de declarar a los que no saben letras, como yo. (59)

(I shall have to make use of some comparison, although I should like to excuse myself from this since I am a woman and write simply what they ordered me to write. But these spiritual matters for anyone who like myself has not gone through studies are so difficult to explain [1:80].)

Teresa, like other mystics, founds her authority on the mystical experience itself; it is God who empowers her to speak and inspires her to write. However, her first task is to establish the authenticity of such extraordinary spiritual phenomena.

Saint Teresa expresses great anguish over the question of whether her experiences might be due to demonic instigation. This concern was almost never voiced in the utterances of her forerunners. They were probably aware of the problem—it had become codified in patriarchal texts—but the question of diabolical deception is not manifested as an acute preoccupation in their writings. In this respect, Saint Teresa's experience was rather different from that of her predecessors, for only María de Ajofrín had serious problems in convincing those in power of the authenticity of her supernatural messages. Although some of María de Santo Domingo's detractors alleged that her mystical raptures were feigned, the majority of her accusers attacked not her credibility as a mystic but her controversial life-style. For her part, Saint Teresa was obsessed by the possibility that her experiences might be inspired by the devil, for she internalized the patriarchal notion that women are particularly susceptible to diabolical delusion. Observing that beginners in the spiritual life should not overly rely on their own efforts but wait for divine illumination, Teresa remarks that it "would be especially bad for women to try to raise up the spirit because the devil would be able to cause some illusion" (1:88).[18]

Teresa's predecessors are not only free of the concern that their visions might be the result of diabolic suggestion; they also possess a certain unreflecting fluency that enables them to narrate their experiences at great length with barely a hint of the difficulties of expression that Teresa faced in describing her own encounters with the supernatural. Juana de la Cruz, for example, dictated more than nine hundred pages of expansive narratives that show little self-consciousness of the mystical experience or reflection on it.[19] Saint Teresa, however, is acutely aware of the fundamental ineffability of her experiences, and for that reason she is self-conscious in her expression, constantly seeking to do justice to an experience that defies human language and weighing her own effectiveness in the choice of images and similes: "This comparison, I think, gets to the point" (1:115),[20]

"And even though the comparison may be a coarse one I cannot find another that would better explain what I mean" (2:354),[21] and so forth.

By Teresa's standards, the female mystics who preceded her could be said to belong to the "minor leagues" of mysticism. Reflecting classic orthodox statements on the subject,[22] Teresa distinguishes among three kinds of visions: intellectual, imaginary, and corporeal. Teresa describes an intellectual vision as a strong and undeniable sense of Christ's presence, but in an imageless way, that is, "seen" with neither the eyes of the body (as in corporeal visions) nor with those of the soul (as in imaginative visions).[23] Teresa was familiar not only with such terminology, but also with the hierarchy traditionally ascribed to the three types of visions. She says: "Those who know more about these matters than I say that the intellectual vision is more perfect than this one [the imaginative vision] and that this one is much more perfect than visions seen with the bodily eyes" (1:182). Teresa goes on to remark that "corporeal visions, they say, are the lowest and the kind in which the devil can cause more illusions" (1:182).[24] If her precursors appear to have had only corporeal and imaginative visions,[25] perhaps that explains why Teresa makes no reference to them. She might have been expected to allude to them, for Juana de la Cruz was quite celebrated, María de Santo Domingo only somewhat less so. Did Teresa really not know of them? Was their experience irrelevant to hers? Or, at a time when female visionaries were being subjected to such scrutiny, did she perhaps find her forerunners' experiences of the suspect "lower" kinds of visions embarrassing or at least reflecting negatively, if only by association, on her own project?

Although this study focuses on the writing nuns and visionaries who preceded Saint Teresa, it would be incomplete without considering a representative text of the celebrated Carmelite. I have chosen for commentary a relatively little-studied work, usually known as the *Meditations on the Song of Songs*.[26] Teresa completed a first version between 1566 and 1567; a second redaction dates from around 1574.[27] The text is ostensibly a treatise on prayer written for the other nuns in her community.[28] Most scholars who have considered the *Meditations* agree that it was a daring enterprise. Alison Weber observes that Teresa exposed herself "to the charge of interpreting Scripture," an activity expressly prohibited by the Index of Forbidden Books of 1559, which proscribed scriptural commentaries written in the vernacular. Moreover, Teresa's commentaries did not "shy away from the eroticism inherent in the language" of the biblical verses.[29] Although Domingo Báñez, Teresa's confessor, gave his approbation to the text in

1575, a later confessor, Diego de Yanguas, ordered that it be burned. Teresa's editor, Gracián de la Madre de Dios, described the incident in the following terms:

> El cual libro (como pareciesse a un su confessor cosa nueva y peligrosa que muger escriviesse sobre los Cantares) se le mandó quemar, movido con zelo de que (como dize San Pablo) *Callen las mugeres en la Iglesia de Dios*, como quien dize, no prediquen en púlpitos, ni lean en cáthedras, ni impriman libros. . . . Y como en aquel tiempo que le escrivió, hazía gran daño la heregía de Luthero, que abrió puerta a que mugeres y honbres idiotas leyessen y explicassen las divinas letras, por la cual han entrado inumerables almas a la heregía, y con- denádose al infierno, parecióle que le quemasse. Y así al punto que este padre se lo mandó, ella hechó el libro en el fuego, exercitando sus dos tan heroicas virtudes de la humildad y obediencia.[30]

> (She was ordered to burn this book, since it seemed to a certain confessor of hers very unorthodox and dangerous for a woman to write about the *Song of Songs*. He was moved by his pious concern that, as St. Paul says, women should be silent in God's church, which is to say: they should not preach from the pulpit, or teach at universities, or print books. And since at the time Luther's heresy was doing much harm, for it had opened the doors for igno- rant women and men to read and explicate divine works . . . it seemed to him that the book should be burned. And so, as soon as this priest ordered it, she threw her book into the fire, practicing her two heroic virtues of humility and obedience.) [31]

The second confessor's hostile reading of Teresa's text points to an impor- tant facet of its reception. When Father Yanguas recalls I Corinthians 14:34, it is an indication that the question of women speaking—and writing—in public was as much a problem in Teresa's time as it had been for her medi- eval mothers.[32] Fortunately, Teresa's treatise was preserved because some nuns disobeyed the order to burn all the copies of the *Meditations*.[33] The work was finally published in Brussels, that is, outside of Spain but within the Spanish empire, in 1611.

The *Meditations* boldly assert women's right to enjoy the Scriptures, declaring: "Nor must we make women stand so far away from enjoyment of the Lord's riches" (2:220).[34] Teresa never argues that women should be allowed to explicate the Bible; indeed, she admits that they do not have the intellectual equipment to do so. Addressing her companions, Teresa says: "Thus I highly recommend that when you read some book or hear a sermon or think about the mysteries of our sacred faith you avoid tiring yourselves or wasting your thoughts in subtle reasoning about what you cannot properly understand" (2:216).[35] She goes on to say that what women may perceive of the Scriptures is a gift that they receive from God with no effort on their part:

> Cuando el Señor quiere darlo a entender, Su Majestad lo hace sin travajo nuestro. A mujeres digo esto. . . . Mas nosotras con llaneza tomar lo que el Señor nos diere; y lo que no, no nos cansar, sino alegrarnos de considerar qué tan gran Dios y Señor tenemos, que una palabra suya terná en sí mil misterios, y ansí su principio no entendemos nosotras. . . . Ansí que siempre os guardad de gastar el pensamiento con estas cosas, ni cansaros, que mujeres no han menester más que para su entendimiento bastare; con esto las hará Dios merced. Cuando Su Majestad quisiere dárnoslo sin cuidado ni travajo nuestro, lo hallaremos sabido. (334–335)

> (When the Lord desires to give understanding, His Majesty does so without our effort. I am saying this to women. . . . But we should accept with simplicity whatever the Lord gives us; and what He doesn't we shouldn't tire ourselves over, but rejoice in considering what a great Lord and God we have. . . . Thus always guard against wasting your thoughts on these things or tiring yourselves, for women have need of no more than what is sufficient for their meditations. With this, God will favor them. When His Majesty desires to give us understanding of the words, without worry or work on our part, we shall surely find it [2:216–217].)

Teresa argues that women may have an experience of the Scriptures different from that of men, an experience based on a passive receptivity and dependent less on the intellect than on the emotions. Elsewhere she says: "It matters little if what I say is not what the passage means provided, as I said, we benefit from the thoughts" (2:229).[36] Teresa thus takes negative stereotyped categories ascribed to women—that women are passive, while men are active; that women are carnal and emotional, while men are rational—and turns them around, arguing that in the case of the mystical experience, female passivity and emotivity can be viewed as positive categories that predispose women to receive divine favors.

Teresa's subversion of the conventional patriarchal interpretation of the Virgin's reaction to the Annunciation likewise ends up demonstrating the point that both men and women should be permitted to respond to the Scriptures, albeit in different ways. When in the first chapter of Luke the angel Gabriel told Mary that she would conceive a son, she answered: "How shall this be done, because I know not man?" After Gabriel explained that the deed would be accomplished through the agency of the Holy Spirit, Mary responded: "Behold the handmaid of the Lord: be it done to me according to thy word." Biblical exegetes used this passage to justify the virtue of female silence. Women were to take Mary as a model, imitating her taciturnity, for as such commentators were quick to observe, the Annunciation is one of the very few occasions on which the Virgin spoke.[37]

Teresa maintains the Virgin as a model for women, or at the very least, as a model for the nuns in her charge:

> ¡Oh secretos de Dios! Aquí no hay más de rendir nuestros entendimientos y pensar que para entender las grandezas de Dios, no valen nada. Aquí viene bien el acordarse cómo lo hizo con la Virgen nuestra Señora. (356)

> (Oh, secrets of God! Here there is no more to do than surrender our intellects and reflect that they are of no avail when it comes to understanding the grandeurs of God. It is good to recall here how God acted with the Blessed Virgin, our Lady [2:253].)

However, instead of proposing the Virgin's comportment at the Annunciation as a model of female silence, Teresa views the episode as a paradigm of women's nonintellectual encounter with Christ. Moreover, noting that the Virgin engaged in no further discussion, Teresa uses the episode to take a poke at males whose exegetical lucubrations become useless exercises in pride:

> No como algunos letrados, que no les lleva el Señor por este modo de oración ni tienen principio de espíritu, que quieren llevar las cosas por tanta razón y tan medidas por sus entendimientos, que no parece sino que han ellos con sus letras de comprender todas las grandezas de Dios. ¡Si deprendiesen algo de la humildad de la Virgen sacratísima! (356)

> (She did not act as do some learned men [whom the Lord does not lead by this mode of prayer and who haven't begun a life of prayer], for they want to be so rational about things and so precise in their understanding that it doesn't seem anyone else but they with their learning can understand the grandeurs of God. If only they would learn something from the humility of the most Blessed Virgin! [2:253])

Thus, while the Blessed Virgin remains a model for women, in Teresa's hands she becomes even more a model for men, Mary's humility serving to deflate the vanity of learned male clerics. Implicit in such observations is the notion that some women, while lacking the intellectual ability of some men, nonetheless, through God's grace, are able to arrive at a nonintellectual, mystical understanding of God. Such an understanding is a gift, a gift

that Teresa and many other women have received from the Lord. Therefore, Teresa implicitly scoffs at learned men who would presume to judge or
to question divine gifts that they themselves have not been deemed worthy
to receive.

Like her predecessors, Teresa finds positive role models in women
who appear in the Scriptures. We have already seen how she subverts the
episode of the Annunciation to the Virgin in order to contrast men's and
women's approaches to the Scriptures. Later on, Teresa uses another scriptural figure, the Samaritan woman, as an emblem of a privileged woman's
direct experience of Christ. Teresa recalls the Samaritan woman in the context of her discussion of the intimate relationship between the active and
the contemplative lives. Teresa declares that, ideally, supernatural experiences should be a stimulus for acts of charity toward one's neighbors. Thus,
the Samaritan woman, who shared her knowledge of Christ as the Messiah
with others, is an appropriate example of someone who performed a good
work for the benefit of her neighbors (2:258).

Patristic interpretations of the episode of the Samaritan woman are
quite different from Saint Teresa's. For Saint Augustine, for example, the
woman represents the Church, and specifically, the Church that was to
come from the gentiles.[38] Although Augustine interprets Eve's creation
from Adam's rib as a sign of her strength (the weakness of Adam/Christ is
the strength of Eve/the Church [234]), the Samaritan woman, by virtue of
her gender, is associated with carnality and ignorance (237) and must therefore be enlightened by the intellect as the husband rules the wife (240).
For Saint John Chrysostom the Samaritan woman likewise represents the
gentiles,[39] but he provides a more consistently positive view of her. The
Samaritan woman is "manly" in her belief (268), and by spreading the word
of Christ's presence, "she exhibited the actions of an Apostle, preaching
the Gospel to all" (268).[40] Chrysostom praises the Samaritan woman for
her wisdom[41] and exhorts his readers to imitate her comportment (264,
288). Although he does not relate the episode to the mystical experience,
significantly, Chrysostom asserts that the woman "was made dizzy by His
discourse, and fainted at the sublimity of what He said" (278). With this
allusion to women's "weakness," that is, becoming dizzy and faint before
God, Chrysostom argues, perhaps unwittingly, their "strength," that is,
their receptivity to the experience of God. Several of these patristic interpretations were enshrined in works like the *Glossa ordinaria*, which calls
attention to the Samaritan woman's literal-minded carnality as well as to
her role as teacher.[42]

Despite the potentially useful implications of Chrysostom's comments on the Samaritan woman as an apostle, Teresa turns her back on such standard patristic interpretations and personalizes the biblical narrative, establishing a kinship—even a sisterhood—between herself and the Samaritan woman. The Bible merely states that the woman recognized Christ as the Messiah and communicated that realization to others, who believed her testimony: "Now of that city many of the Samaritans believed in him, for the word of the woman giving testimony: He told me all things whatsoever I have done" (John 4:39). Teresa echoes that passage when she says:

> Iva esta santa mujer con aquella borrachez divina dando gritos por las calles. Lo que me espanta a mí es ver cómo la creyeron, una mujer. . . . En fin, le dieron crédito, y por solo su dicho salió gran gente de la ciudad al Señor. (360–361)

> (This holy woman, in that divine intoxication, went shouting through the streets. What amazes me is to see how the people believed her—a woman. . . . In sum, the people believed her; and a large crowd, on her word alone, went out of the city to meet the Lord [2:258–259].)

Now the Bible makes no mention of shouting or of divine inebriation. However, "divine intoxication" ("borrachez divina") is an expression that Teresa has used previously to refer to the mystical experience (2:244) in the context of her exegesis of Song of Songs 1:1 ("for thy breasts are better than wine"). Elsewhere (2:252), Teresa speaks of a "holy inebriation" ("embebecimiento santo"). Divine inebriation as the Samaritan woman's reaction to her encounter with Christ is not authorized by the Bible, but Teresa's use of the term appears to reflect her identification with the scriptural figure, who becomes an emblem of Teresa's own mystical experience of God.[43] Moreover, by focusing on the question of the credibility of a divine message delivered by a woman, Teresa authorizes herself, and perhaps all women, as instruments of God's revelation.[44]

Ostensibly, Teresa is describing her method of prayer; she is not interpreting the Scriptures. The Song of Songs would appear to be merely a springboard for a discussion of the mystical experience, for Teresa's meditations deal substantively with but five verses. However, the Scriptures are omnipresent in the *Meditations*, whether Teresa is quoting them, reacting to them, or appropriating them. Despite the declaration that she is merely sharing her meditations with her sisters (2:220), Diego de Yanguas obviously thought that she was engaging in scriptural exegesis when he ordered the text to be burned. The *Meditations* is not to be found in the 1588 edition of Teresa's collected works. Tomás Alvarez assumes that Teresa's editor, Fray Luis de León, must have been acquainted with the *Meditations*, recognized its problematic nature, and decided not to publish it.[45] On the other hand, Gracián de la Madre de Dios defended Teresa, insisting in the introduction to his edition of the text that it was not a question of exegesis but of meditations.[46] Nonetheless, his defensive attitude toward the work is indicated by the fact that he appended to each chapter his own annotations that seem designed to uphold the text's orthodoxy. In any case, pretext (the Song of Songs) and text (Teresa's meditations on prayer) become conflated, and Teresa's readers are left with the doubt: is she or is she not engaging in scriptural exegesis? Thus, Teresa ends up both describing her mystical experiences and explicating the Scriptures, and she is empowered to engage in both activities by the text's purposefully ambiguous generic identity.

Teresa's meditations lead her to appropriate the image of Christ as mother.[47] Clearly, the image is suggested by one of the biblical verses that inspires her contemplations as well as by the traditional identification of Christ as the bridegroom of the Song of Songs:

> Mas cuando este Esposo riquísimo la quiere enriquecer y regalar más, conviértela tanto en Sí, que, como una persona que el gran placer y contento la desmaya, le parece se queda suspendida en aquellos divinos brazos y arrimada a aquel sagrado costado y aquellos pechos divinos. No sabe más de gozar, sustentada con aquella leche divina, que la va criando su Esposo y mejorando para poderla regalar y que merezca cada día más. Cuando despierta de aquel sueño y de aquella embriaguez celestial, queda como cosa espantada y embovada y con un santo desatino. . . . Porque ansí como un niño no entiende cómo crece ni sabe cómo mama—que, aun sin mamar él ni hacer nada, muchas veces le echan la leche en la boca—, ansí es aquí, que totalmente el alma no sabe de sí ni hace nada ni sabe cómo ni por dónde—ni lo puede entender—le vino aquel bien tan grande. . . . No sabe a qué lo comparar, sino a el regalo de la madre que ama mucho al hijo y le cría y regala. (349–350)

> (But when this most wealthy Bridegroom desires to enrich and favor the soul more, He changes it into Himself to such a point that, just as a person is caused to swoon from great pleasure and happiness, it seems to the soul it is left suspended in those divine arms, leaning on that sacred side and those divine breasts. It doesn't know how to do anything more than rejoice, sustained by the divine milk with which its Spouse is nourishing it and making it better so that He might favor it, and it might merit more each day. When it awakens from that sleep and that heavenly inebriation, it remains as though stupefied

and dazed and with a holy madness. . . . An infant doesn't understand how it grows nor does it know how it gets its milk, for without its sucking or doing anything, often the milk is put into its mouth. Likewise, here, the soul is completely ignorant. It knows neither how nor from where that great blessing came to it, nor can it understand. . . . It doesn't know what to compare His grace to, unless to the great love a mother has for her child in nourishing and caressing it [2:244–245].)

Is it an accident that it is precisely in her *Meditations* that Teresa formulates the motif of Jesus as mother? To be sure, this is the text in which she argues that men and women should be permitted to approach the Scriptures differently. Both have a right to do so, she contends, and both approaches are valid. Nonetheless, despite her declarations to the contrary, Teresa ends up engaging in the "masculine" activity of scriptural exegesis. Perhaps this accounts for her strategy of feminizing Christ by virtue of the Christ-as-mother motif. By feminizing the ultimate male authority figure, Teresa creates an authority that is feminine, and that strategy empowers her in turn to perform the privileged male task of explicating the Scriptures. Yet she remains female and retains her feminine authority. As the author of a work on her method of prayer, Teresa is a nurturing mother to the nuns in her charge even as she fulfills the masculine role, prohibited to women by Saint Paul, of teacher. In arguing the legitimacy of her experience, Teresa acquires not only female and male attributes, but the attributes of a child as well. The soul as child turns out to be a particularly apt image for expressing the passive and dependent relation between Christ and the soul. To the extent that women, like nursing babies, were considered weak and passive, Teresa once again turns such negative commonplaces on their heads; female passivity and dependency become positive attributes that point up the experience of God as a divine gift that requires no special effort on the part of the recipient.

Teresa of Avila, like the nuns who preceded her, had to deal with a patriarchal society that opposed women writing. As a result, both she and her predecessors often adopted similar rhetorical strategies. Nonetheless, socioreligious circumstances were not constant and, as Alison Weber has shown, Teresa also had to develop new or alternative strategies to deal with those changed circumstances. Over time, the Inquisition sought to discredit the type of unmediated experience of the divine embodied in mystics and visionaries. Women, in particular, were branded as the victims of a delusion, a move that effectively discredited their extraordinary religious experiences.[48] But even such strong opposition failed to halt women's desire to participate in all aspects of the religious life and to enjoy an unmediated access to the divine; visionary nuns proliferated in the late sixteenth and seventeenth centuries.

The particular circumstances of inquisitorial Spain and the powerful influence of Saint Teresa combined to make her *Vida* the primary model for the writing nuns who came after her. Significantly, if previously it was above all apparitions of Jesus and the Virgin Mary that served to authorize the writings of visionaries, in the seventeenth century Teresa joined Christ and his mother as authority figures that validate the texts produced by nuns. Electa Arenal and Stacey Schlau observe that in the writings of María de San Alberto (1568–1640) and Cecilia del Nacimiento (1570–1646), "representations of Saint Teresa overshadow those of the Virgin."[49] Saint Teresa, who herself experienced difficulty in founding her reformed convents, became a role model who appears to have offered encouragement to the seventeenth-century Peruvian nun Madre Antonia Lucía when she had similar problems.[50] Thus, despite the repressive spiritual atmosphere of Counter-Reformation Spain and Spanish America, the seventeenth-century daughters of Saint Teresa had precisely what Teresa's own medieval mothers lacked, a more or less contemporary role model to authorize and otherwise validate their experiences.

Notes

Introduction

1. Manuel Serrano y Sanz, *Apuntes para una biblioteca de escritoras españolas desde el año 1401 al 1833*, 2 vols. (Madrid: Sucesores de Rivadeneyra, 1903–1905).

2. Many such religious women are discussed in Electa Arenal and Stacey Schlau, *Untold Sisters: Hispanic Nuns in Their Own Works* (Albuquerque: University of New Mexico Press, 1989).

3. For this phenomenon, see Sonja Herpoel, "Bajo la amenaza de la inquisición: escritoras españolas en el Siglo de Oro," in *España, teatro y mujeres. Estudios dedicados a Henk Oostendorp*, ed. Martin Gosman and Hub. Hermans (Amsterdam and Atlanta: Rodopi, 1989), 123–131.

4. A single work, the *Camino de perfección*, had already been published separately, albeit still posthumously, in 1583.

5. For a convenient overview, see Alan Deyermond, "Spain's First Women Writers," in *Women in Hispanic Literature: Icons and Fallen Idols*, ed. Beth Miller (Berkeley and Los Angeles: University of California Press, 1983), 27–52, and Francisco López Estrada, "Las mujeres escritoras en la Edad Media castellana," in *La condición de la mujer en la Edad Media* (Madrid: Casa de Velázquez and Universidad Complutense, 1986), 9–38.

6. For Leonor López de Córdoba, see Reinaldo Ayerbe-Chaux, "Las memorias de Doña Leonor López de Córdoba," *Journal of Hispanic Philology* 2 (1977): 11–33; Arturo Firpo, "Un ejemplo de autobiografía medieval: Las *Memorias* de Leonor López de Córdoba (1400)," *Zagadnienia Rodzajów Literackich* 23 (1980): 19–31, and "L'idéologie du lignage et les images de la famille dans les *Memorias* de Leonor López de Córdoba (1400)," *Moyen Age* 87 (1981): 243–262; Clara Estow, "Leonor López de Córdoba: Portrait of a Medieval Courtier," *Fifteenth-Century Studies* 5 (1982): 23–46; Amy Katz Kaminsky and Elaine Dorough Johnson, "To Restore Honor and Fortune: *The Autobiography of Leonor López de Córdoba*," in *The Female Autograph*, ed. Domna C. Stanton and Jeanine Parisier Plottel (New York: New York Literary Forum, 1984), 77–88; Ruth Lubenow Ghassemi, "La 'crueldad de los vencidos': Un estudio interpretativo de *Las memorias de doña Leonor López de Córdoba*," *La Corónica* 18 (1989): 19–32; Louise Mirrer, "Leonor López de Córdoba and the Poetics of Women's Autobiography," *Mester* 20 (Fall 1991): 9–18; María-Milagros Rivera Garretas, "Leonor López de Córdoba: La autorrepresentación," in her *Textos y espacios de mujeres (Europa, siglos IV–XV)* (Barcelona: Icaria, 1990), 159–178; Reinaldo Ayerbe-Chaux, "Leonor López de Córdoba y sus ficciones históricas," in *Historias y ficciones: Coloquio sobre la literatura del siglo XV*, ed. R. Beltrán

et al. (Valencia: Universitat de València, 1992), 17–23; Esther Gómez Sierra, "La experiencia femenina de la amargura como sustento de un discurso histórico alternativo: Leonor López de Córdoba y sus *Memorias*," in *La voz del silencio, I: Fuentes directas para la historia de las mujeres (siglos VIII–XVIII)*, ed. Cristina Segura Graiño (Madrid: Asociación Cultural Al-Mudayna, 1992), 111–129; and Aurora Lauzardo, "El derecho a la escrita: Las *Memorias* de Leonor López de Córdoba," *Medievalia* 15 (diciembre 1993): 1–13. I refer briefly to Leonor López de Córdoba in Chapter 2 of this book.

7. Pinar wrote courtly love poetry that critics have viewed as in some ways atypical in comparison with the poems of her male contemporaries. See Alan Deyermond, "The Worm and the Partridge: Reflections on the Poetry of Florencia Pinar," *Mester* 7 (1978): 3–8; Joseph Snow, "The Spanish Love Poet: Florencia Pinar," in *Medieval Women Writers*, ed. Katharina M. Wilson (Athens: University of Georgia Press, 1984), 320–332; Barbara Fulks, "The Poet Named Florencia Pinar," *La Corónica* 18 (1989): 33–44; and Constance L. Wilkins, "Las voces de Florencia Pinar," in *Studia Hispanica Medievalia II*, ed. Rosa E. Penna and María A. Rosarossa (Buenos Aires: Universidad Católica Argentina, 1990), 124–130. On other female poets of the fifteenth century, see Jane Whetnall, "*Lírica femenina* in the Early Manuscript *Cancioneros*," in *What's Past Is Prologue: A Collection of Essays in Honour of L. J. Woodward* (Edinburgh: Scottish Academic Press, 1984), 138–150, 171–175; *Poesía femenina en los cancioneros*, ed. Miguel Angel Pérez Priego (Madrid: Castalia, 1989); and Jane Whetnall, "Isabel González of the *Cancionero de Baena* and Other Lost Voices," *La Corónica* 21 (1992): 59–82.

8. Representative studies include: *La condición de la mujer en la Edad Media*, ed. Yves-René Fonquerne and Alfonso Esteban (Madrid: Casa de Velázquez and Universidad Complutense, 1986); María del Carmen García Herrero, *Las mujeres en Zaragoza en el siglo XV*, 2 vols. (Zaragosa: Ayuntamiento de Zaragosa, 1990); Marta González Vázquez, *Las mujeres de la Edad Media y el Camino de Santiago* (Santiago de Compostela: Xunta de Galicia, 1989); *La imagen de la mujer en el arte español* (Madrid: Universidad Autónoma, 1984); *Las mujeres en el cristianismo medieval*, ed. Angela Muñoz Fernández (Madrid: Asociación Cultural Al-Mudayna, [1989]); *Las mujeres en las ciudades medievales*, ed. Cristina Segura Graiño (Madrid: Universidad Autónoma, 1984); *Las mujeres medievales y su ámbito jurídico* (Madrid: Universidad Autónoma, 1983); *Ordenamiento jurídico y realidad social de las mujeres*, ed. María Carmen García-Nieto París (Madrid: Universidad Autónoma, 1986); María Carmen Pallares Méndez, *A vida das mulleres na Galicia Medieval (1100–1500)*, trans. Carme Hermida (Santiago de Compostela: Universidade, 1993); María Isabel Pérez de Tudela y Velasco, *La mujer castellano-leonesa durante la Alta Edad Media* (Madrid: Fundación Juan March, 1983?); *Realidad histórica e invención literaria en torno a la mujer*, ed. María T. López Beltrán et al. (Málaga: Diputación Provincial, 1987); *Religiosidad femenina: expectativas y realidades (ss. VIII–XVIII)*, ed. Angela Muñoz and María del Mar Graña (Madrid: Asociación Cultural Al-Mudayna, 1991); Paloma Rojo y Alboreca, *La mujer extremeña en la Baja Edad Media: amor y muerte* (Cáceres: Diputación Provincial, 1987); Cristina Segura, *Las mujeres en el medievo hispano* (Madrid: Marcial Pons, 1984); Cristina Segura Graiño, *Los espacios femeninos en el Madrid medieval* (Madrid: Comunidad de Madrid, 1992); and *El trabajo de las*

mujeres en la Edad Media hispana, ed. Angela Muñoz Fernández and Cristina Segura Graiño (Madrid: Asociación Cultural Al-Mudayna, 1988).

9. Heath Dillard, *Daughters of the Reconquest: Women in Castilian Town Society, 1100–1300* (Cambridge: Cambridge University Press, 1984), 214.

10. Joan Morris, *The Lady Was a Bishop: The Hidden History of Women with Clerical Ordination and the Jurisdiction of Bishops* (New York: Macmillan, 1973), 85–86. See also José María Escrivá, *La Abadesa de Las Huelgas* (Madrid: Luz, 1944).

11. Liber V, Tit. XXXVIII, Cap. X. See *Corpus iuris canonici,* ed. Aemilius Friedberg, 2 vols. (Graz: Akademische Druck-u.Verlagsanstalt, 1955), II, cols. 886–887.

12. Morris, 85.

13. Carvajal, *Poesie,* ed. Emma Scoles (Rome: Ateneo, 1967), 128–129.

14. Fray Martín de Córdoba, *Jardín de nobles donzellas,* ed. Harriet Goldberg (Chapel Hill: University of North Carolina Press, 1974), 244.

15. "Ideo, exceptis illis horis, quibus orationi, lectioni, vel provisioni divini officii, seu cantus seu eruditioni litterarum debent intendere, operibus manuum omnes attente insistant, prout visum fuerit priorisse" ("Regesta romanorum pontificum pro s. ordine fratrum praedicatorum," *Analecta Sacri Ordinis Fratrum Praedicatorum* 3 [1897–1898]: 634).

16. "Sorores postquam officium ecclesiasticum didicerint diligenter, addiscere poterunt tantum ut quod legitur intelligant, ut maiorem habeant devotionem" (Raymond Creytens, O.P., "Les constitutions primitives des soeurs dominicaines de Montargis [1250]," *Archivum Fratrum Praedicatorum,* 17 [1947]: 80).

17. "Ut exceptis illis horis et temporibus, quibus oracioni vel officio vel alii occupacioni necessarie debent intendere, operibus manuum ad utilitatem communem omnes attente insistant, prout fuerit ordinatum" ("Vetera monumenta legislativa Sacri Ordinis Praedicatorum, IV: *Liber constitutionum sororum Ordinis Praedicatorum,*" *Analecta Sacri Ordinis Fratrum Praedicatorum* 3 [1897–1898]: 346).

18. A. H. Thomas, O.P., *De oudste Constituties van de Dominicanen* (Louvain: Universiteitsbibliotheck, 1965), 361–362.

19. Edward T. Brett, "Humbert of Romans and the Dominican Second Order," in *Cultura e istituzioni nell'Ordine Domenicano tra Medioevo e Umanesimo: Studi e testi* (Pistoia: Memorie Domenicane, 1981), 23–24.

20. Anne Bagnall Yardley, "'Ful weel she soong the service dyvyne': The Cloistered Musician in the Middle Ages," in *Women Making Music: The Western Art Tradition, 1150–1950,* ed. Jane Bowers and Judith Tick (Urbana and Chicago: University of Illinois Press, 1986), 19.

21. ". . . aqueles sors les quals sabran cantar e liger, deyen cantar lo offici divinal segons la custuma del orde dels frares menors. . . . E les sors que no saben letres diguen .XX. e .IIII. pater noster per matines, per laudes .V." (Ambrosio de Saldes, "Una versión catalana de la Regla de las Clarisas. Siglo XIV," *Estudios Franciscanos* 8 [1912]: 221).

22. In England, vernacular literacy among nuns seems to have decreased in the later Middle Ages. Certainly, English nuns were more known for their learning in the Anglo-Saxon age than in later periods. See Eileen Power, *Medieval English Nunneries, c. 1275 to 1535* (Cambridge: Cambridge University Press, 1922), 237–246.

For the decline in the Latin literacy of French nuns in the late twelfth and thirteenth centuries, see Charles Jourdain, "Mémoire sur l'éducation des femmes au Moyen Age," *Mémoires de l'Institut National de France: Académie des Inscriptions et Belles Lettres* 28 (1874): 103–104.

23. The queen's teacher may have been Beatriz Galindo, whose knowledge of Latin earned her the nickname "la Latina." See *Las Memorias de Gonzalo Fernández de Oviedo*, ed. Juan Bautista Avalle-Arce, 2 vols. (Chapel Hill: University of North Carolina Press, 1974), 1:339.

24. See José García Oro, O.F.M., *La reforma de los religiosos españoles en tiempo de los Reyes Católicos* (Valladolid: Instituto Isabel la Católica, 1969), and José García Oro, O.F.M., *Cisneros y la reforma del clero español en tiempo de los Reyes Católicos* (Madrid: CSIC, 1971).

25. See Vicente Beltrán de Heredia, O.P., *Cartulario de la Universidad de Salamanca*, 6 vols. (Salamanca: Universidad de Salamanca, 1970–1972), 3:307.

26. Paul Saenger, "Books of Hours and the Reading Habits of the Later Middle Ages," *Scrittura e civiltà* 9 (1985): 240–241.

27. This is evinced from a letter of June 22, 1524, that forms part of his inquisitorial trial. See José C. Nieto, *Juan de Valdés and the Origins of the Spanish and Italian Reformation* (Geneva: Droz, 1970), 73, n. 83.

28. "Reading and writing were not automatically coupled at the end of the twelfth century, nor was a minimal ability to perform these actions described as literacy. Writing was a skill distinct from reading because the use of parchment and quills made it difficult. Likewise the traditional emphasis on the spoken word caused reading to be coupled more often with speaking aloud than with eyeing script. Although the average medieval reader had been taught to form the letters of the alphabet with a stylus on a writing tablet, he would not necessarily have felt confident about penning a letter or a charter on parchment. Scholars and officials employed scribes, particularly for drafting formal legal documents, just as typists are employed today" (M. T. Clanchy, *From Memory to Written Record, England, 1066–1307* [Cambridge, Mass.: Harvard University Press, 1979], 183).

29. "Et pour ce que aucuns gens dient que ilz ne vouldroient pas que leurs femmes ne leurs filles sceussent bien de clergie ne d'escripture, je dy ainsi que, quant d'escripre, n'y a force que femme en saiche riens; mais, quant à lire, toute femme en vault mieulx de le sçavoir" (*Le Livre du Chevalier de La Tour Landry pour l'enseignement de ses filles*, ed. Anatole de Montaiglon [Paris: Jannet, 1854], 178). Philippe de Navarre (d. 1261/64) excepts nuns from his warnings against the dangers of women learning to read and write: "A fame ne doit on apanre letres ne escrire, se ce n'est especiaument por estre nonnain; car par lire et escrire de fame sont maint mal avenu" (*Les Quatre âges de l'homme*, ed. Marcel de Fréville [Paris: Didot, 1888], 16). The prejudice against women learning to write persisted even in late sixteenth-century Spain. The Jesuit Gaspar Astete writes that "la donzella christiana, y verdadera hija de sus padres, para el aprovechamiento de su alma se contente con solo saber leer, y piense que aunque no sepa escrevir no perderá de su honor ni de su reputación" (*Tratado del gobierno de la familia y estado de las viudas y donzellas* [Burgos, 1603], 171). The first edition of Astete's *Tratado* was published in 1597. (I would like to thank Anne Cruz for calling my attention to Astete's treatise.)

30. "Numerous other examples of using 'dictate' where a modern literate would use 'write' could be given. Dictating was the usual form of literary composition" (Clanchy, 218–219).

31. "The commonest way of committing words to writing was by dictating to a scribe. . . . Exceptions to the rule that authors dictated their works are usually monks, as distinct from secular clerics. Monks wrote more of their own works because they were expected to be humble and also because some had training in a *scriptorium*" (Clanchy, 97). Nonetheless, in the later Middle Ages dictation ceased to be the typical mode of composition for ecclesiastics writing in Latin. Silent composition was much slower to replace dictation in the case of vernacular texts. See Paul Saenger, "Silent Reading: Its Impact on Late Medieval Script and Society," *Viator* 13 (1982): 387–388, 404–405.

32. Mary's *taciturnitas* was praised by Richard of Saint Laurent, who contrasts woman's unthinking loquaciousness, which led Eve to be tempted by the serpent, with Mary's reflection, when the angel Gabriel appeared to her: "Notorium enim est et vulgatum muliebrem sexum de multiloquio et minori circumspectione redargui: nec mirum, cum ad primas suggestiones noxias loquela poenitus sit adempta serpenti, et aliquatenus inhibita mulieri. Hic poteris assignare de propera responsione Hevae sine discussione verborum serpentis, unde ortum est omne malum: et cogitatione Mariae qualis esset angelica salutatio, unde ortum est omne bonum" (*De laudibus B. Mariae Virginis*, Book IV, chap. 32, in Albertus Magnus, *Opera omnia*, ed. Auguste Borgnet and Emile Borgnet, vol. 36 [Paris: Vivès, 1898], 267).

33. "Beloved brides of Jesus Christ, look upon your Lady and mine; behold Mary, the mirror of all virtues, and learn from her the discipline of silence. It is easy to see from the Gospels how quiet the Blessed Virgin was, speaking very little, and with few people; it is recorded that she talked to four, and spoke seven times: twice to the angel, twice to Elizabeth, twice to her Son, and once to the attendants at the wedding" ("On the Perfection of Life, Addressed to Sisters," chap. 4, in *The Works of Bonaventure, I: Mystical Opuscula*, trans. José de Vinck [Patterson, N.J.: St. Anthony Guild Press, 1960], 229).

34. For the iconographic motif of Saint Anne teaching the Blessed Virgin to read, see Manuel Trens, *María: Iconografía de la Virgen en el arte español* (Madrid: Plus Ultra, 1947), 136–139, and Gertud Schiller, *Ikonographie der christlichen Kunst, IV, 2: Maria* (Gütersloh: Mohn, 1980), 75–76. For the considerably rarer case of the Virgin depicted as writing, see Trens, 577.

35. Richard of Saint Laurent comments: "De taciturnitate commendatur Maria, quae omnia verba conferens in corde suo, tacite conservabat" (*De laudibus*, Book IV, chap. 32, ed. cit., p. 267).

36. Quoting Luke 2:19, Saint Thomas Aquinas comments that Mary "had the use of wisdom in contemplation," but "she had not the use of wisdom as to teaching; since this befitted not the female sex" (*Summa theologica*, III, Q. 27, art. 5). See *Summa theologica*, trans. Fathers of the English Dominican Province, 3 vols. (New York: Benziger Brothers, 1947–1948), 2:2169.

37. Teresa de Cartagena, *Arboleda de los enfermos. Admiraçión operum Dey*, ed. Lewis Joseph Hutton, *Boletín de la Real Academia Española*, anejo 16 (Madrid, 1967), 48.

38. "Mi grosero juyzio mugeril haze mis dichos de pequeña o ninguna abtoridad" (ibid., 96).

39. "E yo haziendo cuenta con mi pobre juyzio, estando presente la espirençia, la qual en esta çiençia me haze saber más de lo que aprendo" (ibid., 69).

40. Steven E. Ozment has argued that medieval mysticism is an inherently dissident ideology: "It is a receptacle for more intimate communications from God than those which the eyes and ears behold in the sermons, sacraments, ceremonies, and writings of the Church" (*Mysticism and Dissent: Religious Ideology and Social Protest in the Sixteenth Century* [New Haven, Conn. and London: Yale University Press, 1973], 3). Ozment goes on to observe that, because the mystical enterprise is transrational and transinstitutional, "it bears a potential *anti*-intellectual and *anti*-institutional stance, which can be adopted for the critical purposes of dissent, reform, and even revolution" (8). Nonetheless, women's visions, for all their parenthesizing of the Church hierarchy, tended to be conservative with regard to their messages, emphasizing the veneration of the Eucharist and the need for penance. Since both communion and confession were firmly under the control of the male clergy, such visions ended up supporting the ecclesiastical establishment.

41. *Summa theologica*, 3:2698.

42. Donald Weinstein and Rudolph M. Bell, *Saints and Society: The Two Worlds of Western Christendom, 1000–1700* (Chicago and London: University of Chicago Press, 1982), 229. See also Caroline Walker Bynum, *Holy Feast and Holy Fast: The Religious Significance of Food to Medieval Women* (Berkeley and Los Angeles: University of California Press, 1987), 26.

43. Juana de la Cruz, *El libro del conorte*, Escorial, MS J-II-18, fol. 369ᵛ.

44. Christ's words are a paraphrase of Matthew 11:25 ("I confess to thee, O Father, Lord of heaven and earth, because thou hast hid these things from the wise and prudent, and hast revealed them to little ones") and of Luke 10:21.

45. A similar notion is articulated in the sermon devoted to the pains of hell, where the Lord says that sometimes the learned read the Scriptures without understanding them only later to hear them explicated by an unlettered person, and then they understand: "E dixo su divina magestad que algunas vezes permite El que lean los letrados las Santas Escrituras e no las entiendan, e después las oigan dezir algunas personas sinples y entonçes las entienden mejor. E que por eso no deven despreçiar a ninguno que diga la palabra de Dios e la denunçie con caridad e amor de los próximos e deseo de su salvaçión" (*Conorte*, fol. 407ᵛ). The passage suggests a relation between Mother Juana and those who preach the Word of God for the benefit of their neighbors. In any case the sermon discredits book learning and exalts the infused wisdom closely associated with the unlettered and particularly with women.

46. See the facsimile edition with an introductory study by José Manuel Blecua (Madrid: Hauser y Menet, 1948), sig. a 2ʳ.

47. Mary E. Giles, *The Book of Prayer of Sor María of Santo Domingo: A Study and Translation* (Albany: State University of New York Press, 1990), 124.

48. "Non despreçies el consejo de los synples . . . Que muchas vezes enbía Dios su graçia en personas que non se podría pensar, e los consejos son graçia de Dios, e non leys escriptas" (*El libro de los doze sabios o Tractado de la nobleza y*

lealtad, ed. John K. Walsh, *Boletín de la Real Academia Española*, anejo 29 [Madrid, 1975], 107).

49. "Los aldeanos han instintos que los letrados non los podrían conprehender, así en consejos súbitos como en pronosticar las cosas futuras. Esto es por qué las mugeres han buenos consejos súbitos, es a saber, porque non son tan bivas en razón, como los honbres e han más instintos" (Martín de Córdoba, *Compendio de la fortuna*, Book 1, chap. 18, in *Prosistas castellanos del siglo XV (2)*, ed. Fernando Rubio, O.S.A., Biblioteca de Autores Españoles, 171 [Madrid: Atlas, 1964], 34).

50. "El que procura vivir / a la llana y simplemente / sin trabajo y sin mentir / suele a veces adquirir / más que el sabio y diligente. // Y a los que mal les pareçe / de imbidia y malenconía / dicen, segun aconteçe / que a los bobos apareçe / la Virgen Santa María" (Sebastián de Horozco, *Teatro universal de proverbios*, ed. José Luis Alonso Hernández [Universidad de Groningen and Universidad de Salamanca, 1986], 103).

51. "A los que el mundo desprecia / y tiene por insipientes / los desdeña y menosprecia / a los tales Dios los precia / y da graçias excelentes. // A los que desfaborece / el mundo que desvaría / y ser bobos le pareçe / a los tales aparece / la Virgen Santa María" (ibid., 104).

52. "Esto es muy mal dicho en el sentido que el vulgo lo toma, que es quando a una persona poco activa y encogida le sucede una buena fortuna sin que la busque. Lo cierto es que Dios ama mucho el coraçón senzillo y humilde, y no mora en el sobervio y malicioso, y por el consiguiente la Sacratíssima Reyna de los Angeles, la qual muchas vezes se ha aparecido a gente rústica y simple, y reveládoles su voluntad, y la de su preciosíssimo hijo Jesús" (Sebastián de Covarrubias, *Tesoro de la lengua castellana o española* [Madrid: Turner, 1977?], 221).

53. "Breve memorial de los oficios activos y contemplativos de la religión de los frailes menores," ed. Fidel Lejarza and Angel Uribe, O.F.M., in "Escritos villacrecianos," *Archivo Ibero-Americano*, 2ª época, 17 (1957): 691. Likewise, a story from a popular manual for preachers, Sánchez de Vercial's *Libro de los exenplos*, cautions that wisdom (*sciençia*) can exist without formal education (*letras*). Saint Anthony is said to have warned that "before there was booklearning, men were wise." And even now, recalls Sánchez de Vercial, they can be so for that very same reason ("ante que oviesse letras fueron los ombres sabios. E ahun agora syn letras pueden ser por essa misma razón"). See Clemente Sánchez de Vercial, *Libro de los exenplos por a.b.c.*, ed. John Esten Keller (Madrid: CSIC, 1961), 303.

54. " 'Más aprendí en la cella llorando en tiniebra, que en Salamanca, o en Tolosa, e en París estudiando a la candela.' . . . 'Más quisiera ser una vejezuela simple con caridad de amor de Dios e del prójimo, que saber la teología de San Agustín e del Doctor Sutil Escoto.' E por tanto, el primer estudio que él enseñaba a sus discípulos era el llorar e aborrescer el estudio de las letras" ("Segundas satisfacciones," ed. Fidel Lejarza and Angel Uribe, O.F.M., in "Escritos villacrecianos," 862–863).

55. "Memorial contra las laxaciones y abusiones de prelados y súbditos," in "Escritos villacrecianos," 928.

56. "Síguense algunas avisaciones spirituales del santo padre fray Lope," in Angel Uribe, O.F.M., "Nuevos escritos inéditos villacrecianos," *Archivo Ibero-Americano*, 2ª época, 34 (1974): 330–334.

57. *Biografía y escritos de San Vicente Ferrer*, ed. José M. de Garganta, O.P., and Vicente Forcada, O.P. (Madrid: Editorial Católica, 1956), 514–522.

58. Julio Caro Baroja, *Las formas complejas de la vida religiosa* (Madrid: Akal, 1978), 37–42. When Saint Bernardino of Siena warns against false revelations, he begins by referring to both men and women ("quanti e quante"), but then the first adjective is in the feminine and the examples that follow all refer to women who claim to have had supernatural experiences: "O quanti e quante ne so' ingannate! Quante so' di quelle che dicono:—oh, elli m'è venuta una bella visione stanotte. Io viddi così e così, e dissemi ch'io àrei la tale e la tale cosa.—L'altra dice:—elli m'è aparita la Vergine Maria.—L'altra dice: elli m'è apparito uno angelo.—L'altra dice:— e' m'è aparita la luna;—e l'altra,—il sole,—e l'altra—la stella nella mia camara che tutta riluceva" ("Predica XXVIII," in Bernardino of Siena, *Le prediche volgari*, ed. Piero Bargellini [Milan and Rome: Rizzoli, 1936], 622). And when the *Libro de los exenplos* tells an exemplary tale warning that not all visions are to be believed, the protagonist turns out to be a woman ("Visionibus non omnibus est credendum," in Sánchez de Vercial, *Libro de los exenplos*, 329–330).

59. In the *Epistola solitarii* that he attached to Book VIII of his edition of the revelations of Saint Bridget, Alfonso Pecha seeks to defend the authenticity of Bridget's revelations while simultaneously stressing the need to submit such extraordinary phenomena to a careful examination. See Edmund Colledge, "*Epistola solitarii ad reges*: Alphonse of Pecha as Organizer of Birgittine and Urbanist Propaganda," *Mediaeval Studies* 18 (1956): 40–41.

60. Colledge, 46.

61. Paschal Boland, O.S.B., *The Concept of "Discretio spirituum" in John Gerson's "De probatione spirituum" and "De distinctione verarum visionum a falsis"* (Washington, D.C.: Catholic University of America Press, 1959), 30.

62. "Omnis doctrina mulierum, maxime solemnis verbo seu scripto, reputanda est suspecta, nisi prius fuerit altero sex modorum quos supra tetigimus diligenter examinata, et multo amplius quam doctrina virorum. Cur ita? Patet ratio, quia lex communis nec qualiscumque sed divina tales arcet. Quare? quia levius seductibiles, quia pertinacius seductrices, quia non constat eas esse sapientiae divinae cognitrices" (Jean Gerson, *Oeuvres complètes*, ed. Mgr. Glorieux, 10 vols. [Paris: Desclée, 1960–1973], 9:468).

63. And perhaps even—to the extent that visionary experiences were typically associated with women in the Middle Ages—the more "feminine" aspects of religion, for *blandura* (see note 64 below) could have connotations of weakness and effeminacy.

64. "Es la gente (como todos saben) de su natural belicosa, y ocupada en continuas guerras con los Moros que viven juntos con ellos, estava en esta parte como bárbara, desaficionada a esta blandura, y regalo divino, tan importante para las almas" (Fray José de Sigüenza, *Historia de la Orden de San Jerónimo*, ed. Juan Catalina García, vol. 1, Nueva Biblioteca de Autores Españoles, 8 [Madrid, 1907], 316–317).

65. This messianic atmosphere was created in part by royal propagandists. See Américo Castro, *Aspectos del vivir hispánico* (1949; Madrid: Alianza, 1970), 13–45, and José Cepeda Adán, "El providencialismo en los cronistas de los Reyes Católicos," *Arbor* 17 (1950): 177–190.

66. Francisco Jiménez de Cisneros became Queen Isabella's confessor in 1492 and Archbishop of Toledo in 1495. In 1507 he became both inquisitor general and a cardinal.

67. Alvaro Huerga, "La edición cisneriana del *Tratado de la vida espiritual* y otras ediciones del siglo XVI," *Escritos del Vedat* 10 (1980): 297–313.

68. For the relations between Cisneros and the holy women of his time, see Marcel Bataillon, *Erasmo y España*, trans. Antonio Alatorre, 2d ed. (Mexico City: FCE, 1966), 68–71; Alvaro Huerga, O.P., "Los pre-alumbrados y la Beata de Piedrahíta," in Fliche-Martin, *Historia de la Iglesia, vol. 17: El Renacimiento* (Valencia: EDICEP, 1974), 523–546; and José García Oro, *El Cardenal Cisneros: Vida y empresas*, 2 vols. (Madrid: Editorial Católica, 1992–1993), 1:239–256. Cisneros had dealings with the two visionaries discussed in this book who were his contemporaries when he was archbishop of Toledo. Cisneros visited Juana de la Cruz and gave economic help to her convent. Likewise, he was very impressed by his meeting with María de Santo Domingo and protected her from her detractors.

69. Felipe Fernández-Armesto, "Cardinal Cisneros as a Patron of Printing," in *God and Man in Medieval Spain: Essays in Honour of J. R. L. Highfield*, ed. Derek W. Lomax and David Mackenzie (Warminster: Aris and Phillips, 1989), 149–168.

70. "Paresce que en esta muger fuerte claramente se muestra lo que estava abscondido aun a los varones muy especulativos, pero ciegos con sus carnales exposiciones y entendimientos" (*Libro de la bienaventurada Sancta Angela de Fulgino* [Toledo, 1510], fol. 1^r).

71. "A la qual recurría el pueblo en oprobrio e denuesto de los varones e doctores de la ley, que por ser quebrantadores e traspassadores de los mandamientos, la prophecía fue trasladada a sexo femíneo" (ibid., fol. 1^v).

72. Raymond of Capua, *Vida y milagros de la bienaventurada Sancta Catherina de Sena, trasladada de latín en castellano por el reverendo maestro fray Antonio de la Peña* (Medina del Campo, 1569), sig. a 3^r. The first edition of this translation was published in 1511.

73. Apropos of visions of the Passion, F. P. Pickering observes: "It is a fact of textual and iconographical history that what the many visionaries of the later Middle Ages saw, coincides for the greater part with what Anselm in his *Dialogue* and Bonaventura in the *Meditations* had already related, and the artists had meantime drawn or carved" (*Literature and Art in the Middle Ages* [London: Macmillan, 1970], 279–280).

74. Carl A. Keller, "Mystical Literature," in *Mysticism and Philosophical Analysis*, ed. Steven T. Katz (London: Sheldon Press, 1978), 86.

75. For the custom of reading aloud in the Middle Ages, see H. J. Chaytor, *From Script to Print: An Introduction to Medieval Vernacular Literature* (New York: October House, 1967), 10–13.

76. For example, in the constitutions that Saint Dominic wrote for the nuns of San Sisto in Rome, he stipulates: "In refectorio semper ad mensam legatur, et sorores devote cum silentio audiant lectionem" ("Regesta romanorum pontificorum," 629).

77. Ramón F. Pousa, "Catálogo de una biblioteca española del año 1331: el monasterio de San Clemente, de Toledo," *Revista de Bibliografía Nacional* 1 (1940): 50.

78. Olegario González Hernández, "Fray Hernando de Talavera. Un aspecto nuevo de su personalidad," *Hispania Sacra* 13 (1960): 157–158.

79. Ignacio Omaechevarría, O.F.M., *Orígenes de la Concepción de Toledo* (Burgos: Imprenta de Aldecoa, 1976), 168, 217.

80. *Vida y fin de la bienabenturada virgen sancta Juana de la Cruz*, Escorial, MS K-III-13, fol. 15ʳ.

81. *Vida y fin*, fol. 82ᵛ.

82. See S. Berger, "Les Bibles castillans," *Romania* 28 (1899): 360–408, 508–567; Margherita Morreale, "Apuntes bibliográficos para la iniciación al estudio de las traducciones bíblicas medievales al castellano," *Sefarad* 20 (1960): 66–109; and Margherita Morreale, "Vernacular Scriptures in Spain," in *The Cambridge History of the Bible*, vol. 2, ed. G. W. H. Lampe (Cambridge: Cambridge University Press, 1969), 465–491. A Castilian translation of the Bible was printed in 1478. See Encarnación Marín Padilla, "Pablo Hurus, impresor de biblias en lengua castellana en el año 1478," *Anuario de Estudios Medievales* 18 (1988): 591–603.

83. Alfonso Martínez de Toledo, *Arcipreste de Talavera o Corbacho*, ed. J. González Muela (Madrid: Castalia, 1970), 135.

84. Teresa de Cartagena, *Arboleda de los enfermos*, 38. In his testament of October 8, 1464, Gonzalo de Illescas left a glossed Psalter in the vernacular to the nuns of the convent of Santa María de las Dueñas. See Carmen Alvarez Márquez, "Las lecturas de Fray Gonzalo de Illescas, obispo de Córdoba (1454–1464)," in *Las fiestas de Sevilla en el siglo XV: Otros estudios*, ed. José Sánchez Herrero (Madrid: Deimos, 1991), 322.

85. Pousa, "Catálogo," 50.

86. The edict promulgated by the Inquisition of Valencia in 1497 ordered that all Hebrew books and vernacular translations of the Bible were to be turned in and burned. A document from 1498 specifies that this is because it is almost impossible to translate the Bible into a modern language without making errors that could lead the unlearned and especially recent converts to have doubts about their faith. See José E. Serrano y Morales, *Reseña histórica en forma de diccionario de las imprentas que han existido en Valencia desde la introducción del arte tipográfico en España haste el año 1868* (Valencia: F. Domenech, 1898–99), 151–152.

87. "Siempre se tuvo miramiento a los colegios y monesterios y a las personas nobles que estaban fuera de sospecha, y se les daba licencia que las tuviesen y leyesen" (Bartolomé Carranza de Miranda, *Comentarios sobre el Catechismo christiano*, ed. José Ignacio Tellechea Idígoras, 2 vols. [Madrid: Editorial Católica, 1972], 1:110).

88. "La qual obra se fizo a fin que los que la lengua latina ignoran, no sean privados de tan excelente e maravillosa doctrina, qual fue la de Christo nuestro redemptor escripta en los evangelios, e por que cada uno retraído en su casa, despenda el tiempo ante en leer tan altos misterios, que en otros libros de poco fruto" (William of Paris, *Evangelios e epístolas con sus exposiciones en romance*, trans. Gonzalo García de Santa María, ed. Isak Collijn and Erik Staaff [Uppsala: Akademiska Bokhandeln, and Leipzig: Harrassowitz, 1908], 490–491).

89. Margherita Morreale, "Las *Epístolas y evangelios* de Ambrosio Montesino, eslabón entre los romanceamientos medievales y la lectura de la Biblia en el Siglo de Oro," in *Studi in onore di Antonio Corsano*, ed. Mario Sansone (Manduria: Lacaita, 1970), 453.

90. The four-volume Castilian translation by Ambrosio Montesino was published at Alcalá in 1502–1503 under the auspices of Cardinal Cisneros.

91. Sister Mary Immaculate Bodenstedt, *The "Vita Christi" of Ludolphus the Carthusian* (Washington, D.C.: Catholic University of America Press, 1944), 30, 94.

92. Francisco Rico, *Predicación y literatura en la España medieval* (Cádiz: UNED, 1977), 10–11.

93. *Les oeuvres de Marguerite d'Oingt*, ed. Antonin Duraffour, Pierre Gardette, and Paulette Durdilly (Paris: Les Belles Lettres, 1965), 140–143.

94. Teresa de Cartagena, *Arboleda*, 96.

95. *Meditations on the Life of Christ: An Illustrated Manuscript of the Fourteenth Century*, trans. and ed. Isa Ragusa and Rosalie B. Green (Princeton, N.J.: Princeton University Press, 1961), 5.

96. The Castilian poet Juan Alvarez Gato (d. 1510/12) sent certain Christmas meditations (*contenplaçiones*) to a convent of nuns. Afterward, in a poem Alvarez Gato asked the nuns to tell him what they felt when they saw the Redeemer born and when they accompanied the shepherds to adore the Child. The poet thus expected the nuns to use the meditations to react emotionally and to participate imaginatively in the Nativity. For the poem, see *Obras completas de Juan Alvarez Gato*, ed. Jenaro Artiles Rodríguez (Madrid: Nueva Biblioteca de Autores Españoles, 1928), 77–78.

97. *Libro de la casa y monasterio de Nuestra Señora de la Cruz*, Biblioteca Nacional (Madrid), MS 9661, fols. 42^r–44^r, 48^v–51^v.

98. "Secondo che veduti gli avea per le chiese dipinti" (quoted in Millard Meiss, *Painting in Florence and Siena after the Black Death* [New York: Harper and Row, 1964], 105, n. 2). For other examples, see Chiara Frugoni, "Le mistiche, le visioni e l'iconografia: Rapporti ed influssi," in *Temi e problemi nella mistica femminile trecentesca* (Rimini: Maggioli, 1983), 137–179. Nonetheless, in later centuries the resemblances between visions and the pictorial arts could have quite a different meaning. For the Carmelite Juan de Jesús María the resemblance between the sacred figures that appear in visions and the traditional iconographic representations of such figures is a sign that the visions are false. Chapter 10 of his *Guía interior* (1636) is headed: "En que se trata de cómo, cuando se aparece la Santísima Trinidad u otros santos o santas como las pintan, de ordinario, son ilusiones o embustes" (ed. Daniel de Pablo Maroto [Madrid: Fundación Universitaria Española and Universidad Pontificia de Salamanca, 1987], 222–223).

99. Chiara Frugoni, "Il linguaggio dell'iconografia e delle visioni," in *Culto dei santi, istituzioni e classi sociali in età preindustriale*, ed. Sofia Boesch Gajano and Lucia Sebastiani (L'Aquila and Rome: Japadre, 1984), 527–536.

100. See Ronald E. Surtz, *"El libro del conorte" (1509) and the Early Castilian Theater* (Barcelona: Puvill, 1982).

101. Apropos of later manifestations of this unusual combination of motifs, Emile Mâle observes that they were most likely intelligible only to persons who had received sophisticated theological instruction: "Ces images semblaient faites pour des théologiens plutôt que pour le commun des fidèles; elles étaient à leur place à Saint-Pierre de Rome ou chez les Franciscains de l'Aracoeli, familiers avec les plus hautes spéculations, mais, ailleurs, elles risquaient de n'être pas comprises de tous"

(*L'Art religieux de la fin du XVIe siècle, du XVIIe siècle et du XVIIIe siècle*, 2d ed. [1932; Paris: Armand Colin, 1951], 44).

102. Jacob Ornstein, "Misogyny and Pro-feminism in Early Castilian Literature," *Modern Language Quarterly* 3 (1942): 221–234.

103. William A. Christian, Jr., *Apparitions in Late Medieval and Renaissance Spain* (Princeton, N.J.: Princeton University Press, 1981), 4.

104. Technically speaking, the Castilian nuns who had supernatural experiences are not mystics but visionaries and prophets. Classic formulations of the mystic experience focus on the notion of union of the soul with God and the processes that lead up to that moment of union. Nonetheless, to the extent that the visions of the nuns discussed here appear to originate in that direct experience of the Divinity that constitutes the core of the mystic experience, I will continue to refer to them indifferently as both mystics and visionaries.

105. Penelope D. Johnson, "*Mulier et monialis*: The Medieval Nun's Self-Image," *Thought* 64 (1989): 242–253.

106. I use writing in a very loose sense in the case of María de Ajofrín, whose words are inscribed in the biography written by her confessor.

Chapter 1: The New Judith

1. Francisco Cantera Burgos, *Alvar García de Santa María y su familia de conversos. Historia de la judería de Burgos y de sus conversos más egregios* (Madrid: Instituto Arias Montano, 1952), 538.

2. "Teresie moniali centum fl. ad aliquod subsidium sustentacionis" (Cantera Burgos, 537).

3. For Teresa's family see Cantera Burgos, *Alvar García de Santa María y su familia de conversos*.

4. At one point Teresa says that she was young when her deafness became exacerbated: "Pues en la joventut doblar el açote, la obra da testimonio, ca en esta propia hedat se acresçentó mi pasión en la manera que vedes." See Teresa de Cartagena, *Arboleda de los enfermos. Admiraçión operum Dey*, ed. Lewis Joseph Hutton, *Boletín de la Real Academia Española*, anejo 16 (Madrid, 1967), 53. Future references to the works of Teresa de Cartagena will be indicated by the page number in parentheses.

5. "La niebla de tristeza tenporal e humana cubrió los términos de mi bevir e con un espeso torvellino de angustiosas pasiones me llevó a una ínsula que se llama 'Oprobrium hominum et abiecio plebis'" (37). "Oprobrium hominum et abiecio plebis" is a quotation from Psalm 21:7.

6. "Que me acuerdo de un tienpo, el qual era antes que mis orejas çe[r]rasen las puertas a las bozes humanas, aver oído en los sermones" (96). In another passage Teresa states that her deafness began to manifest itself twenty years previous to the time when she is writing: "Que oy son veinte años que este freno ya dicho començó a costreñir la haz de mis vanidades" (51).

7. The probability that Teresa was a Franciscan nun is suggested by the phrase "our most glorious father Saint Francis" ("muy glorioso padre nuestro Sant Françisco" [81]) in the *Arboleda*.

8. Lewis J. Hutton, "Teresa de Cartagena: A Study in Castilian Spirituality," *Theology Today* 12 (1955–1956): 480.

9. "Los amigos nos olvidan, los parientes se enojan, e aun la propia madre se enoja con la hija enferma, y el padre abor[r]esçe al hijo que con continuas dolençias le ocupare la posada" (63).

10. "Non digo que solamente los amigos e parientes le⟨s⟩ avrán en despreçio, mas su mesmo padre y madre dispornán de le desenpachar prestamente de su casa y poner donde ningund detrimento e confusión les pueda venir" (76–77).

11. ". . . los pocos años que yo estudié en el estudio de Salamanca" (103).

12. It appears that in the early years of the fifteenth century a female student did manage to attend the University of Krakow, albeit in male attire. See Michael H. Shank, "A Female University Student in Late Medieval Kraków," *Signs* 12 (1987): 373–380. In 1508 Luisa de Medrano taught—although perhaps only as a substitute—at the University of Salamanca. See Therese Oettel, "Una catedrática en el siglo de Isabel la Católica: Luisa (Lucía) de Medrano," *Boletín de la Real Academia de la Historia* 107 (1935): 334.

13. Alan Deyermond sees the *Arboleda*, at least to some extent, as a work of auto-consolation. See his "'El convento de dolençias': The Works of Teresa de Cartagena," *Journal of Hispanic Philology* 1 (1976): 22. For Juan Marichal, Teresa seeks less to communicate with others than to achieve self-knowledge through communication with herself. See his *La voluntad de estilo* (Madrid: Revista de Occidente, 1971), 43.

14. On Teresa's alleged feminism, see Luis Miguel Vicente García, "La defensa de la mujer como intelectual en Teresa de Cartagena y Sor Juana Inés de la Cruz," *Mester* 18 (1989): 95–103, and María-Milagros Rivera Garretas, "La *Admiración de las obras de Dios* de Teresa de Cartagena y la Querella de las mujeres," in *La voz del silencio, I: Fuentes directas para la historia de las mujeres (siglos VIII–XVIII)*, ed. Cristina Segura Graiño (Madrid: Asociación Cultural Al-Mudayna, 1992), 277–299.

15. Deyermond, "El convento," 25.

16. Teresa observes that Gómez Manrique was also a reader of her *Arboleda*: "E porque me dizen, virtuosa señora, que el ya dicho bolumen de papeles bor[r]ados aya venido a la notiçia del señor Gómez Manrique e vuestra" (114). Rivera Garretas ("La *Admiración*," 279) remarks that, like Christine de Pizan and other fifteenth-century humanists, Teresa seeks to enlist the support of the nobility in her intellectual endeavors.

17. We should keep in mind, however, that writing out of obedience and the claim of divine inspiration can be literary topoi. For the topos of writing by command, see Ernst Robert Curtius, *European Literature and the Latin Middle Ages*, trans. Willard R. Trask (New York: Harper and Row, 1963), 85.

18. Representative examples include such phrases as "diré lo que a mi sinpleza me presenta" (49), "mi pobre e mugeril y⟨e⟩ngenio" (69), "mi grosero juizio mugeril" (96), "el entendimiento flaco e mugeril" (112), "mi flaco mugeril entendimiento" (113), and "mi angosta capaçidad e mugeril entendimiento" (124).

19. When Hildegard sent a copy of her last major work, the *Liber divinorum operum*, to Ludwig, abbot of St. Eucharius, in the accompanying letter (1174) she refers to herself as a "poor little womanly creature." See Peter Dronke, *Women Writers of the Middle Ages: A Critical Study of Texts from Perpetua (†203) to Marguerite*

Porete (†1310) (Cambridge: Cambridge University Press, 1984), 195. As Dronke observes in the case of the German nun Hrotsvitha, the topos of the *vilis muliercula* can be used ironically to indicate anything but humility: "Her insistences on her frailty, lowly submissiveness, and incompetence all contain an element of deliberate over-acting: they can be seen as so many ironic glances at the double standards of the world she knew, and especially of the powerful male-dominated world" (82).

20. For the relation between exemplarity and autobiography in Teresa's *Arboleda*, see Gregorio Rodríguez Rivas, "La autobiografía como *exemplum*: *La arboleda de los enfermos*, de Teresa de Cartagena," in *Escritura autobiográfica*, ed. José Romera Castillo et al. (Madrid: Visor, 1993), 367–370.

21. I have studied the imagery of the *Arboleda* in "Image Patterns in Teresa de Cartagena's *Arboleda de los enfermos*," in *La Chispa '87. Selected Proceedings*, ed. Gilbert Paolini (New Orleans: Tulane University Press, 1987), 297–304.

22. Stephen L. Wailes, *Medieval Allegories of Jesus' Parables* (Berkeley and Los Angeles: University of California Press, 1987), 162–166.

23. Teresa's choice of an Old Testament figure may also reflect an awareness of her Jewish heritage.

24. "Mulier vero a mollitie, tamquam mollier, detracta littera vel mutata, appellata est mulier. Utrique enim fortitudine et inbecillitate corporum separantur" (*Isidori hispalensis episcopi Etymologiarum sive originum Libri XX*, ed. W. M. Lindsay [Oxford: Clarendon Press, 1911], Book XI, chap. ii, 18–19).

25. "Vir nuncupatus, quia maior in eo vis est quam in feminis" (ibid., Book XI, chap. ii, 17).

26. The inside-outside dichotomy is a patriarchal commonplace. Martín de Córdoba writes: "Notá que segund los philósofos en el regimiento doméstico e casero, los oficios del varón e de la muger son repartidos, ca el marido ha de procurar lo de fuera de casa e la muger lo de dentro de casa; ca natural cosa es a la muger estar sienpre en casa." See his *Jardín de nobles donzellas*, ed. Harriet Goldberg (Chapel Hill: University of North Carolina Press, 1974), 206. Writing in 1477, Hernando de Talavera observes that "comúnmente las mujeres están y fueron hechas para estar encerradas e ocupadas en sus casas, y los varones para andar e procurar las cosas de fuera" (*De vestir y de calzar*, in *Escritores místicos españoles*, ed. Miguel Mir, Nueva Biblioteca de Autores Españoles, 16 [Madrid: Bailly-Baillière, 1911], 61). Teresa herself in a later passage in the *Admiración* refers in a negative light to lazy lower-class women who leave their homes all too often to go visiting, neglecting the household duties appropriate to their gender: "mugeres comunes que salen de su casa a menudo e andan vagando por c[a]sas ajenas, las quales, por esta mala costunbre, se fazen así nigligentes e perezosas en el exerçiçio fimíneo e obras domésticas e caseril" (138). Note that Teresa here gives her implicit approval to the enclosure of women—especially aristocratic women—in the domestic sphere.

27. C. B. Bourland, "*La dotrina que dieron a Sarra*. Poema de Fernán Pérez de Guzmán," *Revue Hispanique* 22 (1910): 679. In another strophe Pérez de Guzmán warns women to avoid sermons and pilgrimages in order to not raise suspicions regarding their chastity. Then he cites the case of the Virgin Mary, who was visited by the angel while she was modestly staying home: "La que fue eçelençia de virginidat, / origo e primiçia e forma de aquella, / antes del parto e despúes donzella, /

estando en su casa en toda onestad, / la visitó el ángel con grant homilidat" (vv. 233–237, p. 668). Does the poet wish his readers to conclude that had the Blessed Virgin been gallivanting about at the time, she would have missed the Annunciation? In any case, the need for women to remain at home, particularly in order to safeguard their chastity, is a commonplace of medieval marriage manuals. For example, the fifteenth-century *Castigos y dotrinas que un sabio dava a sus hijas* warns women to go outside the home only when absolutely necessary: "Lo otro que avés de guardar para ser onestas es que no curéis de salir a menudo fuera de vuestras casas, especialmente a los juegos o justas o toros o cosas semejantes, ca la muger que mucho quiere andar por las plaças muestra de sí poca cordura y no pone buen recabdo en su casa, y quando ovierdes de sallir sea a cosas honestas y adó fueren personas honestas y no a semejantes burlas" (in *Dos obras didácticas y dos leyendas*, ed. Hermann Knust [Madrid: Sociedad de Bibliófilos Españoles, 1978], 276).

28. George W. Corner, *Anatomical Texts of the Earlier Middle Ages: A Study in the Transmission of Culture, with a Revised Latin Text of "Anatomia Cophonis" and Translations of Four Texts* (Washington, D.C.: Carnegie Institution, 1927), 103. See also Joan Cadden, *Meanings of Sex Difference in the Middle Ages: Medicine, Science, and Culture* (Cambridge: Cambridge University Press, 1993), 177.

29. In his *Triunfo de las donas* of around 1440, Juan Rodríguez del Padrón writes: "A la muger ninguna cosa se puede ver de las secretas partes, e al onbre por el contrario" (*Obras completas*, ed. César Hernández Alonso [Madrid: Editora Nacional, 1982], 222).

30. Danielle Jacquart and Claude Thomasset, *Sexuality and Medicine in the Middle Ages*, trans. Matthew Adamson (Princeton, N.J.: Princeton University Press, 1988), 81.

31. For a complementary study of the ways in which Teresa subverts gendered notions of masculinity and femininity in the *Admiraçión*, see Dayle Seidenspinner-Núñez, "'El solo me leyó': Gendered Hermeneutics and Subversive Poetics in *Admiraçión operum Dey* of Teresa de Cartagena," *Medievalia* 15 (1993): 14–23.

32. "Este potentísimo Hazedor hizo el sexu beril primeramente, e segunda e por adjutorio de aquél fizo al fimíneo" (116).

33. Saint Thomas Aquinas, *Summa theologica*, trans. Fathers of the English Dominican Province, 3 vols. (New York: Benziger Brothers, 1947–1948), 1:466.

34. Saint Augustine's commentary on Genesis 2:18 similarly reduces woman as helper to a reproductive role, utilizing a rather different sort of natural image: "If one should ask why it was necessary that a helper be made for man, the answer that seems most probable is that it was for the procreation of children, just as the earth is a helper for the seed in the production of a plant from the union of the two" (*The Literal Meaning of Genesis*, Book IX, chap. 3, trans. John Hammond Taylor, S.J. [New York: Newman Press, 1982], 2:73).

35. The *locus classicus* for the image in medieval Castilian literature is the prologue to Gonzalo de Berceo's miracles of the Virgin, concretely, the moment when Berceo as teacher begins to gloss for his readers his allegorical description of heaven: "Sennores e amigos, lo que dicho avemos, / palabra es oscura, esponerla queremos; / tolgamos la corteza, al meollo entremos, / prendamos lo de dentro, lo de fuera dessemos" (*Milagros de Nuestra Señora*, ed. A. G. Solalinde [Madrid: Espasa-Calpe, 1964], 5).

36. Although the instances of Teresa's direct address to her patroness may have a completely arbitrary distribution, it does often appear that Teresa uses such occasions to call attention to a particularly important passage. In that case, the vocatives function as a sort of underlining, exhorting not only the dedicatee but also other readers to pay attention to a significant point.

37. Elena Ciletti observes that a popular tradition transformed Judith from widow to virgin, thus strengthening her identification with the Virgin Mary. See her "Patriarchal Ideology in the Renaissance Iconography of Judith," in *Refiguring Woman: Perspectives on Gender and the Italian Renaissance*, ed. Marilyn Migiel and Juliana Schiesari (Ithaca, N.Y., and London: Cornell University Press, 1991), 43. Virginity was seen as a source of strength, as when Leander of Seville writes that virginity gives a woman a manly vigor that enables her to overcome her natural weakness: "Forgetful of her natural feminine weakness, she lives in manly vigor and has used virtue to give strength to her weak sex, nor has she become a slave to her body, which by natural law should be subservient to a man" (*The Training of Nuns and the Contempt of the World*, Prologue, in *Iberian Fathers, I: Martin of Braga, Paschasius of Dumium, Leander of Seville*, trans. Claude W. Barlow [Washington, D.C.: Catholic University of America Press, 1969], 192).

38. "Behold the head of Holofernes the general of the army of the Assyrians; and behold his canopy, wherein he lay in his drunkenness, where the Lord our God slew him by the hand of a woman" (Judith 13:19).

39. When Clement of Rome is about to cite the cases of Judith and Esther, he echoes the Vulgate, remarking that many women, "invested with power through the grace of God, have accomplished many a manly deed" (*First Epistle to the Corinthians*, 55, in *The Epistles of St. Clement of Rome and St. Ignatius of Antioch*, trans. James A. Kleist, S.J. [Westminster, Md.: The Newman Bookshop, 1946], 42). Martín de Córdoba juxtaposes his approval of the daring and strength of Judith with an excursus on the daring, strong, and likewise chaste Amazons (*Jardín de nobles donzellas*, 249).

40. The sword-phallus connection is not an invention of modern psychoanalysis, for *vagina*, the Latin word for the female genitalia, literally means "a sheath or scabbard for a sword."

41. When it comes time to speak of the proper activities for a noblewoman in Pérez de Guzmán's *La dotrina que dieron a Sarra*, the poet singles out arms and letters as being the least appropriate: "que no en armas ni en cavallería / porque la flaqueza de su coraçón no sufrirá miedo, ni la conplisión / tierna los trabajos conportar podría. // Ni es convenible a ella ciençia / por el grant trabajo del estudiar, / ni sería onesto a ella la presençia / de los escolares, ni su conversar" (vv. 421–428, ed. Bourland, pp. 678–679). A hundred years later in an assessment (1558–1559) of Carranza's *Catechismo*, in order to belittle the participation of women in biblical interpretation, Melchor Cano quotes the proverb "Armas y dineros, quieren buenas manos," leading his readers to conclude that scriptural exegesis is as inappropriate for the female gender as is participation in warfare and business. See the *Qualificación hecha por los maestros Cano y Cuevas del Catechismo [de Carranza]*, in *Fray Bartolomé Carranza: Documentos históricos, VI = Audiencias III*, ed. J. Ignacio Tellechea Idígoras, Archivo Documental Español, 33 (Madrid: Real Academia de la Historia, 1981), 234.

42. By placing Judith in the company of classical heroes like Horatius Cocles, Publius Decius Mus, and Scipio Africanus, who sacrificed themselves for the good of the state, Alvaro de Luna suggests such a "political" reading of the biblical heroine in his *Libro de las claras e virtuosas mugeres*, ed. Manuel Castillo, 2d ed. (Valencia: Prometeo, [1917]), 37–41.

43. The fourteenth-century *Speculum humanae salvationis* juxtaposes Judith severing Holofernes's head with the Blessed Virgin spearing a bound devil. See Marina Warner, *Monuments and Maidens: The Allegory of the Female Form* (New York: Atheneum, 1985), 164.

44. Warner, 169.

45. Warner, 167–168.

46. Apparently, readers of both sexes shared not only the same assumptions concerning gender roles, but also a certain wonderment at Teresa's composition of the *Arboleda*: "Muchas vezes me es hecho entender, virtuosa señora, que algunos de los prudentes varones e así mesmo henbras discretas se maravillan o han maravillado de un tratado que, la graçia divina administrando mi flaco mugeril entendimiento, mi mano escrivió" (113).

47. Ciletti, "Patriarchal Ideology," 35–36, esp. n. 2.

48. "El solo me consoló, e El solo me enseñó, e El solo me leyó" (131). Here, "leyó" ("read") seems to have the meaning of "taught," as when in medieval universities the professor taught by reading aloud the texts of canonical authors, supplying his own commentary.

49. Deyermond, "The Convent," 25.

50. Gregory the Great, *Forty Gospel Homilies*, trans. Dom David Hurst (Kalamazoo, Mich.: Cistercian Publications, 1990), 94–95.

51. "Caecus significat humanum genus, quod a superna claritate exclusum damnationis suae patitur tenebras, sed a Domino appropinquante Hiericho curatur" (*Glossa ordinaria*, IV: 204).

52. Other patristic interpretations of the biblical episode offer a similarly collective meaning. For example, the blind man represents the gentiles for Rupert of Deutz (*In Evangelium S. Joannis commentariorum Libri XIV*, *Patrologia Latina*, 169, col. 587).

53. "Que vea yo luz por la qual la mi tinebrosa e mugeril inorançia sea alunbrada de los rayos de la tu muy alta prudençia" (133).

54. For the concept of sex-linked male languages, see Walter J. Ong, S.J., *Interfaces of the Word: Studies in the Evolution of Consciousness and Culture* (Ithaca, N.Y., and London: Cornell University Press, 1977), 25. On Teresa's use of Latin, see also Seidenspinner-Núñez, "'El solo me leyó'," 17.

55. Walter J. Ong, S.J., "Latin Language Study as a Renaissance Puberty Rite," in *Rhetoric, Romance, and Technology: Studies in the Interaction of Expression and Culture* (Ithaca, N.Y., and London: Cornell University Press, 1971), 120.

56. Martín de Córdoba quotes Valerius Maximus to prove this point: "Que hornamento e compostura graciosa de la muger es el silencio" (*Jardín de nobles donzellas*, 156). In another pasage, referring to women's natural loquacity, he observes: "Y esto tiene buen remedio: que la muger ponga silencio e guarda en su lengua e quando quisiere hablar que se muerda primero la lengua e los labros, por que no salga palabra que no sea limada por juyzio de razón" (211).

57. "Çerró las puertas de mis orejas por donde la muerte entrava al ánima mía e abrió los ojos de mi entendimiento, e vi e seguí al Salvador" (137).

58. "E desta manera el mi çego entendimiento ⟨acatar con diligencia⟩ vio, e seguió e sigue al Salvador, manificando a Dios" (137).

59. Teresa's strategy here is at best ambiguous, if only from the perspective of recent attempts to portray her as a feminist writer and her *Admiración* as a feminist text. Teresa can be said to be egotistical to the extent that her own case is what matters. The *Admiración* is above all a self-defense, an effort to disarm the critics of her *Arboleda*; it is anything but a vindication of the rights of all women to express themselves by writing, for it never occurs to Teresa, for example, to advocate education for women or to suggest that any woman has the right to compose a spiritual treatise.

Chapter 2: Constanza de Castilla and the Gynaeceum of Compassion

1. J. B. Sitges, *Las mujeres del rey don Pedro I de Castilla* (Madrid: Sucesores de Rivadeneyra, 1910), 408–409. For Pedro's marriage to Juana, see also Pero López de Ayala, *Corónica del rey don Pedro*, ed. Constance L. Wilkins and Heanon M. Wilkins (Madison, Wis.: Hispanic Seminary of Medieval Studies, 1985), 52–53. Prince Juan's mother may have actually been a commoner, for the assertion that she was Juana de Castro occurs only in a sixteenth-century chronicle falsely attributed to Pedro Gracia Dei (see note 6). The spurious chronicle was intended to exalt Prince Juan's descendants, the Castilla clan, by enhancing the status of Prince Juan as King Pedro's legitimate heir. See Nancy F. Marino, "Two Spurious Chronicles of Pedro *el Cruel* and the Ambitions of His Illegitimate Successors," *La Corónica* 21:2 (1993): 7–10. What is important, however, is that, whoever Prince Juan's mother may have been, King Pedro recognized the prince as his son.

2. Sitges (448) supposes that he was brought there by his maternal uncle, Fernando de Castro, one of King Pedro's staunchest supporters. England supported King Pedro, and Gascony, being under English control, was thus a safe haven. It was also at Bayonne in Gascony where King Pedro and his daughters (Beatriz, Constanza, and Isabel) sought refuge in 1366. See P. E. Russell, *The English Intervention in Spain and Portugal in the Time of Edward III and Richard II* (Oxford: Clarendon Press, 1955), 57–59.

3. In 1372 King Pedro I's daughter Constanza had married John of Gaunt, the duke of Lancaster (Sitges, 440).

4. Sitges, 447–448.

5. Sitges, 448.

6. *Historia del Rey Don Pedro, y su descendencia, que es el linage de los Castillas. Escrita por Gracia Dei, glosado y anotado por otro autor, quien va continuando la dicha descendencia*, ed. Antonio Valladares de Sotomayor, in *Semanario Erudito* 28 (1790): 259. Sister C. de Jesús states that Constanza professed in 1408. See *Breve reseña histórica del Convento de Santo Domingo el Real de Madrid desde su fundación por el mismo santo patriarca Domingo de Guzmán año del Señor de 1218* (Santiago de Compostela: Seminario Conciliar, 1946), 28.

7. One of Catherine's first actions upon her husband's death was to enlist Fernando's support so that she could take personal charge of raising her son. The queen's effort went against the wishes of her late husband, whose testament had stipulated that Diego López de Astúñiga, Juan de Velasco, and the bishop of Cartagena take charge of the Prince until he should reach the age of fourteen, that is, the age when he could legally rule. Catherine shut herself up in the royal castle at Segovia with the prince and her other children and refused to turn the heir over to López and Velasco. Efforts to mediate the dispute were unsuccessful at first, but Catherine won out in 1407, when López and Velasco agreed to accept a consolatory sum of six thousand florins a year (Alvar García de Santa María, *Crónica de Juan II de Castilla*, ed. Juan de Mata Carriazo y Arroquia [Madrid: Real Academia de la Historia, 1982], 23–24, 31, 49, 88). Although Queen Catherine was no doubt motivated by maternal concerns, keeping her son in her personal care was also a source of power, for it meant that she would not be relegated to a marginal position in Castilian politics. The queen managed to keep her son with her for ten years, but after the death of her co-regent Fernando in 1416, Catherine agreed to comply with her husband's testament and handed the prince over to López and Velasco (*Crónicas de los reyes de Castilla*, ed. Cayetano Rosell, Biblioteca de Autores Españoles, 68 [Madrid, 1877], 372).

8. As supporters of King Pedro I, Leonor López de Córdoba's family was on the losing side in the civil war, but Leonor managed to restore the family fortunes and to become the favorite of Catherine of Lancaster. Leonor is the author of an interesting autobiographical memoir in which she recounts her travails and efforts to rehabilitate her family. For the text, see Reinaldo Ayerbe-Chaux, "Las memorias de Doña Leonor López de Córdoba," *Journal of Hispanic Philology* 2 (1977): 11–33.

9. "La qual dueña [Leonor] hera muy privada de la Reyna, en tal manera que cosa del mundo non fazía sin su consejo" (García de Santa María, *Crónica de Juan II de Castilla*, 56).

10. Clara Estow, "Leonor López de Córdoba: Portrait of a Medieval Courtier," *Fifteenth-Century Studies* 5 (1982): 37.

11. In a letter dated September 28, 1408, Fernando expresses his dismay at Leonor's control over the queen. He accuses Leonor of accepting bribes, for anyone who wants to see the queen must first deal with Leonor. See the "Relación que enbió el infante don Ferrando de lo pasado en el reino desde que el rey don Enrrique murió fasta agora" in Juan Torres Fontes, "La regencia de don Fernando de Antequera," *Anuario de Estudios Medievales* 1 (1964): 427.

12. Adolfo de Castro quotes the corresponding passage from Alvar García de Santa María's *Crónica de Juan II de Castilla*, a passage not included in the manuscript of the chronicle edited by Carriazo. See Adolfo de Castro, "Memorias de una dama del siglo XIV y XV (de 1363 a 1412): Doña Leonor López de Córdoba," *La España Moderna* 164 (August 1902): 120.

13. Adolfo de Castro (120–121) quotes a letter from Catherine to Leonor in which the queen refers to Leonor as "very beloved" and "mother." When in 1410 the co-regent Fernando needed funds from Catherine to pay his troops during the siege of the Moorish city of Antequera, he called upon Leonor, who was still in exile, to support his request, and she did so (García de Santa María, *Crónica de*

Juan II de Castilla, 353). However, when in 1412 Leonor herself sought Fernando's help to enable her to return to the court, the queen became angry, believing that Leonor was now on Fernando's side. In a letter to Fernando, Catherine threatened to have Leonor burned if she came near her (*Crónicas de los reyes de Castilla*, 344). In another letter to her son's chief harbinger, Catherine ordered Leonor's person and property to be seized should she approach Toledo (C. García Rey, "La famosa priora doña Teresa de Ayala. Su correspondencia íntima con los monarcas de su tiempo," *Boletín de la Real Academia de la Historia* 96 [1930]: 754).

14. *Crónicas de los reyes de Castilla*, 372.

15. Jeremy N. H. Lawrance, *Un episodio del proto-humanismo español: Tres opúsculos de Nuño de Guzmán y Giannozzo Manetti* (Salamanca: Diputación de Salamanca, 1989), 38.

16. *Crónicas de los reyes de Castilla*, 372.

17. *Crónicas de los reyes de Castilla*, 372. Meanwhile, Inés had been the mistress of Luis de Guzmán, the master of the military order of Calatrava, by whom she had had seven children. The couple could not regularize their union, for the master of Calatrava was required to take a vow of celibacy. See Jeremy N. H. Lawrance, "Nuño de Guzmán and Early Spanish Humanism: Some Reconsiderations," *Medium Aevum* 51 (1982): 64. Lawrance hypothesizes that "the pair had contracted an illegal chivalric 'secret marriage'" (84). A *Crónica de Juan II* says that Inés had been *desposada* (formally engaged to be married) before she arrived at court (*Crónicas de los reyes de Castilla*, 372). No social stigma seems to have been attached to such liaisons among the nobility—Lawrance cites a number of other notorious cases; obviously, it made no difference to Queen Catherine. Although Inés and Luis eventually married, the couple did not live together during the infancy of their offspring, and it was to Inés alone that fell the task of raising the children (Lawrance, "Nuño de Guzmán," 65–66). Inés was herself well educated and a patron of learning; in 1445 she had her chaplain copy out a Castilian translation of Seneca's *De ira* (Lawrance, "Nuño de Guzmán," 57). This "single mother" *avant la lettre* sought to assure that her children were likewise well educated; indeed, one of her sons, Nuño de Guzmán, became a noted humanist and patron of learning.

18. When Inés de Torres was exiled from the court, she took refuge in the convent of Santo Domingo el Real in Toledo. An affectionate letter from Queen Catherine to the prioress, Teresa de Ayala, begs her to receive Inés as she would Catherine herself (García Rey, 755–756). García Rey (726) states that Inés became a nun at Santo Domingo, whose archive preserves the testament she dictated on May 31, 1442. While Inés may have lived there for a time, it seems unlikely that she ever professed. A *Crónica de Juan II* states that when Inés was exiled from the court, the queen ordered her to become a nun in Toledo, but when the former favorite's supposed paramour begged her not to go to Toledo, she did as he wished (*Crónicas de los reyes de Castilla*, 372). Inés and Luis de Guzmán finally married in 1440, but Inés was widowed in 1443. It is improbable that she became a nun at that time because the copy of the Senecan treatise that she commissioned in 1445 indicates that she had a personal chaplain and thus was living outside the convent.

19. García Rey, 703. García Rey (705) hypothesizes that it was precisely this blot on the family honor that led the Ayalas to switch their support from Pedro

to his bastard half-brother Enrique during the civil war. In 1374 Teresa's family married her off to the Portuguese nobleman Juan Núñez de Aguilar (García Rey, 708–709). She was widowed in 1384; by 1393 the former royal concubine, along with her daughter María, had entered the Dominican convent of Santo Domingo el Real in Toledo.

20. García Rey, 709–710.

21. With the permission of the officials of the Dominican order, Teresa was present when Queen Catherine gave birth to Princess María (García Rey, 736–738). Later, during the illness of another daughter, Princess Catherine, the queen wrote to Teresa, begging her and the other nuns to pray for health of the princess (García Rey, 715–716). Teresa, along with her daughter María, was again summoned to be present at the birth of Catherine's son Prince Juan (García Rey, 738–741). The king himself consulted with Teresa regarding the selection of wet nurses for the prince (García Rey, 742). When the queen dared to set up the newborn prince's household without consulting the king, the angry monarch ordered Teresa and her daughter María to tell his wife Catherine not to interfere in such matters (García Rey, 745). The queen was soon to have a freer hand, for the king died nine months after the birth of Prince Juan.

22. She was the wet nurse of the king's son, Prince Alfonso, and with her Pedro I fathered two illegitimate offspring, Princes Diego and Sancho. Lady Isabel's children spent the greater part of their lives as prisoners of their uncle, the bastard usurper King Enrique II. Sancho died in prison at an early age, and Teresa had his body buried in her own convent of Santo Domingo el Real, an action that earned her a letter of profuse thanks from Queen Catherine, who addresses Teresa affectionately as her "mother" and María as her "aunt" (García Rey, 747–749). Queen Catherine sent the imprisoned Prince Diego clothing, calling him her "dear uncle" (García Rey, 749–750). Teresa's daughter, María de Ayala, whom Diego addresses as his "sister," helped the prince to obtain certain funds that Queen Catherine had assigned to him (García Rey, 750–753). Meanwhile, Diego had fathered five children with the daughter of his jailor; Teresa de Ayala raised three of them (García Rey, 723–725).

23. In a letter dated February 16, 1464, Constanza recounts how she sent her young niece, who had been ill for three and a half months, to the tomb of Blessed Diego of Alcalá (d. 1463), where she was cured. See Lucio María Núñez, O.F.M., "Carta de una nieta del Rey D. Pedro I," *Archivo Iberoamericano* 2 (1915): 127.

24. Luis G. Alonso Getino, "Centenario y Cartulario de nuestra Comunidad," *La Ciencia Tomista* 20 (1919): 130–131.

25. Alonso Getino (ibid., 132) calculates that Constanza became prioress in 1415. Since her parents married after 1388, if Constanza were the firstborn child, she could have been born at the earliest in 1389. Nonetheless, Prince Juan may not have married so soon after his imprisonment. Moreover, either Constanza's brother Pedro or one of the three other children who died in infancy (Alonso Getino, ibid., 135) could have been born before her, which would place her birth in the mid to late 1390s. This means that Constanza was not over eighteen, and probably even younger, when she took the veil and in her low to mid-twenties when she became prioress.

26. The constitutions for Dominican sisters indicate that the master general of the order or the provincial prior is to appoint a new prioress in those convents where such a practice is customary. Elsewhere, the community of nuns is to elect the prioress, but that choice must be ratified by the master general, provincial, or vicar. See "Vetera monumenta legislativa Sacri Ordinis Praedicatorum, IV: *Liber constitutionum sororum Ordinis Praedicatorum*," *Analecta Sacri Ordinis Fratrum Praedicatorum* 3 (1897): 346. In a letter (May 1220) to the sisters of Santo Domingo el Real in Madrid, the future Saint Dominic authorizes his half-brother Mames, "if necessary, to remove the prioress from office, provided that a majority of the nuns agree" (*Early Dominicans: Selected Writings*, trans. Simon Tugwell, O.P. [New York: Paulist Press, 1982], 394).

27. "Doña Constanza, fija de don Juan e nieta del Rey don Pedro, . . . Priora del Monesterio de Santo Domingo de Madrid" (Alonso Getino, "Centenario y Cartulario," 131–132).

28. Ibid., 133–134.

29. Ibid., 134–135.

30. Ibid., 139–141.

31. Ibid., 141–142.

32. For the date, see ibid., 141.

33. Ricardo del Arco, *Sepulcros de la casa real de Castilla* (Madrid: CSIC, 1954), 299. Constanza thus lived well into her eighties. Perhaps her status as nun was a factor in achieving such longevity, for married women had to contend with the dangers of childbirth. In her study of members of the royal family in fourteenth-century Castile and León, Reyna Pastor de Togneri notes that in more than half of the cases studied (twelve out of nineteen), the marriage lasted less than ten years, most likely due to the wife's death in childbirth. See her "Historia de las familias en Castilla y León (siglos X–XIV) y su relación con la formación de los grandes dominios eclesiásticos," *Cuadernos de Historia de España* 43–44 (1967): 99–101.

34. Ana María Huélamo San José, "El devocionario de la dominica Sor Constanza," *Boletín de la Asociación Española de Archiveros, Bibliotecarios, Museólogos y Documentalistas* 42:2 (1992): 136.

35. In one of her prayers Constanza says: "Asimesmo te suplico que enbíes tu graçia sobre todas las dueñas d'este monesterio, acresçientes sus virtudes e les des buena fin, pues sabes tú el grant defecto mío como soy nigligente en su regimiento" (Constanza de Castilla, *Devocionario*, Biblioteca Nacional, Madrid, MS 7495, fol. 30^r). Future references to MS 7495 will be indicated by the folio number in parentheses.

36. Constanza also prays for "King ***," the name being left blank. Presumably, the lacuna corresponds to the name of Enrique III, the husband of Catherine of Lancaster (Huélamo San José, 140).

37. The same prayer ("Domine Jesu Christe, qui hanc sacratissimam carnem") is found in the book of hours published in Paris by Simon Vostre in 1498. See Félix Soleil, *Les Heures gothiques et la littérature pieuse aux XVe et XVIe siècles* (Rouen: Augé, 1882), 83. The prayer that opens "Otórgame, Señor, misericordioso Dios, aquellas cosas que a ti son placenteras codiciar con grande ardor et verdaderamente conoscer e cuerdamente las buscar et perfectamente las acabar" (MS

7495, fol. 99^r) is obviously translated from the same Latin original as the fifteenth-century French prayer that begins: "Sire Dieux de misericorde, donne moy ce qui te plaist ardemment convoiter, sagement encerchier, vraiement congnoistre et perfaittement acomplir." See No. 3636 in Keith V. Sinclair, *French Devotional Texts of the Middle Ages: A Bibliographic Manuscript Guide* (Westport, Conn.: Greenwood Press, 1979), 164.

38. *Ordenar* can be related to the technical term, *ordinatio*, which involved the organization and presentation of texts by means of the systematic use of descriptive rubrics, subheadings, marginal numbers, an analytical table of contents, and so on. Closely related is the notion of *compilatio*, the arrangement of the texts of recognized authorities in the form of a systematized anthology. See M. B. Parkes, "The Influence of the Concepts of *Ordinatio* and *Compilatio* on the Development of the Book," in *Medieval Learning and Literature: Essays Presented to Richard William Hunt*, ed. J. J. G. Alexander and M. T. Gibson (Oxford: Clarendon Press, 1976), 115–141. Janet Coleman observes that different manuscripts of the *Canterbury Tales* group the stories differently and that in several manuscripts the work is called a *compilatio*. For example, the colophon of the Ellesmere Manuscript reads: "Here is ended the book of the tales of Canterbury compiled by Geoffrey Chaucer." See her *Medieval Readers and Writers, 1350–1400* (New York: Columbia University Press, 1981), 199. Although Constanza mixes her own texts with those of other authors, she can nonetheless be considered a kind of *compilator*.

39. ". . . que tú, Señor, non acates salvo mi deseo que fue de te loar e servir" (fol. 82^v).

40. For example, Hildegard of Bingen refers to herself with the humility formula *ego paupercula feminea forma* ("a poor little figure of a woman"). See Barbara Newman, *Sister of Wisdom: St. Hildegard's Theology of the Feminine* (Berkeley and Los Angeles: University of California Press, 1987), 2.

41. When the authors of the *Hammer of Witches* seek to explain "Why Superstition is chiefly found in Women," they observe that women "are more credulous; and since the chief aim of the devil is to corrupt faith, therefore he rather attacks them." Furthermore, "women are naturally more impressionable, and more ready to receive the influence of a disembodied spirit." Quoting Terence with obvious approval, they note: "Women are intellectually like children" (Heinrich Kramer and James Sprenger, *The Malleus maleficarum*, trans. Montague Summers [1928; New York: Dover, 1971], 43–44).

42. Archivo Histórico Nacional, Clero, Carpeta 1364, nos. 2, 3, and 19.

43. Perhaps the daughters of noble families were also accepted as pupils, as was often the case in sixteenth-century Italy. See Paul F. Grendler, *Schooling in Renaissance Italy: Literacy and Learning, 1300–1600* (Baltimore and London: Johns Hopkins University Press, 1989), 96–97. For the same phenomenon in medieval France, see Charles Jourdain, "Mémoire sur l'éducation des femmes au Moyen Age," *Mémoires de l'Institut National de France: Académie des Inscriptions et Belles Lettres* 28 (1874): 94–95.

44. In the case of England, Eileen Power concludes that few nuns knew Latin and that most must have sung the offices by rote. See *Medieval English Nunneries, c. 1275 to 1535* (Cambridge: Cambridge University Press, 1922), 246. Thomas

Gascoigne (1403–1458) wrote his *Miroure of Oure Ladye*, which contains English translations of the hours and masses of the Virgin Mary, for the nuns of Syon so that they could understand what they were singing in Latin (Power, 253–254).

45. Since the translation is done in rhyme, Alonso Getino concludes that it was intended to be sung. See Luis G. Alonso Getino, "Los primeros versos castellanos acerca de Santo Tomás de Aquino," *La Ciencia Tomista* 23 (1921): 146.

46. In his *On the Formation of Preachers*, the master general Humbert of Romans (ca. 1200–1277) offered four reasons why women should not be permitted to preach: "First, lack of understanding, because a man is more likely to have understanding than a woman. Secondly, the inferior status imposed on women; a preacher occupies a superior position. Thirdly, if a woman were to preach, her appearance would inspire lustful thoughts. . . . And fourthly, as a reminder of the foolishness of the first woman, of whom Bernard says, 'She taught once and wrecked the whole world.'" (*Early Dominicans*, 223).

47. The forms "Costanza" and "Constanza" coexist in the manuscript.

48. A. J. Minnis, *Medieval Theory of Authorship: Scholastic Literary Attitudes in the Later Middle Ages*, 2d ed. (Philadelphia: University of Pennsylvania Press, 1988), 170.

49. Christiane Marchello-Nizia, "L'Historien et son prologue: forme littéraire et stratégies discursives," in *La Chronique et l'histoire au Moyen Age*, ed. Daniel Poirion (Paris: Presses de l'Université de Paris-Sorbonne, [1984]), 13–25.

50. Don Juan Manuel, *El conde Lucanor*, ed. José Manuel Blecua (Madrid: Castalia, 1969), 47.

51. "Yo, don Johan, fijo del infante don Manuel" (ibid., 51)

52. Gonzalo de Berceo, *La "Vida de San Millán de la Cogolla" de Gonzalo de Berceo: Estudio y edición crítica*, ed. Brian Dutton (London: Tamesis, 1967), 158–159. Similarly, Berceo's *Poema de Santa Oria* ends: "Gonçalo li dixieron al versificador, / que en su portalejo fizo esta labor; / ponga en él su graçia Dios el Nuestro Señor, / que vea la su Gloria en el Regno Mayor. Amen" (ed. Isabel Uría Maqua [Madrid: Castalia, 1981], 140). In the case of Berceo's *Vida de Santo Domingo de Silos*, the poet's signature occurs likewise near the end of the poem: "Yo, Gonçalo por nonbre, clamado de Berceo, / de Sant Millán crïado, en la su merçed seo, / de fazer est' travajo ovi muy gran deseo, / riendo gracias a Dios quando fecho lo veo. // Sennor Sancto Domingo, yo bien estó creído / por est' poco servicio que en él é metido, / que fará a don Christo por mí algún pedido, / que me salve la alma quando fuere transido" (ed. Aldo Ruffinatto [Logroño: Diputación Provincial, 1978], 266). In the nineteen strophes that follow, the poet first requests that his audience pray for him; then, as the poem ends, he prays to Saint Dominic himself that he protect and give succor to Berceo and to all Christians (266–271).

53. Ayerbe-Chaux, "Las memorias," 16.

54. Amy Katz Kaminsky and Elaine Dorough Johnson, "To Restore Honor and Fortune: *The Autobiography of Leonor López de Córdoba*," in *The Female Autograph*, ed. Domna C. Stanton (New York: New York Literary Forum, 1984), 80.

55. The term is probably of biblical origin, for elsewhere (fol. 1ᵛ) Constanza

appropriates Psalm 21:7 ("But I am a worm and no man: the reproach of men and the outcast of the people").

56. Letter of April 10, 1420. Archivo Histórico Nacional, Clero, Carpeta 1364, no. 19.

57. "E suplico a ti, en cuya memoria de tu encarnación e Pasión yo conpuse las cosas sobredichas, que me faga parçionera en los méritos de las personas que lo rezaren" (fol. 83ʳ). Cf. "E ruega a cuantas personas la rezaren que le den parte de su devoçión" (fol. 1ʳ).

58. For a very early (ca. 200), but representative, example, see Edmond Martène, *De antiquis ecclesiae ritibus libri*, 4 vols. (Antwerp, 1736; facsimile reprint: Hildesheim: Georg Olms, 1967), I, cols. 954–955. These interrogations were later incorporated into Part III of the various versions of the *Ars moriendi*. See Sister Mary Catharine O'Connor, *The Art of Dying Well: The Development of the "Ars moriendi"* (New York: Columbia University Press, 1942), 31–36. For a Spanish instance that is textually very close to Constanza's interrogations, see *Arte de bien morir*, Biblioteca Nacional (Madrid), MS 6485, fols. 8ᵛ–10ʳ.

59. Later, Constanza briefly envisions her work as being used by a wider audience that includes both sexes: "E aunque estas preguntas sobredichas se deven fazer a todas presonas, más conveniblemente se deven fazer a religiosos e a presonas devotas" (fol. 98ʳ).

60. J. B. Lightfoot, *The Apostolic Fathers*, Part 2 (London: Macmillan, 1885), 590.

61. ". . . que sienpre a El fuste junta, familar e sabidora de los secretos d'El" (fol. 94ʳ).

62. Lightfoot (2:1, 224) hypothesizes that the phrase may refer to Ignatius's letter to one Mary of Cassola, who is addressed as *Christofera filia Maria*, that is to say, "Christ-bearing daughter Maria." Although Ignatius used that phrase in a spiritual sense, it would have been easy to interpret it literally and to assume that the letter was addressed to the Blessed Virgin. Indeed, that phrase may have inspired the forger of Ignatius's apocryphal letter to the Virgin to enlarge the correspondence.

63. Jacob, that is, Saint James the Less, was generally identified with the James that Saint Paul mentions as "James the brother of the Lord" (Galatians 1:19). According to the *Golden Legend* (I:270), Christ and James were often mistaken for one another. Although the two were not really brothers, the resemblance was explained in genealogical terms: their mothers, the Blessed Virgin (the daughter of Saint Anne and Joachim) and Mary Cleophas (the daughter of Saint Anne and Cleophas) were half sisters, and their fathers (foster father in the case of Christ) were brothers, Joseph and Alpheus (*Golden Legend*, I:270 and II:150). Christ and James were often represented iconographically as similar in appearance.

64. Lightfoot, 2:1, 224.

65. Botticelli's "Madonna of the Magnificat" depicts the Virgin holding the Child with one arm and writing out the Magnificat with her free hand. See Caterina Caneva, *Botticelli: catalogo completo dei dipinti* (Florence: Cantini, 1990), 66–67.

66. Caroline Walker Bynum, *Holy Feast and Holy Fast: The Religious Signifi-*

cance of Food to Medieval Women (Berkeley and Los Angeles: University of California Press, 1987), 269.

67. Bynum, *Holy Feast*, 269.

68. I use the title *Hours of the Nails*, translating the rubric of the vernacular version of this office, *Oras de los clavos*. The office also contains a votive mass in commemoration of the nails.

69. The semicloistered life that the Virgin led is one of the virtues for which she was traditionally praised. The *Vita Beate Virginis Marie et Salvatoris rhythmica*, from the first half of the thirteenth century, states that when Mary was a young girl living in the temple, she seldom went out: "In hoc autem collegio Maria morabatur / Iugiter et rarius egrediebatur" (ed. Adolf Vögtlin [Tübingen: Litterarischen Verein in Stuttgart, 1888], 37).

70. One example concerns the Virgin's *compassio*: "O Lady, what are you doing? You stay at the feet of the most wicked of men; you pray to the inexorable" (*Meditations on the Life of Christ: An Illustrated Manuscript of the Fourteenth Century*, trans. and ed. Isa Ragusa and Rosalie B. Green [Princeton, N.J.: Princeton University Press, 1961], 339).

71. Walter J. Ong, S.J., "Latin Language Study as a Renaissance Puberty Rite," in *Rhetoric, Romance, and Technology: Studies in the Interaction of Expression and Culture* (Ithaca, N.Y., and London: Cornell University Press, 1971), 113–141.

72. Here I discuss only the *Hours of the Nails*, the office that Constanza composed in Latin and then translated into Castilian. She also wrote a liturgical office in honor of the Incarnation: "Este oficio ordenó la mesma so[r]or sobredicha" (fol. 31ᵛ). This office appears only in Latin (fols. 31ᵛ–44ʳ).

73. Sabina Flanagan, *Hildegard of Bingen, 1098–1179: A Visionary Life* (London and New York: Routledge, 1989), 107.

74. Saint Hildegard of Bingen, *"Symphonia": A Critical Edition of the "Symphonia armonie celestium revelationum" [Symphony of the Harmony of Celestial Revelations]*, ed. and trans. Barbara Newman (Ithaca, N.Y., and London: Cornell University Press, 1988), 17–18.

75. An official historian of the Dominican order notes that the *Hours of the Nails* were celebrated with the permission of the popes and the masters general of the order. See Fray Juan López, *Tercera parte de la historia general de Sancto Domingo y de su orden de predicadores* (Valladolid, 1613), 128.

76. "La terçera es la que comúnmente los católicos, así eclesiásticos como seglares [fazemos] que tiende en Dios, fazen pediéndole con toda humildat la vida perdurable e algunos otros bienes espirituales e tenporales que desseamos en cuanto conviene a lo eterno poder alcançar" (*El "Oracional" de Alonso de Cartagena*, ed. Silvia González-Quevedo Alonso [Valencia: Albatros Ediciones, and Chapel Hill, N.C.: Hispanófila, 1983], 50).

77. " 'La oración es una petición' en que pedimos a Dios las cosas que nos son convenibles" (ibid., 115).

78. Clemente Sánchez de Vercial, *Libro de los exenplos por a.b.c.*, ed. John Esten Keller (Madrid: CSIC, 1961), 256–257.

79. For the prevalence of this indulgenced prayer in French books of hours, see A. Wilmart, O.S.B., *Auteurs spirituels et textes dévots du Moyen Age latin* (Paris:

Bloud et Gay, 1932), 378, n. 10. For a Spanish instance, see Biblioteca Nacional (Madrid), MS 6539, fol. 51^r.

80. Leonor López de Córdoba furnishes several examples of this mentality. She believes that Mary answered her request for a favor when she said a certain prayer to the Virgin and three hundred Ave Marias nightly for a period of thirty days (Ayerbe-Chaux, "Las memorias," 21). On another occasion she believes she was rewarded after reciting a prayer to the Virgin sixty-three times and sixty-six Ave Marias daily over a period of thirty days (22).

81. Margherita Morreale, "Los *Gozos* de la Virgen en el *Libro* de Juan Ruiz (II)," *Revista de Filología Española* 64 (1984): 7.

82. V. Leroquais, *Les Sacramentaires et les missels manuscrits des bibliothèques publiques de France*, 3 vols. (Paris, 1924), 2:77.

83. Wilmart, 327–329.

84. The symbolic relation between the Fifteen Joys and the fifteen steps is also found in the mid-thirteenth-century *Meditationes de gaudiis beate et gloriose semper virginis Marie* of Stephen of Salley (Wilmart, 339).

85. *Golden Legend*, II:152–153.

86. For the text, see V. Leroquais, *Les Livres d'Heures manuscrits de la Bibliothèque Nationale*, 3 vols. (Paris, 1927), 2:310–311. Leroquais (1:xxvii) observes that this version of the Fifteen Joys is found in most books of hours produced in northern France.

87. For the text, see Iñigo López de Mendoza, Marqués de Santillana, *Obras completas*, ed. Angel Gómez Moreno and Maximilian P. A. M. Kerkhof (Barcelona: Planeta, 1988), 373–376.

88. Pious tradition errs here. Since Pedro was murdered in 1369 and Constanza's parents did not marry until after 1388, the king never met his granddaughter.

89. C. de Jesús, *Breve reseña*, 28–29.

90. Christiane Klapisch-Zuber, "Holy Dolls: Play and Piety in Florence in the Quattrocento," in her *Women, Family, and Ritual in Renaissance Italy*, trans. Lydia Cochrane (Chicago: University of Chicago Press, 1985), 324.

91. "Esta oración que se sigue conpuso una soror de la Orden de Sancto Domingo de los Predicadores, la cual es grant pecadora. E ruega a cuantas personas la rezaren que le den parte de su devoçión. E suplica a Nuestro Señor que la faga partiçionera de sus mereçimi[en]tos. Dévese dezir esta oración ante de la comunión" (fol. 1^r).

92. Paul Saenger observes that the silent recitation of vernacular prayers during Mass was a significant innovation of the fourteenth and fifteenth centuries. In contrast to the liturgical uniformity of the Latin missal, such private vernacular prayers varied greatly according to individual desires and circumstances. See "Books of Hours and the Reading Habits of the Later Middle Ages," *Scrittura e civiltà* 9 (1985): 263–266.

93. The prototype of such novelization was, of course, the *Meditations on the Life of Christ* of the Pseudo-Bonaventure.

94. "E *posumus credere* que Sant Juan, tu amado diçípulo, que presente fue a todos los tormentos que reçebiste, sufrió tan grant pesar que perdería todos sus sentidos, mesaría sus cabellos, daría fuertes golpes en su rostro e pechos con espe-

sos gemidos, abondosas lágrimas en tanto grado que aquel día fue mártir" (fols. 17ᵛ–18ʳ).

95. "La Madalena con sobrepujante amor e dos hermanas de la gloriosa con deudo natural, Marta obligada de beneficios, todos con grandísimo amor e dolor mesarían sus cabellos, rasgarían sus caras, braços, manos, pechos e con agudos gritos lloraron amargosamente la cruel e desonrada muerte que padesçías, timientes que la gloriosa daría su ánima ese mesmo día" (fol. 18ʳ).

96. "But I am a worm and no man: the reproach of men and the outcast of the people" (Psalm 21:7).

97. In the final chapter on Pentecost, Constanza juxtaposes the motif of the Descent of the Holy Spirit with the request that God compensate her lack of wisdom in leading her charges (fol. 30ʳ).

98. Del Arco, *Sepulcros de la casa real de Castilla*, 299. While such gisants were commonly portrayed with the hands joined in prayer or the arms crossed on the breast, sometimes the dead were represented with some emblem of their earthly life. Thus, a clergyman could appear holding a chalice or a sacred book in his hands. An architect might hold a pair of compasses and a square. See Henriette s'Jacob, *Idealism and Realism: A Study of Sepulchral Symbolism* (Leiden: Brill, 1954), 19–20. The tombs of Eleanor of Aquitaine and Henry the Lion at Fontevrault show them holding a prayer book and a sword respectively. See Erwin Panofsky, *Tomb Sculpture: Four Lectures on Its Changing Aspects from Ancient Egypt to Bernini*, ed. H. W. Janson (New York: Abrams, [1964]), 57.

99. Huélamo San José, 139. John Gower's tomb (1408) depicts him lying prone with his head resting on three of his works (s'Jacob, 206).

Chapter 3: María de Ajofrín

1. Fray Juan de Corrales, *Vida de María de Ajofrín*, Escorial, MS C-III-3, fols. 193ʳ–231ᵛ. References to this manuscript will be indicated by "Corrales" and the folio number in parentheses.

2. Fray José de Sigüenza, *Historia de la Orden de San Jerónimo*, ed. Juan Catalina García, vol. 2, Nueva Biblioteca de Autores Españoles, 12 (Madrid, 1909), 358. Succeeding references to Sigüenza's chronicle will be indicated by "Sigüenza" and the page number in parentheses.

3. For a study of Dominican friars who were the confidants of female saints and either wrote or contributed their testimony to the biographies of those women, see John Coakley, "Friars as Confidants of Holy Women in Medieval Dominican Hagiography," in *Images of Sainthood in Medieval Europe*, ed. Renate Blumenfeld-Kosinski and Timea Szell (Ithaca, N.Y., and London: Cornell University Press, 1991), 222–246.

4. Coakley (223, n. 3) cautions that such biographies actually bear witness to the hagiographers' experience of their saints rather than to the saints' experience itself.

5. Sigüenza rounds out his narrative with a hagiographic commonplace. For the motif of precocious sanctity, see Donald Weinstein and Rudolph M. Bell,

Saints and Society: The Two Worlds of Western Christendom, 1000–1700 (Chicago and London: University of Chicago Press, 1982), 29.

6. The same criterion prevailed at the end of the sixteenth century, for Alonso de Villegas (*Adición a la tercera parte del Flos sanctorum* [Toledo, 1588], fol. 62ʳ) and Sigüenza (358) use the same adverb. This is a hagiographic commonplace. For example, Book I, chap. 4, of the life of Lutgard of Aywières (d. 1246) tells how she rejected the unwelcome wooing of a certain knight, and the chapter heading notes that she "manfully repulsed and confounded him" ("viriliter repulit eum, et confudit [sic]"). See *Acta Sanctorum*, June 16 (1867), 189. For the application of the metaphor of "becoming male" to outstanding women in the Christian West, see Margaret R. Miles, *Carnal Knowing: Female Nakedness and Religious Meaning in the Christian West* (1989; rpt. New York: Vintage, 1991), 55–56.

7. "Tanta fue la fuerça que a los padres y hermanos hizo que de todos fue aborrezida" (Corrales, 194ʳ). The motif of familial opposition is a traditional hagiographic formula. See Michael Goodich, "The Contours of Female Piety in Later Medieval Hagiography," *Church History* 50 (1981): 24–25.

8. William A. Christian, Jr., *Local Religion in Sixteenth-Century Spain* (Princeton, N.J.: Princeton University Press, 1981), 16.

9. A modern historian of the order gives 1510 as the year of the official incorporation of the convent. See Josemaría Revuelta Somalo, *Los jerónimos: Una orden religiosa nacida en Guadalajara* (Guadalajara: Institución Provincial de Cultura, 1982), 305.

10. "Abrí, que viene el Señor a posar en [v]uestra casa" (Corrales, 196ʳ).

11. The Sunday within the octave of Easter seems like an odd moment to have a vision that rewrites a Christmas episode. While there may be no necessary connection between the octave of Easter and the content of the vision, it is pertinent to note that the readings in the Roman Breviary for that Sunday include the biblical episode in which the apostles were gathered together "and the doors were shut" for fear of the Jews. Nonetheless, Jesus "came and stood in the midst" (John 20:19), passing miraculously through the closed doors.

12. Corrales's narration reads: "su ángel e con azotes y a unos fiera a unos." I have amended the passage in the light of Pedro de la Vega's version: "Venido es el tiempo en que es tan menospreciado el hijo de Dios, mas tiempo es que embíe el Señor su ángel para que a unos hiera con açotes y a otros con espada y a otros con fuego" (*Chronicorum fratrum hieronymitani ordinis* [Alcalá, 1539], Book III, fol. 95ᵛ).

13. Cf. Deuteronomy 17:8.

14. "Aqueste es mi Hijo muy amado" (Corrales, 197ᵛ). These are the words spoken by the Heavenly Father at Christ's baptism (Matthew 3:17) and then again at Christ's transfiguration (Matthew 17:5).

15. According to Sigüenza (361), the reference is to unworthy priests.

16. "Ve y di por horden todo lo que viste a tu confesor, para que lo diga al deán y al capellán mayor para que de todos sea sabido por que no carezcan estas cosas de muy grandes méritos" (Corrales, 197ᵛ). A notarial document later quoted by Corrales (231ʳ) identifies the dean and the *capellán mayor* as Pedro [Jiménez] de Préxano and Diego de Villaminaya, respectively.

17. André Vauchez observes that in the late Middle Ages female visionaries

tended to address their messages to the upper ecclesiastical hierarchy, rather than to the masses of the faithful: "Si divers que puissent être leur tempérament et leur sensibilité, les voyantes de cette époque, une fois convaincues de l'importance de leur tâche et de la réalité de leur élection, adoptent une démarche commune. Elles ne cherchent pas à s'adresser au peuple, mais à promouvoir la réforme de l'Eglise par en haut, comme si à leurs yeux la *reformatio in capite* commandait la *reformatio in membris*. D'où, l'aspect socialment élitique de ces interventions qui se traduisent par des messages adressés aux papes, cardinaux, souverains et grands de ce monde, et par des démarches visant à rencontrer ces personnalités influentes pour les admonester et les inviter à agir dans le sens voulu par Dieu" ("Prophétesses, visionnaires et mystiques en Occident aux derniers siècles du Moyen Age," in *Les Réformes: enracinement socio-culturel*, ed. Bernard Chevalier and Robert Sauzet [Paris: Editions de la Maisnie, 1985], 67).

18. "La sierba del Señor, fuerte ansí como león, lo increpó muy duramente de la tal dureza e incredulidad de su coraçón, mostrándole por razones muy duras que creyese sin dubda que ninguno escribió las cartas sino ella por su mano con el ángel" (Corrales, 200^V). Obviously, the comparison of María to a lion is an editorial embellishment on the part of Corrales, as is the likening of her doubting confessor to the apostle Thomas.

19. The notarial document asserts that the wound was in the same place as the lance wound in Christ's side (Corrales, 231^V). The late Middle Ages developed a special devotion to the wound in Christ's side, which was represented in prayer books in drawings that purported to reproduce its exact size and shape. According to L. Gougaud, O.S.B. ("La prière dite de Charlemagne et les pièces apocryphes apparentées," *Revue d'Histoire Ecclésiastique* 20 [1924]: 224), the wound was depicted as six to nine or ten centimeters long and three to four centimeters wide. Since a man's thumb could fit into María's wound, it was presumably a smaller version of Christ's. See also W. Sparrow Simpson, "On the Measure of the Wound in the Side of the Redeemer, Worn Anciently as a Charm, and on the Five Wounds as Represented in Art," *Journal of the British Archaeological Association* 30 (1874): 357–374.

20. "De la corona de dolores que sintió en su cabeza en remenbranza de la corona de Nuestro Señor" (Corrales, 203^V).

21. For this important political and ecclesiastical figure, see F. Javier Villalba Ruiz de Toledo, *El cardenal Mendoza (1428–1495)* (Madrid: Rialp, 1988).

22. It is not clear exactly when Juan de Velma stopped being María's confessor, but it appears that he was still fulfilling that function when she received the sign of the sword wound, for Corrales's narrative (202^V) speaks of her confessor in the third person. Previously, chapter 11 (199^{rv}) specified that it was Juan de Velma who suggested to María that she ask for a divine sign.

23. Perhaps this document corresponded to the first twenty-nine or so chapters of Corrales's extant biography, for at the end of chapter 29 Corrales comments: "Y para dezir estas cosas se hizo muy gran fuerza porque le avíais mandado por obediençia que a ninguno las dixese salvo a mí, que ninguna cosa me encubría de las que el Señor le mostrava" (212^V) ("And she had to force herself to reveal these things because you had ordered her out of obedience to reveal them to no one save to me, for she concealed nothing of what the Lord revealed to her"). The "you"

in this passage seems to refer to the archbishop, whom Corrales assumes to be the receiver of his narrative.

24. "... vidi illud testimonium notarii confirmatur de tales testigos, varones y mugeres, a quien toda fe se deve dar" (Corrales, 230^r).

25. William A. Christian, Jr., *Apparitions in Late Medieval and Renaissance Spain* (Princeton, N.J.: Princeton University Press, 1981), 194.

26. María did not know how to write. Chapter 68 of Corrales's narrative describes how she dictated to her secretary, Inés de San Nicolás, a letter for Cardinal Mendoza (228^v). Apparently, however, María could read a little, for her biographer occasionally portrays her with a book of devotions in her hands. In 1489 while María was praying from a book for the health of a nun who had the plague, a skull appeared on the page, which she interpreted as a sign that her companion was to die (Corrales, 221^{rv}). Elsewhere María is seen embracing a book of devotions (Corrales, 215^v) or praying in the oratory of the convent from two books in which her devotions are written (Corrales, 217^r). Thus, while unable to write, she was probably at least phonetically literate and could thus decode devotional prayers.

27. For Italy, see Kate Greenspan, "Matre Donante: The Embrace of Christ as the Virgin's Gift in the Visions of 13th-Century Italian Women," *Studia Mystica* 13:2–3 (1990): 26–37. For Dominican convents in fourteenth-century Germany, see Rosemary D. Hale, "*Imitatio Mariae*: Motherhood Motifs in Devotional Memoirs," *Mystics Quarterly* 16 (1990): 193–203.

28. Gertrud the Great of Helfta, *The Herald of God's Loving-Kindness*, trans. Alexandra Barratt (Kalamazoo, Mich.: Cistercian Publications, 1991), 139.

29. Henry Suso, *The Exemplar, with Two German Sermons*, ed. and trans. Frank Tobin (New York: Paulist Press, 1989), 80.

30. Perhaps because iconographic representations of Luke 2:28 often depicted the Blessed Virgin handing the Child to Simeon.

31. *Il libro della beata Angela da Foligno*, ed. Ludger Thier, O.F.M., and Abele Calufetti, O.F.M., 2d ed. (Grottaferrata: Collegium S. Bonaventurae ad Claras Acquas, 1985), 587–589.

32. Manuel Trens mentions a fifteenth-century painting belonging to the school of Nice in which Mary stands before an altar, dressed in the priestly garb of the Old Testament. The Virgin extends her hand toward the Child Jesus as if to offer him upon the altar. For Trens, the allusion to the Eucharistic sacrifice is obvious. See *María: Iconografía de la Virgen en el arte español* (Madrid: Plus Ultra, 1947), 444–445.

33. Eucharistic visions were more typically received by holy women than by their male counterparts. See Caroline Walker Bynum, *Holy Feast and Holy Fast: The Religious Significance of Food to Medieval Women* (Berkeley and Los Angeles: University of California Press, 1987), 76–77.

34. A passage in Saint Bernard's third sermon on the Purification reads: "Offer thy Son, then, O holy Virgin, present to the Lord the 'blessed Fruit of thy womb' (Luke i. 42). Offer for the reconciliation of us all the 'living sacrifice, holy, pleasing unto God' (Rom. xii. 1). Certainly, God the Father will accept this new Oblation, this most precious Victim of Whom He says, 'This is My beloved Son in Whom I am well pleased' (Matt. iii. 17)" (*St. Bernard's Sermons for the Seasons and*

Principal Festivals of the Year, trans. by a priest of Mount Melleray, 3 vols. (Westminster, Md.: The Carroll Press, 1950], 3:99–100). It is worth noting that the biblical verse "This is my beloved Son" is likewise quoted by the Father in María's vision. María de Ajofrín's Ascension vision juxtaposes the sculptures of the Annunciation (which is to say, Christ's Incarnation), the Virgin's offering of her son to the priest, and the Consecration of the Mass. For the association of the Annunciation or the Incarnation with the Consecration in the Middle Ages, see Bynum, *Holy Feast*, 81. For the juxtaposition of the Consecration and the Incarnation and for miracles in which the host changes into the Child Jesus, see Leah Sinanoglou, "The Christ Child as Sacrifice: A Medieval Tradition and the Corpus Christi Plays," *Speculum* 48 (1973): 491–509.

35. Pseudo-Albert the Great, *Mariale*, Quaestio XLI, in Albertus Magnus, *Opera Omnia*, ed. Auguste Borgnet and Emile Borgnet, vol. 37 (Paris: Vivès, 1898), 79–80.

36. "Maria dicto vespere jovis sancto, etsi non fuit insignita caractere sacerdotalis officii dum Judas illum suscepit, nihilominus tunc et antea et postmodum fuit in regale sacerdotium prae consortibus suis inuncta, non quidem ad consecrandum sed ad offerendum hanc hostiam puram, plenam et perfectam in altari cordis sui, in quo semper ignis ardebat holocausti" (Jean Gerson, *Collectorium super Magnificat*, in *Oeuvres complètes*, ed. Mgr. Glorieux, 10 vols. [Paris: Desclée, 1960–1973], 8:384).

37. "De manera que Nuestra Señora hera el sacerdote grande que comulgava e dava a todos el Señor" (Juana de la Cruz, *El libro del conorte*, Escorial, MS J-II-18, fol. 57ᵛ).

38. Caroline Walker Bynum, "The Female Body and Religious Practice in the Later Middle Ages," in *Zone 3: Fragments for a History of the Human Body*, ed. Michel Feher, 3 vols. (New York: Orzone, 1989), 1:182.

39. For a view of the female visionary experience as an alternative to the male authority of office, see Caroline Walker Bynum, *Jesus as Mother: Studies in the Spirituality of the High Middle Ages* (Berkeley and Los Angeles: University of California Press, 1982), 261–262.

40. The notion that the Blessed Virgin suffered a passion parallel to that of Christ first became important in the twelfth century.

41. As Bynum has argued (*Holy Feast*, 263), for many holy women *imitatio Christi* meant identification with Christ's feminine aspect, his suffering humanity.

42. Saint Paul relates the words of God to a two-edged sword: "For the word of God is living and effectual and more piercing than any two-edged sword" (Hebrews 4:12). Elsewhere, Paul refers to "the sword of the Spirit (which is the word of God)" (Ephesians 6:17).

43. On Mendoza's promotion of his personal and family interests, see Helen Nader, *The Mendoza Family in the Spanish Renaissance, 1350 to 1550* (New Brunswick, N.J.: Rutgers University Press, 1979), 119–123.

44. There was a minor meeting of parish priests in 1493, but that meeting was presided over by Mendoza's vicar general. See José Sánchez Herrero, *Concilios provinciales y sínodos toledanos de los siglos XIV y XV* (La Laguna: Universidad de La Laguna, 1976), 73. The brief acts of the meeting deal mostly with liturgical mat-

ters and also order priests to announce the names of the excommunicated from the pulpit on Sundays (339–340).

45. Albert A. Sicroff, *Los estatutos de limpieza de sangre: Controversias entre los siglos XV y XVII* (Madrid: Taurus, 1985), 103–105.

46. Haim Beinart, "The Judaizing Movement in the Order of San Jerónimo in Castile," in *Scripta Hierosolymitana*, VII: *Studies in History*, ed. Alexander Fuks and Israel Halpern (Jerusalem: Magnes Press, 1961), 183. Beinart erroneously gives Gonzalo Manrique as the name of the corregidor of Toledo.

47. Beinart, 167, n. 2.

48. Perhaps he was one of the two Hieronymites from the monastery of La Sisla burned at the stake on July 27, 1488. See F. Fita, "La Inquisición toledana. Relación contemporánea de los autos y autillos que celebró desde el año 1485 hasta el de 1501," *Boletín de la Real Academia de la Historia* 11 (1887): 306.

49. Diego de Zamora, a Hieronymite monk from the monastery of San Bartolomé de la Lupiana near Guadalajara, was in the service of Cardinal Mendoza. Under the cardinal's orders, he acted to remove Jews from those quarters of Alcalá de Henares inhabited by a mixed population of Jews and converted Jews. When Zamora was accused in 1489 of Judaizing, his lawyers argued that he had been falsely denounced by his enemies, and the cardinal himself intervened on behalf of his servant, proving that several Jews testifying against Diego were perjurers. Diego de Zamora was therefore acquitted (Beinart, 183–188).

50. Nader, 122. It must be said that Mendoza preferred less extreme means of resolving the question of the orthodoxy of the converted Jews, seeking to educate the *conversos* in their new faith through preaching and the diffusion of a catechism (Villalba Ruiz de Toledo, 204 and 208).

51. In the Synod of Toledo of 1483 Carrillo likewise opposed the imposition of statutes of blood purity that would have excluded the descendants of Jews from certain religious orders, institutions of higher education, and confraternities (Sicroff, 106).

52. Pilar León Tello, *Judíos de Toledo*, 2 vols. (Madrid: CSIC, 1979), 1:254–256.

53. Sicroff, 106.

54. Sicroff, 107–111.

55. Sicroff, 112.

56. "Y como yo estuviese en la exsaminatión de los procesos de la Inquisitión de Toledo" (Corrales, 222^r). Corrales also traveled to Burgos on Inquisition business ("cuando iba a la Inquisitión a tierra de Burgos" [223^v]). Elsewhere, he says that he was "exsaminando los proçessos de los herejes de Toledo" (224^r).

57. "Me dixo que estuviese fuerte en las batallas del Señor" (Corrales, 222^v).

58. Fita, 300–301.

59. Fita, 303–304.

60. Bynum, *Holy Feast*, 64.

61. Clemente Sánchez de Vercial, *Libro de los exenplos por a.b.c.*, ed. John Esten Keller (Madrid: CSIC, 1961), 48.

62. *Libro de los exenplos*, 233. Similar stories are told in the Dominican preaching manual, *The Gift of Fear*. See *Early Dominicans: Selected Writings*, ed. Simon Tugwell, O.P. (New York: Paulist Press, 1982), 376–381.

Chapter 4. The New Magdalen

1. This was a truly exceptional case. Inquisitorial scrutiny and suspicion of female mystics severely diminished the chances that their writings could be published at all, let alone during their lifetimes. Saint Teresa's works were not published until 1588, that is, six years after her death. Indeed, female revelations were seldom printed, but biographies were considered less controversial, especially if published at a certain chronological distance from the lifetime of the individual. For example, the visions of Mother Juana de la Cruz were never printed, but biographies of her were published in 1610 and 1622, that is, considerably long after her death in 1534.

2. Vicente Beltrán de Heredia observes that the last document that mentions María is dated 1524 and suggests, therefore, that 1524 was the year of her death. See his *Historia de la reforma de la provincia de España (1450–1550)* (Rome: Istituto Storico Domenicano, 1939), 138. Other biographical sources for María de Santo Domingo include: Bernardino Llorca, S.J., *La Inquisición española y los alumbrados (1509–1667)*, Refundición y puesta al día de la edición de 1936 (Salamanca: Universidad Pontificia, 1980), chap. 2, 37–64, and Appendix 1, 259–271; and Alvaro Huerga, O.P., "Los pre-alumbrados y la Beata de Piedrahíta," in Fliche-Martin, *Historia de la Iglesia, vol. 17: El Renacimiento* (Valencia: EDICEP, 1974), 523–546.

3. Beltrán de Heredia, *Historia*, 78.

4. Ibid., 79–81.

5. Ibid., 81–82. For the Beata's relations with King Ferdinand, Cardinal Cisneros, and the duke of Alba, see Jodi Bilinkoff, "A Spanish Prophetess and Her Patrons: The Case of María de Santo Domingo," *Sixteenth Century Journal* 23 (1992): 21–34.

6. Beltrán de Heredia, *Historia*, 82–86.

7. Jodi Bilinkoff, "Charisma and Controversy: The Case of María de Santo Domingo," *Archivo Dominicano* 10 (1989): 55.

8. Ibid., 58.

9. Beltrán de Heredia, *Historia*, 87–93, 100.

10. Jesús G. Lunas Almeida, *La historia del Señorío de Valdecorneja en la parte referente a Piedrahíta* (Avila: S. Martín, 1930), 155.

11. ". . . porque les parece que de esa manera tienen alguna virtud y luego las llevan como reliquia" (Lunas Almeida, 156). Taking as her cue the testimony of Sor María del Cordero, who testified that María wore fine clothing only as a sacred image might wear it (Lunas Almeida, 192), Bilinkoff refers to the Beata's totally passive role, "that of a living statue or icon, dressed by members of the faithful hoping for some contact with the divine" ("Charisma and Controversy," 64).

12. "Que cuando algunas veces, dicha Sor María baila y juega al ajedrez y hace otras cosas de recreación de su espíritu, piensa en cosas divinas y santas, lo cual se demuestra porque se suele arrebatar algunas veces y, estando en tal estado, dice cosas muy divinales y provocativas a gran devoción, dando a entender maravillosamente la limpieza de sus pensamientos" (Lunas Almeida, 156).

13. "Que los varones y religiosos que conversan con dicha María, muchas veces se quedan con ella de día o de noche por ayudarla, consolarla y acompañarla en los dolores, angustias y tormentos que su cuerpo padece y porque algunas veces

son tan grandes y tan recios sus males, que verdaderamente llega a punto de muerte; y también por ayudarla en las persecuciones y tormentos que los demonios la dan muy a menudo, dejándola malamente herida, llagada y toda ensangrentada, pero que dichos varones nunca la acompañan con mal fin" (Lunas Almeida, 157).

14. Beltrán de Heredia, *Historia*, 123–124. For Cajetan's notorious misogyny and its probable repercussion in the case of María de Santo Domingo, see Alvaro Huerga, O.P., "Un problema de la segunda escolástica: la oración mística," *Angelicum* 44 (1967): 21–25.

15. Beltrán de Heredia, *Historia*, 125.

16. Ibid., 135.

17. There is a modern facsimile edition with an introduction by José Manuel Blecua: *"Libro de la oración" de Sor María de Santo Domingo* (Madrid: Hauser y Menet, 1948). Quotations from this edition will be indicated by the signature and folio number in parentheses. The *Libro de la oración* has been recently translated into English: Mary E. Giles, *The Book of Prayer of Sor María de Santo Domingo: A Study and Translation* (Albany: State University of New York Press, 1990). Quotations in English of María's writings will be taken from the Giles translation and indicated by the page number in parentheses. I have occasionally modified the translation in order to reflect more closely the original Spanish.

18. Bilinkoff concludes that the Beata "was either completely illiterate or very nearly so" ("Charisma and Controversy," 56). During María's trial her illiteracy was viewed as a proof of the divine origin of her utterances: "Que dicha Sor María nació en una aldea, de padre y madre ignorantes y ella nunca aprendió letras, ni ciencia alguna, ni sabe leer, ni latín y, por tanto, las cosas que dice en rapto parecen divinalmente enseñadas a ella" (Lunas Almeida, 154).

19. "Levántanse los indoctos y arrebatan el cielo y nosotros con nuestra sciencia çapuzámonos en el infierno" (sig. a 2^r).

20. Adrian of Utrecht, Charles V's former tutor, was inquisitor general of Castile and Aragon at the time of the book's publication.

21. I offer a brief analysis of another of María's revelations in "The 'Sweet Melody' of Christ's Blood: Musical Images in the *Libro de la oración* of Sister María de Santo Domingo," *Mystics Quarterly* 17 (1991): 94–101.

22. For the date when the community moved into the new convent at Aldeanueva, see Manuel María de los Hoyos, O.P., *Registro historial de la Provincia de España*, 3 vols. (Madrid and Villava: Editorial OPE, 1966–1968), 2:177.

23. The late thirteenth-century *Meditationes vitae Christi* is the prototype of this Franciscan tradition of novelizing the biblical narrative with dialogue and verisimilar details. For the *Meditationes* as an archetypically Franciscan work, see John V. Fleming, *An Introduction to the Franciscan Literature of the Middle Ages* (Chicago: Franciscan Herald Press, 1977), 242–251. By the time María was uttering her revelations, the novelization of the Scriptures was no longer a peculiarly Franciscan phenomenon but had become a standard practice. Interesting enough, Beltrán de Heredia (*Historia*, 127) sees the Beata and her followers as being in many ways more "Franciscan" than "Dominican" in their spirituality.

24. In Colossians 3:1, Saint Paul expresses the notion of being risen with Christ.

25. "O piadosa Magdalena, mira que ya estavas como huérfana y estranjera.

Recibe a mí pecadora en la compañía de tu maestro y no me desampares porque me haya yo hecho huérfana y estranjera d'El. Sea yo por medio tuyo allegada a El y recebida d'El. ¿Y cuándo me veré yo tan alegre con El que no me pueda entristecer por ninguna cosa? ¿Cuándo seré yo recebida entre tus braços por que mi alma sea quieta con El y alegrada d'El?" (sig. b 4ʳ).

26. Pious tradition and iconographical convention paired the two Marys. Margaret R. Miles observes: "The *Meditations [on the Life of Christ]* describes Mary Magdalene after her conversion as remaining close to the Virgin for the rest of her life, even living with the Virgin in some stories. Paintings depict the two Marys as leaning on one another for support in their anguish at the crucifixion" (*Image as Insight: Visual Understanding in Western Christianity and Secular Culture* [Boston: Beacon Press, 1985], 81). Another example of Mary Magdalene as mediatrix, an example that highlights the Magdalen's special relationship with Christ, can be found in Saint Anselm of Canterbury's *Prayer to St. Mary Magdalene*: "Turn to my good that ready access that you once had and still have to the spring of mercy. Draw me to him where I may wash away my sins; bring me to him who can slake my thirst; pour over me those waters that will make my dry places fresh. You will not find it hard to gain all you desire from so loving and so kind a Lord, who is alive and reigns and is your friend" (*The Prayers and Meditations of Saint Anselm*, trans. Sister Benedicta Ward [Harmondsworth: Penguin, 1973], 202).

27. The rubric says: "*Tibi soli peccavi, etc.*" ["To thee only have I sinned, etc."], implying that María recited at least the entire verse of the psalm.

28. It is not clear what María's editor means by this observation, since the passage immediately preceding is part of a prayer that María addresses to Christ. Perhaps he means that in quoting the psalm, María is speaking in David's voice.

29. There is no scriptural justification for Christ's appearance to the Blessed Virgin, but the encounter came to be a matter of tradition since it seemed impossible that Christ would not appear to his mother. The *Golden Legend* observes: "Indeed, if this is not to be believed, on the ground that no evangelist testifies to it, we would have to conclude that Jesus never appeared to Mary after his resurrection because no gospel tells us where or when this happened. But perish the thought that such a son would fail to honor such a mother by being so negligent! . . . Christ must first of all have made his mother happy over his resurrection, since she certainly grieved over his death more than the others. He would not have neglected his mother while he hastened to console others" (I:221). See also James D. Breckenridge, " 'Et Prima Vidit': The Iconography of the Appearance of Christ to His Mother," *Art Bulletin* 39 (1957): 9–32.

30. Psalm 56:9 was traditionally seen as a prophecy of Christ's Resurrection. See, for example, Saint Augustine's *Expositions on the Book of Psalms*, trans. A. Cleveland Coxe, in *A Select Library of the Nicene and Post-Nicene Fathers of the Christian Church*, vol. 8 (New York: The Christian Literature Company, 1888), 228–229.

31. "Y ¿qué miras tanto en esse versito: *Exurge gloria mea exurgan diluculo*? Estás mirando lo que buscas. ¿Hállaslo y entristéceste agora?" (sig. b 5ᵛ).

32. In the *Meditationes vitae Christi* the Virgin expresses her faith in the Resurrection during a monologue in which she quotes a prophecy that Christ uttered before the Passion: "O my sweetest Son, how are you? What are you doing? What

causes your delay? I beg you not to wait any longer to come to me, for you said, 'On the third day I will rise again' [Matt. xxvii, 63]. Is not today the third day, my Son?" See *Meditations on the Life of Christ: An Illustrated Manuscript of the Fourteenth Century*, trans. and ed. Isa Ragusa and Rosalie B. Green (Princeton, N.J.: Princeton University Press, 1961), 359.

33. Two French books of hours, one from ca. 1425 and the other from the sixteenth century, depict the Virgin with a book when Christ appears to her. In neither case is it evident what she is reading. See Breckenridge, 24, 30, and figures 7 and 18.

34. According to I Timothy 2:11–14, Eve's sin disqualified women from speaking, teaching, and preaching: "Let the woman learn in silence with all subjection. But I suffer not a woman to teach, nor to use authority over the man, but to be in silence with all subjection. For Adam was first formed, then Eve. And Adam was not seduced, but the woman, being seduced, was in the transgression."

35. In María's fourth trial, the duke of Alba's brother, Fernando de Toledo, testified that "asimismo, había visto también, en su casa de Viloria, que estando en rapto dicha sierva de Dios la propusieron cuestiones sobre los Santos Evangelios, a las cuales respondió como nunca había oído el testigo contestar a los más grandes hombres de letras" (Lunas Almeida, 194).

36. An iconographical motif supposed that Christ appeared to his mother just after the episode of the harrowing of hell and was therefore accompanied by the redeemed of the Old Testament. Breckenridge (28) says that this motif originated in Spain.

37. In Saint Bonaventure's *The Mystical Vine* the wounds of the crucified Christ become so many roses: "See His whole body: is there a single spot where the rose is not found? Examine one hand, then the other; examine one foot and then the other; and see whether you do not find the roses" (*The Works of Bonaventure*, trans. José de Vinck, vol. 1: *Mystical Opuscula* [Paterson, N.J.: St. Anthony Guild Press, 1960], 200).

38. The *Golden Legend* states that "all except the Blessed Virgin lost their faith at the crucifixion" (I:219).

39. Catherine of Siena, *The Dialogue*, trans. Suzanne Noffke, O.P. (New York: Paulist Press, 1980), 60. Catherine's point of departure for her revelation is the parable of the laborers in the vineyard (Matthew 20:1–16). Catherine thereupon urges her readers to use the knife of their free will to "uproot the thorns of deadly sin and to plant the virtues" (60), and then introduces the image of God as gardener: "Indeed I am the gardener, for all that exists comes from me. With power and strength beyond imagining I govern the whole world: Not a thing is made or kept in order without me. I am the gardener, then, who planted the vine of my only-begotten Son in the earth of your humanity so that you, the branches, could be joined to the vine and bear fruit" (61). God goes on to say that true workers "till their souls well, uprooting every selfish love, cultivating the soil of their love in me" (62).

40. Catherine of Siena, *Obra de las epístolas y oraciones de la bienaventurada virgen sancta Catherina de Sena* (Alcalá, 1512), fol. 139ʳ.

41. Augustine, *Homilies on the Gospel of St. John*, Tractate CXXI, trans. John

Gibb and James Innes, in *A Select Library of the Nicene and Post-Nicene Fathers of the Christian Church*, vol. 7 (New York: The Christian Literature Company, 1888), 437. Obviously, Saint Augustine has in mind the gospel parable of the mustard seed (Matthew 13:31; Mark 4:30–32; and Luke 13:19). Faith is compared to a mustard seed in Matthew 17:19 and Luke 17:6.

42. Gregory the Great, *Forty Gospel Homilies*, trans. Dom David Hurst (Kalamazoo, Mich.: Cistercian Publications, 1990), 192.

43. "Sicut enim hortulani officium est noxias herbas eradicare, ut bonae quaeque proficere valeant; ita Dominus Jesus Christus de horto suo, id est de Ecclesia sua, quotidie vitia eradicat, ut virtutes crescere valeant" (Odo of Cluny, *Sermo II. In veneratione Sanctae Mariae Magdalenae*, in *Patrologia Latina*, 133, col. 720).

44. "O Lord Jesus, true Gardener, effect in us what you demand of us. For without you we cannot do anything. You are the true gardener, the same creator who cultivates and protects your garden. You plant by your word, water with your Spirit, give growth by your power. You were mistaken, Mary, when you thought he was the gardener of that poor and tiny garden in which he was buried. He is the gardener of the whole world, he is the gardener of heaven, he is the gardener of the Church, which he plants and waters here until its growth is completed and he transplants it into the land of the living by streams of living water" (Guerric of Igny, *Liturgical Sermons*, trans. Monks of Mount Saint Bernard Abbey, 2 vols. [Spencer, Mass.: Cistercian Publications, 1971], 2:216).

45. In her unpublished *Revelaciones* (Biblioteca Colombina, códice 83-3-16, fols. 246^r–258^r) María re-creates the biblical parable of the tares among the wheat (Matthew 13:24–30, 36–43), comparing the human heart to a field of wheat that can be choked by the tares of little vices that have not been eradicated: "[A]simismo digo que querría que toviésemos en muncho los viçios que paresçen en sí pequeños como risas, palabras oçiosas y cosas semejantes. Porque los tales viçios, cuando se menospreçian e tienen [en] poco, inpiden muncho a nuestra perfección y cresçimiento, como una çizaña spiritual que no dexa creçer el trigo de las virtudes en el campo de nuestro coraçón. Por lo cual es muy nesçesario los tales viçios arrancarse muy de raíz de manera que no pueda más nasçer ni ser inpedimiento ni estorvo a nuestro aprovechamiento" (fol. 248^r). The same image reappears on fol. 249^r. The need for the gardener of the soul to pull out the weeds of the vices by their roots is reiterated on fol. 253^r: "[L]os que quieren creçer e aprovechar en las cosas spirituales an de ser como los buenos hortelanos, los cuales no solamente en su huerta cortan e siegan someramente todas las yervas malas e inútiles que se crían entre las buenas, mas trabajan de las arrancar de raíz por que no puedan más pulular y renasçer. Y ansí nosotros devemos trabajar y poner todas nuestras fuerças para arrancar de raíz de nosotros todos los viçios y todo nuestro proprio amor y voluntad y seso y paresçer nuestro fasta que no quede gusto ni delectamiento, rastro ni sabor ni vestigio d'ellos en el ánima." On fol. 256^v María observes that just as the gardener must sometimes prune the rosebushes of withered roses, so God will sometimes remove one of his creatures from the number of the elect: "[D]eve muncho temer la criatura de ser del todo dexada de Dios, porque cuando por su oculto e justo juizio El delibera de la dexar, no se le da nada cortarla de entre sus electos, como

hazen los ortolanos que crían rosas en sus huertos, que cuando hallan alguna rosa marchita e seca a par de otra hermosa e fresca, con el plazer de aquella buena no tiene[n] en nada cortar y echar fuera la otra." Finally, María compares Christ to a farmer who tills his fields with the plow of the cross and then takes his ease at the end of the day by dressing up in the festive red clothing of the Passion: "[N]uestro Señor fue como el buen labrador que a la mañana sale de su casa vestido de saco grueso con su arado a cuestas a labrar, el cual, cuando a acabado de trabajar e quiere holgar, se viste de color hermosa. Así Nuestro Señor salió de la casa del vientre virginal a hazer la obra de nuestra redempçión vestido del saco vil de nuestra carne con el arado de la cruz a cuestas. Y en fin de sus trabajos de su mesma sangre se vistió de colorado" (fol. 256ᵛ).

46. As Jodi Bilinkoff observes: "Of course, the metaphor of the soul as a garden has a long pedigree in both the Hebrew and Christian religious traditions, and would have been familiar to María's audience. But, how poignant to have heard it articulated by a labradora, a country woman who had actually worked the land!" ("Ecstatic Text and Historical Context: The Spanish Holy Woman María de Santo Domingo (1485–1524)," unpublished paper delivered at the Bunting Institute Colloquium Series, Radcliffe College, April 11, 1990, 12). Bilinkoff adds: "A rural audience would have, of course, closely identified with the Beata's descriptions of plowing, pruning, and the like, and perhaps also recognized that her pronouncements spiritualized and validated the peasant experience. But the imagery of garden and pasture would have also struck a responsive chord with humanistically educated upper class listeners. Revivals of Virgil's poetry and other literature which idealized the country life enjoyed great popularity in Spain at this time" (16).

47. Gregory the Great says that John represents the synagogue, while Peter represents the Church (*Forty Gospel Homilies*, 165). The same interpretation is privileged by the *Glossa ordinaria* (IV:268) on John 20:4. Significantly, Gregory foregrounds the question of belief versus disbelief, which is, of course, one of the central issues in María's revelation.

48. The *Golden Legend* suggests that this is perhaps why the evangelists fail to mention Christ's appearance to his mother. Her testimony would have been even less credible than that of the other holy women, given her privileged and prejudiced position as Christ's mother: "Still it may be that in this case the evangelists kept silence because their charge was only to present witnesses to the resurrection, and it would not be proper to have a mother testifying for her son. If indeed the words of the other women had been taken for ravings, how much more surely would a mother be thought to be making up stories for love of her son!" (I:221).

49. Saint Stephen rebukes the high priest and elders of the Sanhedrin, saying: "You stiffnecked ['dura cervice'] and uncircumcised in heart and ears, you always resist the Holy Ghost" (Acts 7:51). Michel Join-Lambert observes that, according to Jewish law, the testimony of women was not admissible. See "Marie-Madeleine: Introduction exégétique," in *Marie Madeleine dans la mystique, les arts et les lettres*, ed. Eve Duperray (Paris: Beauchesne, 1989), 17.

50. María refers, of course, to the apostle Thomas.

51. Beltrán de Heredia, *Historia*, 142. Mary Magdalene was the unofficial pro-

tectress of the Dominican order, which had become the guardian of her supposed tomb at Saint-Maximin. See W. R. Bonniwell, O.P., *A History of the Dominican Liturgy, 1215–1945*, 2d ed. (New York: Wagner, 1945), 220.

52. Miles, *Image as Insight*, 80–81.

53. Medieval exegetes, in accordance with John 20:17, viewed Mary Magdalene as a prophetess of the Ascension: "Mary announced to her fellow apostles the good news of the resurrection of the Messiah: 'I have seen the Lord,' and prophesied of the ascension: 'And he said these words to me: "I ascend to my Father and to your Father." ' " (*The Life of Saint Mary Magdalene and of Her Sister Saint Martha*, trans. David Mycoff [Kalamazoo, Mich.: Cistercian Publications, 1989], 74).

54. For María's prophecies, see Beltrán de Heredia, *Historia*, 111–113.

55. The *Golden Legend*, quoting Saint Ambrose, calls the Magdalen an "apostle to the apostles" (I:376). Writing in 1446, Alvaro de Luna observed that the resurrected Christ "apareçió a ella primero, e la hordenó apóstola" (*Libro de las claras e virtuosas mugeres*, ed. Manuel Castillo, 2d ed. [Valencia: Editorial Prometeo, 1917], 226).

56. According to the *Golden Legend*, seeing a crowd of pagans in Marseilles, the Magdalen "preached Christ fervidly to them" (I:376).

57. "Interrogatus si la dicha soror María oye confesiones de algunos, dixit que ha oído y no sabe a quien que la dicha soror María oye confesiones, pero no sacramentaliter, y también ha hecho uno o dos sermones, pero no como a sermonadores, el uno en Viloria, y el otro en Piedrahíta" (testimony of Juan Hurtado, quoted in Beltrán de Heredia, *Historia*, 113–114).

58. Master general Cajetan wrote apropos of the case of María de Santo Domingo that matters of reform should be left to prelates and not to women, who should remain subject to men: ". . . prohibere [praeficere?] sic hae vel illa vel reformationem jubere. Haec enim praelatorum sunt, non feminae, cujus caput vir" (letter of June 29, 1508, to the provincial chapter, quoted in Beltrán de Heredia, *Historia*, 238).

59. Bilinkoff, "Charisma and Controversy," 62.

60. Ibid., 61.

61. Ibid., 60. For hair as a sign of female sexuality in Paul's time, see J. Duncan M. Derrett, "Religious Hair," in his *Studies in the New Testament*, 1 (Leiden: Brill, 1977), 170–175.

62. Saint Augustine observes of the *Noli me tangere* episode of Christ's appearance to the Magdalen that "by this woman the Church of the Gentiles was symbolized" (*Homilies on the Gospel of St. John*, Tractate CXXI, ed. cit., p. 438). For Saint Gregory the Great the sinful woman (that is, the Magdalen) who washed Christ's feet represents the gentiles while the self-righteous Pharisee represents the Jewish people (*Forty Gospel Homilies*, 272). The *Glossa ordinaria*, quoting Bede with reference to Mark 14:3, states: "Devotio Mariae fidem et pietatem designat Ecclesiae" (IV:126).

63. The *Golden Legend* says that Christ appeared first to Mary Magdalene (I:219–220), but then goes on to argue that it is logical that he would have appeared first to his mother (I:221).

64. Adam Easton uses the precedent of Christ's appearances to the two Marys

in his defense (1382/1383) of the divine revelation of the writings of Bridget of Sweden. See James A. Schmidtke, "'Saving' by Faint Praise: St. Birgitta of Sweden, Adam Easton and Medieval Antifeminism," *American Benedictine Review* 33 (1982): 156.

65. Margaret R. Miles remarks that Mary of Magdala "might be seen as the New Testament parallel to Eve. Mary Magdalene, like Eve, was a sinful and repentant woman, bearing her self-imposed penance as Eve bore her punishment, humbly and obediently." See *Carnal Knowing: Female Nakedness and Religious Meaning in the Christian West* (1989; rpt. New York: Vintage, 1991), 120.

66. Gregory the Great, *Forty Gospel Homilies*, 195. The same notion is echoed by the *Glossa ordinaria* on John 20:18: "Mulier mortem viro propinavit, modo mulier vitam nunciat viris, et quae tunc verba serpentis modo narrat verba vivificatoris, ac si ipsis rebus dicat Deus: De qua manu illatus est potus mortis, de ipsa suscipite potum vitae" (IV:268). The *Glossa* is quoted in turn in the *Golden Legend* (I:220).

67. "Quia enim per feminam mors mundo illata fuerat, ne semper in opprobrium sexus femineus haberetur, per sexum femineum voluit nuntiare viris gaudia Resurrectionis; per quem nuntiata fuerat tristitia mortis" (*Patrologia Latina*, 133, col. 721).

68. "Et sicut per beatam Mariam semper virginem quae spes est unica mundi, paradisi portae nobis sunt apertae, et maledictio exclusa Evae; ita per beatam Mariam Magdalenam opprobrium feminei sexus deletum est, et splendor nostrae Resurrectionis in Dominica resurrectione exortus, ab ea propinatus est" (*Patrologia Latina*, 133, col. 721).

69. In *The Tree of Life*, Saint Bonaventure observes that, while the apostles fled, Mary Magdalene overcame her natural feminine weakness (the same weakness that led Eve to be tempted?) and went to the sepulcher: "Such intense fervor burned in her heart, such sweet pity inundated her, such strong bonds of love drew her, that womanly weakness was forgotten and neither the darkness of night nor the brutality of the persecutors could keep her from the tomb. Even the disciples had fled; yet she did not flee, but remained before the sepulcher, drenching the stone with her tears" (*Mystical Opuscula*, 130).

70. Bilinkoff, "Ecstatic Text," 15.

71. In Christine de Pizan's *The Book of the City of Ladies*, Lady Reason uses the Magdalen to defend women's right to speak: "Similarly, God endowed women with the faculty of speech—may He be praised for it—for had He not done so, they would be speechless. . . . If women's language had been so blameworthy and of such small authority, as some men argue, our Lord Jesus Christ would never have deigned to wish that so worthy a mystery as His most gracious resurrection be first announced by a woman, just as He commanded the blessed Magdalene, to whom He first appeared on Easter, to report and announce it to His apostles and to Peter" (trans. Earl Jeffrey Richards [New York: Persea Books, 1982], 28). Later, Reason concludes: "Thus you can understand, fair sweet friend, God has demonstrated that He has truly placed language in women's mouths so that He might be thereby served" (30).

72. Likewise, chapter 243 of Isabel de Villena's *Vita Christi* (1497) takes the

traditional Eva/Ave topos, which contrasted Eve and the Virgin Mary, and applies a variant of that motif to the biblical episode in which Christ greets with "Avete" the Marys who have come from the empty sepulcher, bidding them to tell the disciples that he will meet them in Galilee (Matthew 28:9–10). Isabel de Villena writes that Christ's decision to appear first to women and, specifically, to greet them thus, indicates that he has lifted the curse that was laid upon Eve and her daughters: "No sens gran misteri primerament han meritat les dones oir la tal salutació, ço és: *Avete*; mostrant lo Senyor clarament que la maledicció donada a la primera dona, qui fon Eve, era ja, del tot, de les dones apartada. . . . E quanta gràcia és aquesta que la dona, qui en lo començament del món fon porta e entrada de mort, e ara, per gran dignitat, l'hajau feta novella preïcadora de la vostra maravellosa resurrecció!" (*Protagonistes femenines a la "Vita Christi,"* ed. Rosanna Cantavella and Lluïsa Parra [Barcelona: LaSal, 1987], 153–154).

Chapter 5. Juana de la Cruz and the Secret Garden

1. The principal sources for the life of Juana de la Cruz are: *Vida y fin de la bienabenturada virgen sancta Juana de la Cruz*, Escorial, MS K-III-13 (hereafter, *Vida*); Fray Antonio Daza, *Historia, vida y milagros, éxtasis y revelaciones de la bienaventurada virgen santa Juana de la Cruz* (Madrid, 1610); and Fray Pedro Navarro, *Favores de el rey de el cielo, hechos a su esposa la Santa Juana de la Cruz* (Madrid, 1622).

2. Antonio de Pastrana's letter describing the affair is printed in Manuel Serrano y Sanz, "Pedro Ruiz de Alcaraz, iluminado alcarreño del siglo XVI," *Revista de Archivos, Bibliotecas y Museos* 8 (1903): 2–3.

3. José Luis Domínguez Ruiz, "El cardenal Cisneros y el monasterio de Santa María de la Cruz," diss. Facultad de Derecho Canónico, Universidad Pontificia de Comillas, 1974, includes on pp. 25–37 a photographic reproduction of eighteenth-century copies of the original orders. (I wish to thank Father Jesús Gómez López for obtaining a photocopy of this thesis for me.)

4. *El libro del conorte* exists in two manuscripts, Escorial, MS J-II-18, and Archivio Segreto Vaticano, Congregazione Riti, MS 3074, *Scripta proc. ord.* Unless otherwise indicated, all quotations are from the Escorial manuscript and will be indicated by the folio number in parentheses. I have edited and translated fragments of several sermons from the *Conorte* in *The Guitar of God: Gender, Power, and Authority in the Visionary World of Mother Juana de la Cruz (1481–1534)* (Philadelphia: University of Pennsylvania Press, 1990).

5. Juana's vision shares certain elements with novelesque elaborations of the episode of the Presentation of the Virgin. In the *Vita Beate Virginis Marie et Salvatoris rhythmica*, for example, Mary stands out from the other virgins like a star in the darkest night and like the rose among the thorns (*Vita Beate Virginis Marie et Salvatoris rhythmica*, ed. Adolf Vögtlin [Tübingen: Litterarischer Verein Stuttgart, 1888], vv. 633–640, p. 29). She is elected by lots as queen of all the maidens (vv. 881–900, p. 36). In Juana's celestial beauty pageant, Mary is likewise selected as the most beautiful of all the virgins. The *Vita* also praises the various parts of Mary's body

one by one (vv. 665–760, pp. 30–32). This, of course, is what the Father does in Juana's vision and constitutes a traditional mode of honoring the Virgin, as in the *De laudibus* of Richard of Saint Laurent cited below. The *Golden Legend* recounts that after her Presentation, while Mary lived in the temple, "she enjoyed the vision of God daily" (II:152). A similar motif was elaborated by Isabel de Villena in the chapter that her *Vita Christi* (1497) devotes to the Presentation. Isabel has the Virgin say that the Lord has taken her in his arms and has raised her up to hear his most profound secrets: ". . . e lo Senyor gloriós m'ha pres en los seus braços e m'ha fet muntar a sentir e assaborir los grans secrets seus" (Isabel de Villena, *Protagonistes femenines a la "Vita Christi,"* ed. Rosanna Cantavella and Lluïsa Parra [Barcelona: LaSal, 1987], 10). Villena goes on to say that the Virgin would spend the night with her spirit elevated in the contemplation of heaven: "E en aquella hora ella elevava lo seu esperit en la glòria de paraís; e aquí sentia consolacions tantes, que no basta llengua a recontar-les. E en aquesta contemplació de la glòria e excel·lència divina estava fins a l'alba" (11). In Juana's vision this is what happens when Mary experiences her divine raptures.

6. The incident in the temple and the ensuing conversation with the angel Gabriel are found only in the Vatican manuscript (fol. 554^v). The apocryphal gospels and pious legends state that the Presentation took place when Mary was three or, less often, seven. For the age of three, see Saint Vincent Ferrer, "Sermo Nativitatis Virginis Marie," in *Sermons*, vol. 3, ed. Gret Schib (Barcelona: Barcino, 1975), 259; *Golden Legend* ("The Nativity of Our Lady," II:152); *Meditationes vitae Christi* (chap. 3); Protevangelium of James (chap. 7); Gospel of the Pseudo-Matthew (chap. 4); and Gospel of the Nativity of Mary (chap. 6). For the age of seven, see *Vita Beate Virginis Marie et Salvatoris rhythmica*, 26. According to the *Narrationes de vita et conversatione Beatae Mariae Virginis et de pueritia et adolescentia Salvatoris*, when Mary was three her parents brought her to the temple, dedicated her to God, and then returned with her to Nazareth. It was when she was seven that they left her to be raised in the temple (ed. Oscar Schade, in *Natalicia principis generosissimi Guielielmi Primi* [Königsberg: Academia Albertina, 1870], 8). Either age could correspond to the episode in the allegorical pageant of Juana's vision in which Mary and the other virgins appear as small children. Nonetheless, in the novelesque elaboration of the Virgin's childhood, the Virgin is pubescent at the moment of her Presentation, for the angel Gabriel refers to her as a grown woman. Those two accounts of Mary's age are in a sense juxtaposed in the allegorical pageant at the moment when the Virgin is described as a *niña* ("little girl"), but has the developing breasts of an adolescent.

7. Cf. the Virgin's words at the Annunciation: "Behold the handmaiden of the Lord; be it done to me according to thy word" (Luke 1:38).

8. The vision describes the Virgin as a *niña*. Pastor has pointed out that according to medieval Spanish law, childhood lasted until the age of fourteen for boys, twelve for girls. Those ages corresponded to their sexual maturity, that is, to the ages at which they were legally permitted to marry and physically able to procreate (Reyna Pastor, "Para una historia social de la mujer hispano-medieval. Problemática y puntos de vista," in *La condición de la mujer en la Edad Media*, ed. Yves-René Fonquerne and Alfonso Esteban [Madrid: Casa de Velázquez and

Universidad Complutense, 1986], 188–189). This means that in Juana's allegorical pageant Mary, as a *niña*, can be understood to be under the age of twelve.

9. "Sube acá, fija mía muy amada, e dame tus tetas, que fermosa heres e acabada sobre todas las fijas de Sión e de Gerusalén" (fol. 337^r). Although "dar las tetas" in Spanish can mean "to suckle," in the light of the Father's subsequent request to play with Mary's breasts (fol. 338^r), it appears that "dar las tetas" means "to allow the breasts to be touched or fondled."

10. In the gloss, both the lilies and the roses contain hosts (fol. 337^v).

11. "Dadme vuestras tetas, que quiero jugar con ellas" (fol. 338^r).

12. The office for the Nativity of the Virgin in the Roman Breviary repeats numerous times an antiphon that requests the Virgin's intercession: "Cum jucunditate Nativitatem beatae Mariae celebremus, ut ipsa pro nobis intercedat ad Dominum Jesum Christum."

13. Although the Mary-Eve antithesis is an exegetical commonplace, it is nonetheless significant that the readings in the Roman Breviary for the Nativity of the Virgin highlight that very contrast, first in the vespers hymn *Ave, maris stella* ("Sumens illud Ave / Gabrielis ore, / Funda nos in pace, / Mutans Hevae nomen"), then at matins in the lessons taken from a sermon of the Pseudo-Augustine: "Heva enim luxit, ista exsultavit; Heva lacrimas, Maria gaudium in ventre portavit; quia illa peccatorem, ista edidit innocentem," and so forth.

14. Saint Peter Damian says that just as Eve ate the food (the apple), punishing us with eternal hunger, so Mary gave birth to the food (Christ), opening up the entrance to the celestial banquet: "Cibum comedit Eva, per quem nos aeterni jejunii fame multavit; cibum Maria edidit, qui nobis coelestis convivii aditum patefecit" ("Sermon XLV. In Nativitate Beatissimae Virginis Mariae," *Patrologia Latina*, 144, col. 743).

15. "Así por semejante ninguna persona, por buenas obras e virtudes que tenga, no puede entrar en el reino de los çielos sin los ruegos e plegarias e mereçimientos de Nuestra Señora la Virgen María" (*Conorte*, fol. 421^v). Likewise, Saint Bernardino of Siena, in his sermon on the Ave Maria, declares that no creature can receive any grace not conferred by the Virgin Mary: "Ita quod nulla creatura aliquam a Deo recipit gratiam virtutis, nisi secundum dispensationem ipsius Virginis Matris" (*Opera omnia* [Quaracchi: Collegium S. Bonaventurae, 1950], 2:157).

16. For example, Saint Anthony of Padua compares the virgin birth to the rose and the lily. Just as those flowers give off their fragrance without losing their blossoms, so Mary gave birth to Christ without losing her virginity: "Gloriosae Virginis partus rosae et lilio comparatur, quia sicut ista suavissimum spirando odorem, eorum flos non corrumpitur, sic beata Maria, Dei Filium parturiendo, Virgo permansit" ("In Annuntiatione Beatae Mariae Virginis," in *S. Antonii Patavini Sermones dominicales et festivi*, ed. Beniamino Costa et al., 3 vols. [Padua: Edizioni Messaggero, 1979], 2:121).

17. In Guerric of Igny's "First Sermon for Our Lady's Birthday," Mary is the flower that produces the fruit that is Christ: "'Such is my beloved,' says Mary, 'and he is my Son, O daughters of Jerusalem. He is the blessed fruit of my womb, the fruit my flowers produced'" (*Liturgical Sermons*, trans. Monks of Mount Saint Bernard Abbey, 2 vols. [Spencer, Mass.: Cistercian Publications, 1971], 2:196). Guerric goes on to explain that the flowers represent Mary's virginity.

18. "Tu mater es eucharistiae" and "tu Maria, mater eucharistiae" (Jean Gerson, *Collectorium super Magnificat*, in *Oeuvres complètes*, ed. Mgr. Glorieux, 10 vols. [Paris: Desclée, 1960–1973], 8:413, 454).

19. "Pascit Maria suos convivas. Primo et digniori modo glorioso fructu suo qui est Christus, quem sumimus in sacramento, qui fructus dulcis est super mel et favum, . . . Secundo, carne sua virginali. Unde dicit: *Qui edunt me adhuc esurient*, etc. Similiter in sacramento ubi sumitur caro Christi: quia caro Christi et caro Mariae, sicut caro matris et filii una caro" (Albert the Great [=Richard of Saint Laurent], *De laudibus B. Mariae Virginis Libri XII*, Book XII, chap. 1, in *Opera omnia*, vol. 36, ed. Auguste Borgnet and Emile Borgnet [Paris: Vivès, 1898], 632). Cf. "Pascimur etiam et potamur carne et ejus sanguine in Filii sacramento: quia caro Christi et caro Mariae sicut matris et filii una caro est" (*De laudibus*, Book II, chap. 2, p. 83).

20. "Malus fructus, immo malus morsus, quo Adam per Hevam vitam perdidit et mortem invenit; bonus fructus, quo genus humanum per Mariam mortem perdidit et vitam invenit . . . Ubi tempus venit huiuscemodi fructus edendi, accipiens panem et vinum, et benedicens: *Accipite*, inquit, *et comedite, hoc est corpus meum. Accipite et bibite, hic est sanguis meus*" (Rupert of Deutz, *Commentaria in Canticum canticorum*, ed. Hrabanus Haacke, O.S.B. [Turnhout: Brepols, 1974], 38).

21. "Never again, O Adam, never again shalt thou say to God, 'The woman whom Thou gavest me to be my companion gave me of the forbidden fruit'; but rather let thy words be henceforth: 'The woman whom Thou gavest me fed me with the fruit of benediction.'" ("Sermon for the Feast of the Nativity of the Blessed Virgin Mary," in *St. Bernard's Sermons for the Seasons and Principal Festivals of the Year*, trans. by a priest of Mount Melleray, 3 vols. [Westminster, Md.: The Carroll Press, 1950], 3:286–287).

22. "Quasi mediatrix est inter radicem suam et fructum suum. Radix Mariae genus humanum: quia egresa est *de radice Jesse*. Fructus ejus Jesus Christus, qui nisi ipsa mediante non potest a nobis haberi" (*De laudibus*, Book XII, chap. 6, p. 790).

23. While the verse of the Song of Songs (4:10) that Richard quotes ("Quam pulchrae sunt mammae tuae, soror mea sponsa! Pulchriora sunt ubera tua vino") appears to use *mammae* and *ubera* as synonyms, his commentary specifies that *ubera* are more properly associated with virgins, while *mammae* pertain to matrons. In classical Latin, *mammae* is the more popular form, while *ubera* is more poetical. Nonetheless, Lucretius makes a distinction, referring to the *ubera mammarum*, the "nipples of the breast" (*De rerum natura*, Book V, line 885).

24. *De laudibus*, Book V, chap. 2, p. 311. Strophe 31 of the hymn "Jubilus de singulis membris Beatae Mariae Virginis" ends: "Dulcis Jesu, per mamillas, / Quas suxisti, me per illas / In hora mortis adscipe" (*Analecta Hymnica Medii Aevi*, ed. Guido Maria Dreves, S.J., vol. 15 [Leipzig: Reisland, 1893], 111).

25. *De laudibus*, Book II, chap. 2, p. 87. The milk-blood connection is commonplace. Saint Peter Damian says that the Virgin's milk was changed into Christ's blood: "Manat liquor ex uberibus Virginis, et in carnem vertitur Salvatoris" ("Sermon XLV. In Nativitate Beatissimae Virginis Mariae," *Patrologia Latina*, 144, col. 743). Likewise, in chapter 243 of the *Vita Christi* of Isabel de Villena (1430–1490): "Quanta raó teniu de triumfar e alegrar-vos, car de la llet vostra virginal és feta, certament, la sang de la nostra redempció!" (*Protagonistes femenines a la "Vita Christi"*,

155). For Saint Anthony of Padua, Christ's body underwent the Passion because it was nourished with the Virgin's milk: "Dum enim Christus lac sumebat, salutem nostram agebat. Nostra salus fuit eius Passio; Passionem sustinuit in corpore quod nutritum fuit Virginis lacte." The sweetness of Mary's milk was transformed into the bitterness of the gall, while the same Christ who suckled at the Virgin's breasts allowed his own breast to be pierced with the lance: "Ubera suxit qui in monte Calvariae in ubere lanceari voluit, ut parvuli pro lacte sanguinem sugerent" ("Dominica III in Quadragesima," in *Sermones*, 1:162). See also Caroline Walker Bynum, *Jesus as Mother: Studies in the Spirituality of the High Middle Ages* (Berkeley and Los Angeles: University of California Press, 1982), 132–133.

26. This notion was codified by such authorities as Hippocrates and Galen. See Danielle Jacquart and Claude Thomasset, *Sexuality and Medicine in the Middle Ages*, trans. Matthew Adamson (Princeton, N.J.: Princeton University Press, 1988), 52.

27. In his exegesis of Judges 5:25 ("He asked her water, and she gave him milk and offered him butter in a dish fit for princes") Saint Anthony of Padua explains that Christ's Incarnation remained hidden from the devil because when Satan saw the Madonna married, pregnant, giving birth and suckling, he believed she was no longer a virgin. Just as Jael took up the nail and the hammer and killed Sisera (Judges 5:26), so the Virgin, nursing her son, deceived Satan and killed him with the nail of her virginity and the hammer of her son's Passion: "Sed dum Virgo Filium lactavit, eum fefellit, et sic clavo tabernaculi et malleo interfecit. In clavo tabernaculi, quod clavo clauditur, beatae Mariae virginitas; 'in malleo, qui habet figuram thau, crux Christi designatur.' Iahel ergo, idest beata Maria, clavo tabernaculi, idest virginitate sui corporis, 'et malleo, idest Passione sui Filii, diabolum interfecit'" ("In Purificatione Beatae Mariae Virginis," in *Sermones*, 2:136). The notion that certain sacred mysteries needed to be hidden from Satan through deception is commonplace. For example, in his *Epistle to the Ephesians* Saint Ignatius of Antioch writes: "Mary's virginity was hidden from the prince of this world; so was her child-bearing, and so was the death of the Lord" (*Early Christian Writings: The Apostolic Fathers*, trans. Maxwell Staniforth [Baltimore: Penguin, 1968], 81).

28. *De laudibus*, Book V, chap. 2, p. 311. Cf. the *Sigillum Beatae Mariae* of Honorius of Autun (d. 1136): "*Statura tua assimilata est palmae.* Christus fuit palma in cruce, quia per eum adipiscitur palma victoriae. Cui assimilata est statura, id est alta gloria Mariae, quia sicut ipse Rex coelorum, ita ipsa regina angelorum. *Et ubera tua botris*, id est merita tua assimilantur martyribus, qui velut botri pressi sunt in passionibus. Et ideo contigit, quia ego *dixi*, id est, istud cum Patre statui: De Virgine carnem assumam. *In palmam*, id est in crucem *ascendam*, fructus ejus apprehendam; omnia ad me traham" (*Patrologia Latina*, 172, col. 514).

29. One of the first formulations of the Double Intercession appears in the *Libellus de laudibus B. Mariae Virginis* of Ernaldus of Chartres (d. ca. 1160): "Securum accessum jam habet homo ad Deum, ubi mediatorem causae suae Filium habet ante Patrem, et ante Filium matrem. Christus, nudato latere, Patri ostendit latus et vulnera; Maria Christo pectus et ubera; nec potest ullo modo esse repulsa, ubi concurrunt et orant omni lingua disertius haec clementiae monumenta et charitatis insignia" (*Patrologia Latina*, 189, col. 1726).

30. The quotation is probably derived from Ernaldus of Chartres, but in the Middle Ages it was traditionally ascribed to Saint Bernard.

31. *Golden Legend*, I:298.

32. "Audiamus quomodo Christus ostendit Patri suo pro nobis sua vulnera, / Et Maria ostendit Filio suo pectus et ubera" (*Speculum humanae salvationis*, ed. J. Lutz and P. Perdrizet, 2 vols. [Leipzig: Karl W. Hiersemann, 1907], 1:80).

33. "Quomodo posset talis Filius tali Matri aliquid negare, / Quos constat se mutuo tanquam se ipsos amare?" (*Speculum humanae salvationis*, 1:81). In medieval Spain, one of the Marian poems of Alfonso the Wise begs the Virgin to intercede for sinners before Christ on Judgment Day, showing him the breasts that he suckled: "mostra 'll' as tas tetas santas que ouv' el mamadas" (*Cantigas de Santa Maria*, ed. Walter Mettmann, 2 vols. [Vigo: Edicións Xerais de Galicia, 1981], 2:408). Likewise, in Juan López's mid-fifteenth-century Marian treatise, the faithful are urged to placate the wrath of the Son by mentioning his mother's breasts in their prayers. Speaking in the person of the Virgin herself, López states: "E una de las más excelentes obsecraciones o conjuraciones contra la ira del mi Fijo y para lo aplacar así es deciéndole: 'Señor, por los pechos de la Virgen tu Madre e por la leche que dellos mamaste, plégate de me otorgar tal cosa,' etc." (*Concepción y Nascencia de la Virgen*, ed. Luis G. A. Getino [Madrid: Tipografía de la *Revista de archivos*, 1924], 65).

34. "Ora pro me sancta dei genitrix. . . . Propter ubera que te lactaverunt, sis sibi propicius. . . . Pater per vulnera mea parce ei. . . . Fili, exaudita est oracio tuua [*sic*]" (quoted in Friedrich Gorissen, "Das Stundenbuch der Katharina von Kleve. Ein Beitrag zu seiner Datierung," *Bulletin van de Koninklijke Nederlandsche Oudheidkundige Bond* 64 [1965]: 6). For the miniature, see John Plummer, *The Hours of Catherine of Cleves: Introduction and Commentaries* (New York: George Braziller, [1966]), plate 96.

35. Manuel Trens mentions a thirteenth-century manuscript from the Cathedral of Toledo in which the Virgin shows her breast to Christ seated in judgment. The inscription reads: "Maria ostendit ubera et orat pro peccatoribus" (*María: Iconografía de la Virgen en el arte español* [Madrid: Plus Ultra, 1947], 372).

36. An inscription indicates the words that Christ addresses to the Father: "Padre mio, sieno salvi chostoro pe' quali tu volesti ch'io patissi passione." Another inscription records the words that the Virgin directs to her son: "Dolciximo figliuolo, pel lacte ch'io ti die abbi misericordia di chostoro." See Millard Meiss, "An Early Altarpiece from the Cathedral of Florence," *The Metropolitan Museum of Art Bulletin* 12 (1954): 308.

37. Saint Isidore of Seville, for example, derives *mamillae* from *malae*: "Mamillae vocatae, quia rotundae sunt quasi malae, per diminutionem scilicet" (*Isidori hispalensis episcopi Etymologiarum sive originum Libri XX*, ed. W. M. Lindsay [Oxford: Clarendon Press, 1911], Lib. XI, i, 74). In Mother Juana's vision inspired by the Flight into Egypt, the Holy Innocents appear as children bearing branches with breast-shaped apples: "Y ençima de los mesmos ramos llevavan unas mançanas muy blancas e olorosas hechas a manera de tetas con sus peçones muy colorados" (*Conorte*, fols. 67^v–68^r).

38. Millard Meiss, *Painting in Florence and Siena after the Black Death* (New York: Harper and Row, 1964), 151.

39. These include the attractiveness of symbolic expressions of nourishment and dependence in the context of chronic malnutrition and anxiety of food supply as well as, in the face of a fashionable trend to employ wet nurses, the encouragement of the feeding of infants at the maternal breast in emulation of the Blessed Virgin. See Margaret R. Miles, "The Virgin's One Bare Breast: Female Nudity and Religious Meaning in Tuscan Early Renaissance Culture," in *The Female Body in Western Culture: Contemporary Perspectives*, ed. Susan Rubin Suleiman (Cambridge, Mass. and London: Harvard University Press, 1986), 197–200.

40. Mother Juana in a sense undoes the Double Intercession, concentrating on the singular intercession of the Virgin Mary. In so doing, the nun marginalizes the role of Christ in her vision, for he is but symbolically present in the hosts and physically present only as one of the persons in the Trinity.

41. Margaret R. Miles, *Carnal Knowing: Female Nakedness and Religious Meaning in the Christian West* (1989; rpt. New York: Vintage, 1991), 93.

42. John A. Phillips, *Eve: The History of an Idea* (San Francisco: Harper and Row, 1984), 62–64.

43. Saint Augustine, *Concerning the City of God against the Pagans*, trans. Henry Bettenson (Harmondsworth: Penguin, 1972), 546.

44. Rupert of Deutz interprets the Virgin's breasts in terms of her dual nature, and, speaking in the person of Christ, states that the two breasts represent her virginity and her fertility: "O ubera vere gratissima atque pulcherrima, duo ubera manu Altissimi formata. Haec sunt enim virginitas et fecunditas, quarum pulchritudo in tuis, o dilecta, uberibus castis, uberibus femineis, quae me lactauerunt, maxime spectanda est" (*Commentaria in Canticum canticorum*, 76).

45. Anne Hollander, *Seeing through Clothes* (New York: Penguin, 1988), 186. See also Jacques Berlioz, "Il seno nel Medioevo tra erotismo e maternità," *Storia e dossier* 2:12 (1987): 40–44.

46. In this case, iconic convention is at odds with verbal texts. The banderole corresponding to the Virgin's words in the miniature from the book of hours of Catherine of Cleves speaks of breasts (*ubera*) in the plural.

47. "'E per què ha dat [Déus] mamelles a la dona? Perquè sie celler de la creatura.' E axí ella matexa la volch alletar. Pensau-vos, mes filles, que Déus vos haje donades les mamelles per mostrar les frexures als milans, com a putanes?" ("Sermo Nativitatis Virginis Marie," in *Sermons*, vol. 3, ed. Gret Schib [Barcelona: Barcino, 1975], 256–257).

48. "Mas ya con grand disolución, perdida toda vergüenza, hasta el estómago descubren las que son deshonestas" (Hernando de Talavera, *De vestir y de calzar*, in *Escritores místicos españoles*, ed. Miguel Mir [Madrid: Bailly-Baillière, 1911], 61).

49. Perhaps this anonymous censor should be identified with Miguel de Medina or with another of the theologians whose negative opinions of the *Conorte* resulted in the inquisitorial order of November 6, 1568, that all extant copies be turned over to the Inquisition (Archivo Histórico Nacional [Madrid], Inquisición, libro 576, fol. 264^r).

50. For an overview of these superimposed readings, see Annie Frémaux-Crouzet, "Alegato en favor de 'las mujeres e idiotas': aspectos del franciscanismo

feminista en la *Glosa* de Francisco de Torres a *El Conorte* (1567–1568) de Juana de la Cruz," in *Homenaje a José Antonio Maravall*, ed. María Carmen Iglesias et al., 3 vols. (Madrid: Centro de Investigaciones Sociológicas, 1985), 2:101–102.

51. "Y el no dar sus dichosos pechos luego en público sino querer vergel secreto en la buelta de la oja está declarado y muy bien y provechoso. Y es lo de los cantares: *Ven, amado mío, salgamos y veamos si ay granadas y allí os daré yo mis pechos*" (*Conorte*, fol. 338 ʳ).

52. "Qué bien significada la verdad del sanctíssimo sacramento y cómo no se anegó esta pequeñosa y simple muger en tan immenso mar sino que salió bien, levantada la cabeça sobre tan infinitas aguas, declarando cómo están las incomprehensibles personas de la Santíssima Trinidad tan profundamente como lo pudiera el divino Atanasio o el gran maestro Hierónimo. Bendito sea el gran Padre celestial, que tanto le agradan los pequeños, que sin acceptión de personas ni de sexus, no tiniendo cuenta que esta bendita era muger idiota y otras muchas que [ha] havido en su sancta Iglesia, les reveló sus altíssimos y profundos misterios" (*Conorte*, fol. 338 ʳ).

53. "Y no es cosa muy acertada a los que Dios nos hiço visiones alçarnos con la fe y que a mugeres no les cave buena parte, siendo fe que a ellas les cupo la mayor, pues esta niña de cuyo nascimiento aquí se trata supo más que los apóstoles y mereció engendrarle" (*Conorte*, fol. 338 ʳ).

54. See, for example, Ann W. Astell, *The Song of Songs in the Middle Ages* (Ithaca, N.Y., and London: Cornell University Press, 1990), 42–50, and E. Ann Matter, *The Voice of My Beloved: The Song of Songs in Western Medieval Christianity* (Philadelphia: University of Pennsylvania Press, 1990), 151–167.

55. In the readings in the Roman Breviary for the Nativity of the Virgin, Song of Songs 1:1–16 constitute the lessons for the first nocturn at matins.

56. The first lesson of matins for the Nativity of the Virgin in the Roman Breviary includes the following biblical quotation: "The king hath brought me into his storerooms: we will be glad and rejoice in thee, remembering thy breasts more than wine" (Song of Songs 1:3). The passage unites once again the motif of a secret place and that of breasts. In his commentary on this passage, Saint Bernard establishes a symbolic equivalence between the storerooms and the garden and the bedroom that are mentioned later on. See his Sermon 23 on the Song of Songs in *The Works of Bernard of Clairvaux, III: On the Song of Songs, II*, trans. Kilian Walsh, O.C.S.O. (Kalamazoo, Mich.: Cistercian Publications, 1976), 28–29.

57. "In hac auctoritate ostenditur sollicitudo quam gloriosa Virgo gerit pro Ecclesia Dei" (*De laudibus*, Book V, chap. 2, p. 312).

58. *De laudibus*, Book V, chap. 2, p. 312.

59. Mary was believed to inspire a decidedly nonerotic reaction in those who looked at her. The *Golden Legend* notes that, despite her beauty, the Virgin Mary never aroused the lust of those who gazed at her. On the contrary, her sanctity and chastity were transferred to others, extinguishing in them every carnal desire (I:148–149).

60. "Una puella, nescio quibus blanditiis, nescio quibus cautelis, nescio quibus violentiis, seduxit, decepit et, ut ita dicam, vulneravit et rapuit divinum cor, et

Dei sapientiam circumvenit" (Bernardino of Siena, "Sermo LXI: De superadmirabili gratia et gloria Matris Dei," in *Opera omnia*, ed. Collegium S. Bonaventurae [Quaracchi: Collegium S. Bonaventurae, 1950], 2:376).

61. Childhood is similarly associated with innocence in Juana's sermon on the Flight into Egypt. When the Lord transforms the Holy Innocents into the age they would have reached if they had not been slain, the Innocents beg to become children again, for they prefer to remain innocent and completely free from sin: "Porque bien sabemos nosotros que no ay cosa con que tú más te huelgues que es con las ánimas inoçentes e linpias de pecado. Por tanto, Señor Dios Nuestro, tórnanos inoçentes e ayúntanos a ti que heres gloria de toda ánima que te ama e desea" (*Conorte*, fol. 70^r). In the Syriac tradition and in certain Fathers of the Church, Adam and Eve's innocence is signified by their nakedness and by their state as little children. See Robert Murray, *Symbols of Church and Kingdom: A Study in Early Syriac Tradition* (Cambridge: Cambridge University Press, 1975), 304–306.

62. Ephrem the Syrian (ca. 306–373) contrasts the leaves Eve used to cover her shame with the garment of glory (the resurrected body) that Mary, by making the Redemption possible, gave to humankind: "In her virginity Eve put on / leaves of shame. Your mother put on, / in her virginity, the garment of glory / that suffices for all. I gave / the small mantle of the body to the One who covers all" ("Hymn on the Nativity," 17, in *Hymns*, trans. Kathleen E. McVey [New York: Paulist Press, 1989], 154).

63. The image of Christ assuming his humanity as one who puts on a garment of flesh is traditional. Likewise traditional is the notion that the garment Christ dons is Mary's flesh. In the fifteenth-century *Tresenario de contenplaçiones*, the Blessed Virgin is an advocate for mankind ("asigna la causa por que deve dar favor y sernos buena abogada") precisely because Christ donned her as if she were a garment: "de ti se quiso vestir" ("Le *Tresenario de contenplaçiones por estilo rrimado*. Texte espagnol anonyme du XVe siècle," ed. Maximilian P. A. M. Kerkhof, in *Gesammelte Aufsätze zur Kulturgeschichte Spaniens* 31 [1984]: 308). Elsewhere, the narrator, addressing the Virgin, says that "el fijo se viste / tu vestidura carnal" (311). For the Incarnation as Christ donning a garment of flesh in the Syriac tradition, see Murray, *Symbols*, 69–76.

64. For the development of the iconographic motif of the Madonna of the Cloak, see Paul Perdrizet, *La Vierge de Miséricorde: Etude d'un thème iconographique* (Paris: A. Fontemoing, 1908). In Juana's Assumption sermon the Virgin appears wearing a great mantle decorated with pearls and precious jewels. The mantle protects a great crowd of blessed souls, and the Lord explains that "el manto de su gloriosa e sagrada madre hera tan grande que cabían debaxo d'él más de quinientos mill millares de los que subieron a la postre. E tiniéndolos ella así a todos debaxo de sus alas e manto, estava mayor que todo el mundo" (*Conorte*, fol. 318^r).

65. Emile Mâle, *L'Art religieux de la fin du Moyen Age en France*, 3d ed. (Paris: Armand Colin, 1925), 201. The motif of the protective mantle was transferred to other saints, particularly to Saint Ursula, in order to express a similar confidence in their protective powers (Perdrizet, 220–222).

66. Eloquent testimony is born by the titles of two books that treat this ques-

tion, *The Purchase of Paradise* and *La Comptabilité de l'au-delà*. See Joel T. Rosenthal, *The Purchase of Paradise: Gift Giving and the Aristocracy, 1307–1485* (London: Routledge and Kegan Paul, and Toronto: University of Toronto Press, 1972), and Jacques Chiffoleau, *La Comptabilité de l'au-delà. Les hommes, la mort et la religion dans la région d'Avignon à la fin du Moyen Age (vers 1320-vers 1480)* (Rome: Ecole Française de Rome, 1980).

67. "Advocatam praemisit peregrinatio nostra, quae tamquam Iudicis mater, et mater misericordiae, suppliciter et efficaciter salutis nostrae negotia pertractabit" (Saint Bernard of Clairvaux, "In Assumptione Beatae Mariae: Sermo primus," in *Opera, V: Sermones, II*, ed. J. Leclercq, O.S.B., and H. Rochais [Rome: Editiones Cistercienses, 1968], 229).

68. "Illa mulier, scilicet Eva, nos a paradiso expellit et vendit; ista nos reducit et emit" (Bonaventure, *Collationes de septem donis Spiritus Sancti*, Collatio VI, in *Opera omnia, V: Opuscula varia theologica* [Quaracchi: Collegium S. Bonaventurae, 1891], 486).

69. Caroline Walker Bynum, *Holy Feast and Holy Fast: The Religious Significance of Food to Medieval Women* (Berkeley and Los Angeles: University of California Press, 1987), 236–237.

70. Surtz, *The Guitar of God*, chap. 2, esp. p. 40.

71. Bynum, *Holy Feast*, 120.

72. Hernando de Talavera contrasts the shame that Adam and Eve felt at their nakedness with the innocent nudity of children and Christ's nudity on the cross: "Digo que después del pecado, aquellos primeros padres hovieron vergüenza de se ver así desnudos; porque antes que pecasen no havía deshonestidad de que hoviesen vergüenza, porque los vestía e honestava la inocencia, como no han vergüenza los niños que aún no saben pecar, ni la hovo Jesucristo de ser puesto por nos en la cruz cual su santa Madre lo parió" (*De vestir y de calzar*, 60).

73. "And the Lord put grace upon her and she danced with her feet and all the house of Israel loved her" (*The Apocryphal New Testament*, trans. Montague Rhodes James [Oxford: Clarendon Press, 1924], 42). Later, when the high priest realizes that Mary is pregnant, he chides her, recalling the incident of her dancing: "Mary, wherefore hast thou done this, and wherefore hast thou humbled thy soul and forgotten the Lord thy God, thou that wast nurtured in the Holy of Holies and didst receive food at the hand of an angel and didst hear the hymns and didst dance before the Lord, wherefore hast thou done this?" (45).

74. An anonymous fifteenth-century treatise contains a chapter entitled "Cómo en paraíso ay juegos e bailes e risos," which is intended to justify, according to the appropriate authorities, the presence of such pastimes in heaven. See *Tractado muy devoto e provechoso a todos aquellos que lo bien estudiaren e acataren bien a las cosas en él contenidas*, Biblioteca Nacional, Madrid, MS 5626, fols. 57^v–59^r. The chapter coincides nearly word-for-word with Chap. XXVI ("Que la nostra anima se deu promoure a desijar la gloria de paradis per los balls, iochs e ris qui en ella son") of Book III of the *Scala de contemplació* of Antoni Canals (1352–1418). See the edition by Juan Roig Gironella, S.J. (Barcelona: Fundación Balmesiana, 1975), 184–185. It is probable that both texts are derived from Chap. CCCXCI ("Qui ensenya con,

en Paradís, ha cants e bals e jochs e ris") of *Lo libre de les dones* by Father Francesc Eiximenis (1330/35–1409). See the edition by Frank Naccarato, 2 vols. (Barcelona: Universitat de Barcelona and Curial Edicions Catalanes, 1981), 2:567–568.

75. Erwin Panofsky, *Problems in Titian, Mostly Iconographic* (New York: New York University Press, 1969), 44.

76. A popular medieval schooltext, Prudentius's *Tituli historiarum*, perpetuated the interpretation of the story in terms of female treachery and lust: "The dancing-girl demands a fatal reward, the head of John, cut off so that she may carry it on a platter to her lustful mother's lap. The royal performer is carrying the gift, her hands spattered with the blood of a just man" (*Ten Latin Schooltexts of the Later Middle Ages: Translated Selections*, trans. Ian Thomson and Louis Perraud [Lewiston, N.Y., Queenston, Can., Lampeter, Wales: Edwin Mellen Press, 1990], 103).

77. "Erodias la felennesse, / La desloyal, la traïtresse, / Qui le deable ou corps avoit" (*"La Vie Saint Jehan-Baptiste": A Critical Edition of an Old French Poem of the Early Fourteenth Century*, ed. Robert L. Gieber [Tübingen: Max Niemeyer Verlag, 1978], 91).

78. Likewise, in late medieval Castile Salome's dance was on at least one occasion given a positive interpretation. In Gutierre de Palma's 1479 rendering, Herodias is Castile and Isabella the Catholic is Salome. Salome/Isabella dances before the King of Kings—as did David—in order to obtain the head of Saint Juan, which represents Prince John, the long-awaited male heir to the throne. See *Divina retribución sobre la caída de España en tiempo del noble rey Don Juan el Primero, compuesta por el Bachiller Palma*, ed. J. M. Escudero de la Peña (Madrid: Sociedad de Bibliófilos Españoles, 1879), 78–79. Ramón Gonzálvez Ruiz identifies the author of this treatise as the Gutierre de Palma who wrote a defense of Spain's converted Jews. See "El Bachiller Palma, autor de una obra desconocida en favor de los conversos," in *Simposio "Toledo Judaico"*, 2 vols. (Toledo: Centro Universitario de Toledo, [1973?]), 2:41–43.

79. *The Interpreter's Dictionary of the Bible*, ed. George Arthur Buttrick, 4 vols. (New York and Nashville: Abingdon Press, 1962), 2:118.

80. In mystical visions it is often Christ or the soul that dances. See Wolfgang Riehle, *The Middle English Mystics*, trans. Bernard Standring (London: Routledge and Kegan Paul, 1981), 49–50.

81. Juan López has the Virgin herself observe that as a child she never laughed or shouted or performed any action that was frivolous, licentious, or childish: "Ni en mi niñez vido jamás criatura movimiento en Mí liviano ni disoluto; ni me vido reír ni dar voces, ni moverme de ligero, ni me vido facer cosa que fuese pueril o fecho de niña que fuese enojoso" (*Concepción y Nascencia de la Virgen*, 260).

82. Francesco Barbaro, *On Wifely Duties*, trans. Benjamin G. Kohl, in *The Earthly Republic: Italian Humanists on Government and Society*, ed. Benjamin G. Kohl and Ronald G. Witt (Philadelphia: University of Pennsylvania Press, 1978), 205.

83. This form of what we would now call sexual harassment, in the case of a grown woman, or child abuse, in the case of a young child, was not unknown in the Middle Ages. Book XIX, Chap. CXXXVII ("De illis qui libidinose obtrectaverint puellam aut mulierem") of the *Decretorum libri viginti* (ca. 1008–1012) of Burchard of Worms prescribes the penalties for those who touch the breasts or the

genitals of young girls or women: "Si quis obtrectaverit puellae aut mulieris pectus, vel turpitudinem earum: si clericus est, quinque dies: si laicus, tres dies poeniteat. Monachus vel sacerdos, a ministerio divino suspensi, si aliquid tale fecerint, viginti dies poeniteant" (*Patrologia Latina*, 140, col. 1010). In medieval Spain, the early thirteenth-century municipal charter of Alcalá de Henares sets forth the penalties for touching the breasts or private parts of the women of the town. The penalty was stiffest when the victim was a married woman, less for a widow, and lowest for a young girl. See *Fueros castellanos de Soria y Alcalá de Henares*, ed. Galo Sánchez (Madrid: Centro de Estudios Históricos, 1919), 291. Similarly, a thirteenth-century confessors' manual instructs the priest to ask the penitent if he has touched a woman's breasts or private parts: "si tocó muller en las tetas o en otro lugar de vergonça" (Alfred Morel-Fatio, "Textes castillans inédits du XIIIe siècle," *Romania* 16 [1887]: 381).

84. The late thirteenth- or early fourteenth-century *De Secretis Mulierum* (*On the Secrets of Women*) by the Pseudo-Albert the Great states that women begin to menstruate at the age of "12, 13, or, most frequently, 14" (Helen Rodnite Lemay, *"Women's Secrets": A Translation of Pseudo-Albertus Magnus's "De Secretis Mulierum" with Commentaries* [Albany: State University of New York Press, 1992], 69). One of the commentaries on the *De secretis* links puberty, marriageability, and breast development: "When girls are of marriageable age they grow breasts" (Lemay, 111).

Epilogue

1. Teresa does mention Mari Díaz (ca. 1490–1572), a *beata* who lived in Avila and whom she met and admired. Significantly, Mari Díaz was not a visionary nor did she leave any writings. For Mari Díaz and Teresa's relations with her, see Jodi Bilinkoff, *The Avila of Saint Teresa: Religious Reform in a Sixteenth-Century City* (Ithaca, N.Y., and London: Cornell University Press, 1989), 96–106, 120, and 126.

2. Fray José de Sigüenza, *Historia de la Orden de San Jerónimo*, ed. Juan Catalina García, vol. 2, Nueva Biblioteca de Autores Españoles, 12 (Madrid: Bailly-Baillière, 1909), 357–358.

3. Geraldine McKendrick and Angus MacKay, "Visionaries and Affective Spirituality during the First Half of the Sixteenth Century," in *Cultural Encounters: The Impact of the Inquisition in Spain and the New World*, ed. Mary Elizabeth Perry and Anne J. Cruz (Berkeley and Los Angeles: University of California Press, 1991), 100.

4. José C. Nieto, "The Heretical Alumbrados Dexados: Isabel de la Cruz and Pedro Ruiz de Alcaraz," *Revue de Littérature Comparée* 52 (1978): 295.

5. Antonio Márquez, *Los alumbrados: Orígenes y filosofía (1525–1559)*, 2d ed. (Madrid: Taurus, 1980), 129–130.

6. "La mujer, por sabia que sea, en los misterios de la fe y de la Iglesia ponga un candado de silencio a su boca. Pues es cierto lo que dijeron los antiguos, que la joya que más alinda a la hembra es el candado del silencio a las puertas de sus labios para todas pláticas, y particularmente para los misterios de santidad y para

no ser maestra de doctrinas de Escripturas Santas. . . . El sentido literal dellas [Saint Paul's epistles], cuánto más el espiritual, es muy dificultoso a los sabios; cuánto más a la señora beata e a la mujercilla que se olvida de la rueca por presumir leer a San Pablo" (quoted in Melquíades Andrés, *La teología española en el siglo XVI*, 2 vols. [Madrid: Editorial Católica, 1976–1977], 2:558).

7. See Annie Frémaux-Crouzet, "L'antiféminisme comme théologie du pouvoir chez Melchor Cano," in *Hommage à Louise Bertrand (1921–1979): Etudes ibériques et latino-américaines*, ed. Anne-Marie Couland-Maganuco and Monique Mustapha (Paris: Les Belles Lettres, 1982), 149–156.

8. "Por más que las mugeres reclamen con insaçiable apetito de comer esta fruta, es neçessario vedarlo y poner cuchillo de fuego para que el pueblo no llegue a él" (*Qualificación hecha por los maestros Cano y Cuevas del Catechismo [de Carranza]*, in *Fray Bartolomé Carranza: Documentos históricos, VI = Audiencias III*, ed. J. Ignacio Tellechea Idígoras, Archivo Documental Español, 33 [Madrid, 1981], 238).

9. I borrow the term "Tibetization" from the title of Juan Ignacio Gutiérrez Nieto's article, "La discriminación de los conversos y la tibetización de Castilla por Felipe II," *Revista de la Universidad Complutense* 22:87 (1973): 99–129.

10. J. H. Elliott, *Imperial Spain, 1469–1716* (New York: Mentor, 1963), 222.

11. Richard L. Kagan, *Students and Society in Early Modern Spain* (Baltimore: The Johns Hopkins University Press, 1974), 72.

12. J. M. de Bujanda, *Index des livres interdits, V: Index de l'Inquisition espagnole, 1551, 1554, 1559* (Sherbrooke, Can.: Centre d'Etudes de la Renaissance, 1984), 678, 680.

13. Andrés, *La teología española en el siglo XVI*, 2:627.

14. *The Collected Works of St. Teresa of Avila*, trans. Kieran Kavanaugh, O.C.D., and Otilio Rodríguez, O.C.D., 3 vols. (Washington, D.C.: Institute of Carmelite Studies, 1976–1985), 1:172. The Spanish reads: "Cuando se quitaron muchos libros de romance que no se leyesen, yo sentí mucho, porque algunos me dava recreación leerlos, y yo no podía ya por dejarlos en latín" (Santa Teresa de Jesús, *Obras completas*, ed. Efrén de la Madre de Dios, O.C.D., and Otger Steggink, O. Carm. [Madrid: Editorial Católica, 1982], 117). Future English and Spanish quotations from these editions will be indicated by the page number in parentheses.

15. For inquisitorial scrutiny of Teresa's reform movement and her writings, see Enrique Llamas Martínez, O.C.D., *Santa Teresa de Jesús y la Inquisición española* (Madrid: CSIC, 1972).

16. "Si fuera persona que tuviera autoridad de escrivir, de buena gana me alargara en decir muy por menudo" (42).

17. "Cierto, yo quisiera aquí tener gran autoridad para que se me creyera esto" (86).

18. "En especial para mujeres es más malo, que podrá el demonio causar alguna ilusión" (64).

19. On two occasions, however, Mother Juana at least indicates her awareness of the problem of ineffability: "Hera cosa inefable y enposible—dezía ella—explicar y dezir con lengua humana" (*Vida y fin de la bienabenturada virgen sancta Juana de la Cruz*, Escorial, MS K-III-13, fol. 18ᵛ); "Ya savéis, señoras, que muchas vezes os he dicho que las cosas spirituales y revelaçiones çelestiales no se pueden explicar ni dezir por lengua humana" (*Vida*, fol. 110ᵛ). Nonetheless, when she is

actually dictating her visions, Juana gives no indication that she has any difficulty in narrating what she has seen and experienced.

20. "En estremo me parece le viene a el propio esta comparación" (81).

21. "Y aunque sea grosera comparación, yo no hallo otra que más pueda dar a entender lo que pretendo" (401).

22. See, for example, Saint Augustine's discussion of the three types of visions in Book XII, chapters 6–12 of his *The Literal Meaning of Genesis*, trans. John Hammond Taylor, S.J., 2 vols. (New York: Newman Press, 1982), 2:185–195.

23. "Que siente cabe sí a Jesucristo nuestro Señor, aunque no le ve, ni con los ojos del cuerpo ni del alma. Esta llaman visión intelectual" (427).

24. "Dicen los que lo saben mijor que yo que es más perfecta la pasada que ésta, y ésta más mucho que las que se ven con los ojos corporales; ésta dicen que es la más baja y adonde más ilusiones puede hacer el demonio" (123).

25. Mother Juana's biographer, for example, explicitly states on one occasion that she had received a corporeal vision: "La cual vido e oyó corporalmente estando ella en sus propios sentidos e no estando arrovada" (*Vida*, fol. 9^r).

26. I have found useful the following studies on the *Meditations*: Elizabeth Teresa Howe, "St. Teresa's *Meditaciones* and the Mystic Tradition of the Canticle of Canticles," *Renascence* 33:1 (1980): 47–64; Guido Mancini, *Teresa de Avila: La libertà del sublime* (Pisa: Giardini, 1981), chap. 4; Giovanni M. Bertini, "Interpretación de *Conceptos del Amor de Dios* de Teresa de Jesús," in *Congreso internacional teresiano*, ed. T. Egido Martínez et al., 2 vols. (Salamanca: Universidad de Salamanca, 1983), 2:545–556; Carole Slade, "Saint Teresa's *Meditaciones sobre los Cantares*: The Hermeneutics of Humility and Enjoyment," *Religion and Literature* 18 (1986): 27–44; and Guido Mancini, "Sobre los *Conceptos del amor de Dios* de Santa Teresa," in *Philologica Hispaniensia in honorem Manuel Alvar*, 4 vols. (Madrid: Gredos, 1983–1987), 3:255–266.

27. Santa Teresa, *Obras completas*, 333.

28. Teresa's companions constitute the inscribed audience of the work. At one point, however, she claims to be writing out of obedience (*The Collected Works of St. Teresa of Avila*, 2:215).

29. Alison Weber, *Teresa of Avila and the Rhetoric of Femininity* (Princeton, N.J.: Princeton University Press, 1990), 115.

30. *Conceptos del amor de Dios escritos por la beata madre Theresa de Jesús*, ed. Gerónimo Gracián de la Madre de Dios (Brussels, 1611; facsimile reprint, Burgos, 1979), Prólogo, sig. a 3^v.

31. Translated in Weber, 117.

32. In one of his hostile critiques (1589?) of the posthumous edition of Teresa's collected works Alonso de la Fuente objects to instances in which Teresa seemed to teach men. For De la Fuente such a situation smacks of recent heretical movements: "Venir hombres doctos a aprehender de una muger y reconocerla por cabeça en negocios de oración y doctrina espiritual, como se collige de muchos lugares deste libro, es argumento de la novedad desta doctrina, en que esta muger era savia, y del poco seso de los hombres doctos que se le subiectaron. . . . Y en nuestro tiempo han sucedido cosas graves que se podrían traer en confirmación desta verdad, que callo aquí por evitar proligidad" (quoted in Llamas Martínez, 402).

33. *The Collected Works of St. Teresa of Avila*, 2:212.

34. "Tampoco no hemos de quedar las mujeres tan fuera de gozar las riquezas del Señor" (336).

35. "Y ansí os encomiendo mucho que, cuando leyerdes algún libro y oyerdes sermón, u pensáredes en los misterios de nuestra sagrada fe, que lo que buenamente no pudiéredes entender, no os canséis ni gastéis el pensamiento en adelgazarlo" (334).

36. "Poco va que no sea a este propósito, como he dicho, si de ello nos aprovechamos" (341).

37. To the extent that all roads lead back to Eve, handbooks of female spirituality contrasted Eve's loquaciousness in paradise with Mary's silence at the Annunciation. Thus, the thirteenth-century English guide for anchoresses, *Ancrene Wisse*, states: "Eve in paradise held a long discussion with the serpent, told him the whole lesson about the apple that God had taught her and Adam; and so the enemy understood her weakness right away through her words, and found a way into her for her destruction. Our Lady, St. Mary behaved quite differently: she did not discuss anything with the angel, but asked him briefly about what she did not understand. You, my beloved sister, follow our Lady, and not the cackling Eve" (*Anchoritic Spirituality: "Ancrene Wisse" and Associated Works*, trans. Anne Savage and Nicholas Watson [New York: Paulist Press, 1991], 73).

38. Saint Augustine, *Homilies on the Gospel According to St. John, and His First Epistle*, trans. Members of the English Church, 2 vols. (Oxford: John Henry Parker, 1848–1849), 1:235.

39. *The Homilies of S. John Chrysostom, Archbishop of Constantinople, on the Gospel of St. John*, trans. Members of the English Church, 2 vols. (Oxford: John Henry Parker, 1848–1852), 1:260–261.

40. Chrysostom's notion of the Samaritan woman as an apostle and Augustine's view of her as an image of the Church were codified in such medieval florilegia as the *Catena aurea* of Saint Thomas Aquinas. See *Catena aurea: Commentary on the Four Gospels, Collected out of the Works of the Fathers by S. Thomas Aquinas*, 4 vols. (Oxford: John Henry Parker, 1841–1845), 4:139 and 153.

41. Chrysostom, *Homilies*, 1:284.

42. "Tu sensualis voca rationalem intellectum, quo ut viro regaris, tu quae modo carnaliter sapis, hunc ego lux et caput viri illuminabo" (John 4:16) and ". . . iam habens in intellectu mulier Christum caput viri, reliquit ydriam, id est cupiditatem, et cucurrit aevangelizare" (John 4:28) (*Glossa ordinaria*, IV:233 and 234).

43. In chapter 30 of her *Vida*, Teresa recalls the particular meaning the episode of the Samaritan woman had for her: "Oh, how many times do I recall the living water that the Lord told the Samaritan woman about! And so I am very fond of that gospel passage. Thus it is, indeed, that from the time I was a little child, without understanding this good as I do now, I often begged the Lord to give me the water. I always carried with me a painting of this episode of the Lord at the well, with the words, inscribed: *Domine, da mihi aquam*" (1:202). The Spanish reads: "¡Oh, qué de veces me acuerdo del agua viva que dijo el Señor a la samaritana!, y ansí soy muy aficionada a aquel evangelio. Y es ansí, cierto, que sin entender como ahora este bien, desde muy niña lo era y suplicava muchas veces a el Señor me

diese aquel agua, y la tenía debujada adonde estava siempre con este letrero, cuando el Señor llegó a el pozo: *Domine, da miqui aguan*" (136).

44. Although Teresa expresses surprise that the people believed a woman's testimony, it is significant that she omits any mention of a passage from the same episode that devalues female testimony: "And many more believed in him because of his own word. And they said to the woman: We now believe, not for thy saying: for we ourselves have heard him and know that this is indeed the Saviour of the world" (John 4:41–42). In the 1540s the French preacher François LePicart took care to point out that the story of the Samaritan woman was not to be understood, as it was by the followers of Luther, as a license for women to preach. See Larissa Taylor, *Soldiers of Christ: Preaching in Late Medieval and Reformation France* (New York and Oxford: Oxford University Press, 1992), 177.

45. *Conceptos*, Introduction, v. Alvarez (Introduction, vi) also points out that Fray Luis was probably loath to publish a text that existed in but fragmentary copies, none of them autograph versions.

46. "Bien creo yo, que si este confessor huviera leído con atención todo el libro y considerado la doctrina tan importante que tenía, y que no era declaración sobre los Cantares, sino conceptos de espíritu que Dios le dava, encerrados en algunas palabras de los Cantares, no se lo huviera mandado quemar" (*Conceptos*, sigs. a 3^v–a 4^r).

47. For the theme of Christ as mother and images of lactation in Saint Teresa, see Adriana Lewis Galanes, "La configuración arquetipal Criador-*kourotrophos* en la obra de Santa Teresa," in *Santa Teresa y la literatura mística hispánica*, ed. Manuel Criado de Val (Madrid: EDI-6, 1984), 93–99.

48. See Claire Guilhem, "L'Inquisition et la dévaluation des discours féminins," in *L'Inquisition espagnole, XVe–XIXe siècle*, ed. Bartolomé Bennassar (Paris: Hachette, 1979), 197–240.

49. Electa Arenal and Stacey Schlau, *Untold Sisters: Hispanic Nuns in Their Own Works* (Albuquerque: University of New Mexico Press, 1989), 141.

50. Arenal and Schlau, 303.

References Cited

PRIMARY SOURCES

Alfonso X. *Cantigas de Santa Maria*. Ed. Walter Mettmann. 2 vols. Vigo: Edicións Xerais de Galicia, 1981.

Alonso Getino, Luis G. "Los primeros versos castellanos acerca de Santo Tomás de Aquino." *La Ciencia Tomista* 23 (1921): 145–159.

Alvarez Gato, Juan. *Obras completas*. Ed. Jenaro Artiles Rodríguez. Madrid: Nueva Biblioteca de Autores Españoles, 1928.

Analecta Hymnica Medii Aevi. Ed. Guido Maria Dreves. Vol. 15. Leipzig: Reisland, 1893.

Anchoritic Spirituality: "Ancrene Wisse" and Associated Works. Trans. Anne Savage and Nicholas Watson. New York: Paulist Press, 1991.

Angela of Foligno. *Libro de la bienaventurada Sancta Angela de Fulgino*. Toledo, 1510.

——. *Il libro della beata Angela da Foligno*. Ed. Ludger Thier and Abele Calufetti. Second edition. Grottaferrata: Collegium S. Bonaventurae ad Claras Acquas, 1985.

Anselm of Canterbury. *The Prayers and Meditations of Saint Anselm*. Trans. Sister Benedicta Ward. Harmondsworth: Penguin, 1973.

Anthony of Padua. *S. Antonii Patavini Sermones dominicales et festivi*. Ed. Beniamino Costa et al. 3 vols. Padua: Edizioni Messaggero, 1979.

The Apocryphal New Testament. Trans. Montague Rhodes James. Oxford: Clarendon Press, 1924.

Arte de bien morir. Madrid, Biblioteca Nacional, MS 6485.

Astete, Gaspar. *Tratado del govierno de la familia y estado de las viudas y donzellas*. Burgos, 1603.

Augustine. *Concerning the City of God against the Pagans*. Trans. Henry Bettenson. Harmondsworth: Penguin, 1972.

——. *Expositions on the Book of Psalms*. Trans. A. Cleveland Coxe. In *A Select Library of the Nicene and Post-Nicene Fathers of the Christian Church*. Vol. 8. New York: The Christian Literature Company, 1888.

——. *Homilies on the Gospel According to St. John, and His First Epistle*. Trans. Members of the English Church. 2 vols. Oxford: John Henry Parker, 1848–1849.

——. *Homilies on the Gospel of St. John*. Trans. John Gibb and James Innes. In *A Select Library of the Nicene and Post-Nicene Fathers of the Christian Church*. Vol. 7. New York: The Christian Literature Company, 1888.

——. *The Literal Meaning of Genesis*. Trans. John Hammond Taylor. 2 vols. New York: Newman Press, 1982.

Ayerbe-Chaux, Reinaldo. "Las memorias de Doña Leonor López de Córdoba." *Journal of Hispanic Philology* 2 (1977): 11–33.

Barbaro, Francesco. *On Wifely Duties.* Trans. Benjamin G. Kohl. In *The Earthly Republic: Italian Humanists on Government and Society,* ed. Benjamin G. Kohl and Ronald G. Witt, 189–228. Philadelphia: University of Pennsylvania Press, 1978.

Bernard of Clairvaux. "In Assumptione Beatae Mariae: Sermo primus." In *Opera, V: Sermones, II,* ed. J. Leclercq and H. Rochais, 228–231. Rome: Editiones Cistercienses, 1968.

———. *St. Bernard's Sermons for the Seasons and Principal Festivals of the Year.* Trans. by a priest of Mount Melleray. 3 vols. Westminster, Md.: The Carroll Press, 1950.

———. *The Works of Bernard of Clairvaux, III: On the Song of Songs, II.* Trans. Kilian Walsh. Kalamazoo, Mich.: Cistercian Publications, 1976.

Bernardino of Siena. *Le prediche volgari.* Ed. Piero Bargellini. Milan and Rome: Rizzoli, 1936.

———. *Opera omnia, II,* ed. Collegium S. Bonaventurae. Quaracchi: Collegium S. Bonaventurae, 1950.

Biblia latina cum Glossa ordinaria. Facsimile Reprint of the Editio Princeps: Adolph Rusch of Strassburg 1480/81. 4 vols. Turnhout: Brepols, 1992.

Boland, Paschal. *The Concept of "Discretio spirituum" in John Gerson's "De probatione spirituum" and "De distinctione verarum visionum a falsis."* Washington, D.C.: Catholic University of America, 1959.

Bonaventure. *Collationes de septem donis Spiritus Sancti.* In *Opera omnia, V: Opuscula varia theologica,* 455–503. Quaracchi: Collegium S. Bonaventurae, 1891.

———. *The Works of Bonaventure, I: Mystical Opuscula.* Trans. José de Vinck. Patterson, N.J.: St. Anthony Guild Press, 1960.

Bourland, C. B. "*La dotrina que dieron a Sarra.* Poema de Fernán Pérez de Guzmán." *Revue Hispanique* 22 (1910): 648–686.

Bujanda, J. M. de. *Index des livres interdits, V: Index de l'Inquisition espagnole, 1551, 1554, 1559.* Sherbrooke, Can.: Centre d'Etudes de la Renaissance, 1984.

Burchard of Worms. *Decretorum libri viginti.* In *Patrologia Latina,* 140, cols. 337–1058.

Canals, Antoni. *Scala de contemplació.* Ed. Juan Roig Gironella. Barcelona: Fundación Balmesiana, 1975.

Carranza de Miranda, Bartolomé. *Comentarios sobre el Catechismo christiano.* Ed. José Ignacio Tellechea Idígoras. 2 vols. Madrid: Editorial Católica, 1972.

Cartagena, Alonso de. *El "Oracional" de Alonso de Cartagena.* Ed. Silvia González-Quevedo Alonso. Valencia: Albatros Ediciones, and Chapel Hill, N.C.: Hispanófila, 1983.

Cartagena, Teresa de. *Arboleda de los enfermos. Admiración operum Dey.* Ed. Lewis Joseph Hutton. *Boletín de la Real Academia Española,* anejo 16. Madrid, 1967.

Carvajal. *Poesie.* Ed. Emma Scoles. Rome: Ateneo, 1967.

Castigos y dotrinas que un sabio dava a sus hijas. In *Dos obras didácticas y dos leyendas,* ed. Hermann Knust, 255–293. Madrid: Sociedad de Bibliófilos Españoles, 1978.

Catherine of Siena. *The Dialogue.* Trans. Suzanne Noffke. New York: Paulist Press, 1980.

————. *Obra de las epístolas y oraciones de la bienaventurada virgen sancta Catherina de Sena.* Alcalá, 1512.

Christine de Pizan. *The Book of the City of Ladies.* Trans. Earl Jeffrey Richards. New York: Persea Books, 1982.

Constanza de Castilla. *Devocionario.* Madrid, Biblioteca Nacional, MS 7495.

Corner, George W. *Anatomical Texts of the Earlier Middle Ages: A Study in the Transmission of Culture, with a Revised Latin Text of "Anatomia Cophonis" and Translations of Four Texts.* Washington, D.C.: Carnegie Institution, 1927.

Corpus iuris canonici. Ed. Aemilius Friedberg. 2 vols. Graz: Akademische Druck-u. Verlagsanstalt, 1955.

Corrales, Fray Juan de. *Vida de María de Ajofrín.* Escorial, MS C-III-3, fols. 193^r–231^v.

Covarrubias, Sebastián de. *Tesoro de la lengua castellana o española.* Madrid: Turner, 1977?

Creytens, Raymond. "Les constitutions primitives des soeurs dominicaines de Montargis (1250)." *Archivum Fratrum Praedicatorum* 17 (1947): 41–84.

Crónicas de los reyes de Castilla. Ed. Cayetano Rosell. Biblioteca de Autores Españoles, 68. Madrid, 1877.

Daza, Fray Antonio. *Historia, vida y milagros, éxtasis y revelaciones de la bienaventurada virgen santa Juana de la Cruz.* Madrid, 1610.

Early Christian Writings: The Apostolic Fathers. Trans. Maxwell Staniforth. Baltimore: Penguin, 1968.

Early Dominicans: Selected Writings. Ed. Simon Tugwell. New York: Paulist Press, 1982.

Eiximenis, Francesc. *Lo libre de les dones.* Ed. Frank Naccarato. 2 vols. Barcelona: Universitat de Barcelona and Curial Edicions Catalanes, 1981.

Ephrem the Syrian. *Hymns.* Trans. Kathleen E. McVey. New York: Paulist Press, 1989.

The Epistles of St. Clement of Rome and St. Ignatius of Antioch. Trans. James A. Kleist. Westminster, Md.: The Newman Bookshop, 1946.

Ernaldus of Chartres. *Libellus de laudibus B. Mariae Virginis.* In *Patrologia Latina,* 189, cols. 1725–1734.

"Escritos villacrecianos." Ed. Fidel Lejarza and Angel Uribe. *Archivo Ibero-Americano,* 2ª época, 17 (1957): 661–945.

Fernández de Oviedo, Gonzalo. *Las Memorias de Gonzalo Fernández de Oviedo.* Ed. Juan Bautista Avalle-Arce. 2 vols. Chapel Hill: University of North Carolina, 1974.

Ferrer, Saint Vincent. *Biografía y escritos de San Vicente Ferrer.* Ed. José M. de Garganta and Vicente Forcada. Madrid: Editorial Católica, 1956.

————. *Sermons.* Vol. 3. Ed. Gret Schib. Barcelona: Barcino, 1975.

Fueros castellanos de Soria y Alcalá de Henares. Ed. Galo Sánchez. Madrid: Centro de Estudios Históricos, 1919.

García de Santa María, Alvar. *Crónica de Juan II de Castilla.* Ed. Juan de Mata Carriazo y Arroquia. Madrid: Real Academia de la Historia, 1982.

Gerson, Jean. *Oeuvres complètes.* Ed. Mgr. Glorieux. 10 vols. Paris: Desclée, 1960–1973.

Gertrud the Great of Helfta. *The Herald of God's Loving-Kindness*. Trans. Alexandra Barratt. Kalamazoo, Mich.: Cistercian Publications, 1991.

Gonzalo de Berceo. *Milagros de Nuestra Señora*. Ed. A. G. Solalinde. Madrid: Espasa-Calpe, 1964.

———. *Poema de Santa Oria*. Ed. Isabel Uría Maqua. Madrid: Castalia, 1981.

———. *La "Vida de San Millán de la Cogolla" de Gonzalo de Berceo: Estudio y edición crítica*. Ed. Brian Dutton. London: Tamesis, 1967.

———. *Vida de Santo Domingo de Silos*. Ed. Aldo Ruffinatto. Logroño: Diputación Provincial, 1978.

Gregory the Great. *Forty Gospel Homilies*. Trans. Dom David Hurst. Kalamazoo, Mich.: Cistercian Publications, 1990.

Guerric of Igny. *Liturgical Sermons*. 2 vols. Trans. Monks of Mount Saint Bernard Abbey. Spencer, Mass.: Cistercian Publications, 1971.

Hildegard of Bingen. *"Symphonia": A Critical Edition of the "Symphonia armonie celestium revelationum" [Symphony of the Harmony of Celestial Revelations]*. Ed. and trans. Barbara Newman. Ithaca, N.Y., and London: Cornell University Press, 1988.

Historia del Rey Don Pedro, y su descendencia, que es el linage de los Castillas. Escrita por Gracia Dei, glosado y anotado por otro autor, quien va continuando la dicha descendencia. Ed. Antonio Valladares de Sotomayor. In *Semanario Erudito* 28 (1790): 222–288; 29 (1790): 3–61.

Honorius of Autun. *Sigillum Beatae Mariae*. In *Patrologia Latina*, 172, cols. 495–518.

Horozco, Sebastián de. *Teatro universal de proverbios*. Ed. José Luis Alonso Hernández. Universidad de Groningen and Universidad de Salamanca, 1986.

Isidore of Seville. *Isidori hispalensis episcopi Etymologiarum sive originum Libri XX*. Ed. W. M. Lindsay. Oxford: Clarendon Press, 1911.

Jacobus de Voragine. *The Golden Legend*. Trans. William Granger Ryan. 2 vols. Princeton, N.J.: Princeton University Press, 1993.

John Chrysostom. *The Homilies of S. John Chrysostom, Archbishop of Constantinople, on the Gospel of St. John*. Trans. Members of the English Church. 2 vols. Oxford: John Henry Parker, 1848–1852.

Juan de Jesús María. *Guía interior*. Ed. Daniel de Pablo Maroto. Madrid: Fundación Universitaria Española and Universidad Pontificia de Salamanca, 1987.

Juan Manuel. *El conde Lucanor*. Ed. José Manuel Blecua. Madrid: Castalia, 1969.

Juana de la Cruz. *El libro del conorte*. Escorial, MS J-II-18.

———. *El libro del conorte*. Archivio Segreto Vaticano, Congregazione Riti, MS 3074, *Scripta proc. ord.*

Kaminsky, Amy Katz, and Elaine Dorough Johnson. "To Restore Honor and Fortune: *The Autobiography of Leonor López de Córdoba*." In *The Female Autograph*, ed. Domna C. Stanton and Jeanine Parisier Plottel, 77–88. New York: New York Literary Forum, 1984.

Kramer, Heinrich, and James Sprenger. *The Malleus maleficarum*. Trans. Montague Summers. 1928. New York: Dover, 1971.

Leander of Seville. *The Training of Nuns and the Contempt of the World*. In *Iberian Fathers, I: Martin of Braga, Paschasius of Dumium, Leander of Seville*, trans. Claude W. Barlow, 183–228. Washington, D.C.: Catholic University of America Press, 1969.

Lemay, Helen Rodnite. *"Women's Secrets": A Translation of Pseudo-Albertus Magnus's "De Secretis Mulierum" with Commentaries.* Albany: State University of New York Press, 1992.

Libro de la casa y monasterio de Nuestra Señora de la Cruz. Madrid, Biblioteca Nacional, MS 9661.

El libro de los doze sabios o Tractado de la nobleza y lealtad. Ed. John K. Walsh. *Boletín de la Real Academia Española,* anejo 29. Madrid, 1975.

The Life of Saint Mary Magdalene and of Her Sister Saint Martha. Trans. David Mycoff. Kalamazoo, Mich.: Cistercian Publications, 1989.

Lightfoot, J. B. *The Apostolic Fathers.* Part 2. London: Macmillan, 1885.

Le Livre du Chevalier de La Tour Landry pour l'enseignement de ses filles. Ed. Anatole de Montaiglon. Paris: Jannet, 1854.

López, Juan. *Concepción y Nascencia de la Virgen.* Ed. Luis G. A. Getino. Madrid: Tipografía de la *Revista de archivos,* 1924.

López, Fray Juan. *Tercera parte de la historia general de Sancto Domingo y de su orden de predicadores.* Valladolid, 1613.

López de Ayala, Pero. *Corónica del rey don Pedro.* Ed. Constance L. Wilkins and Heanon M. Wilkins. Madison, Wis.: Hispanic Seminary of Medieval Studies, 1985.

López de Mendoza, Iñigo, Marqués de Santillana. *Obras completas.* Ed. Angel Gómez Moreno and Maximilian P. A. M. Kerkhof. Barcelona: Planeta, 1988.

Luna, Alvaro de. *Libro de las claras e virtuosas mugeres.* Ed. Manuel Castillo. Second edition. Valencia: Prometeo, [1917].

Marguerite d'Oingt. *Les oeuvres de Marguerite d'Oingt.* Ed. Antonin Duraffour, Pierre Gardette, and Paulette Durdilly. Paris: Les Belles Lettres, 1965.

María de Santo Domingo. *The Book of Prayer of Sor María of Santo Domingo: A Study and Translation.* Trans. Mary E. Giles. Albany: State University of New York Press, 1990.

——— . *"Libro de la oración" de Sor María de Santo Domingo.* Ed. José Manuel Blecua. Madrid: Hauser y Menet, 1948.

——— . *Revelaciones.* Seville, Biblioteca Colombina, códice 83–3-16, fols. 246^r–258^r.

Martín de Córdoba. *Compendio de la fortuna.* In *Prosistas castellanos del siglo XV* (2). Ed. Fernando Rubio, 3–65. Biblioteca de Autores Españoles, 171. Madrid: Atlas, 1964.

——— . *Jardín de nobles donzellas.* Ed. Harriet Goldberg. Chapel Hill: University of North Carolina, 1974.

Martínez de Toledo, Alfonso. *Arcipreste de Talavera o Corbacho.* Ed. J. González Muela. Madrid: Castalia, 1970.

Meditations on the Life of Christ: An Illustrated Manuscript of the Fourteenth Century. Trans. and ed. Isa Ragusa and Rosalie B. Green. Princeton, N.J.: Princeton University Press, 1961.

Morel-Fatio, Alfred. "Textes castillans inédits du XIIIe siècle." *Romania* 16 (1887): 364–382.

Narrationes de vita et conversatione Beatae Mariae Virginis et de pueritia et adolescentia Salvatoris. Ed. Oscar Schade. In *Natalicia principis generosissimi Guielielmi Primi,* 1–28. Königsberg: Academia Albertina, 1870.

Navarro, Fray Pedro. *Favores de el rey de el cielo, hechos a su esposa la Santa Juana de la Cruz.* Madrid, 1622.

Odo of Cluny. *Sermo II. In veneratione Sanctae Mariae Magdalenae.* In *Patrologia Latina,* 133, cols. 713–721.

Palma, Gutierre de. *Divina retribución sobre la caída de España en tiempo del noble rey Don Juan el Primero, compuesta por el Bachiller Palma.* Ed. J. M. Escudero de la Peña. Madrid: Sociedad de Bibliófilos Españoles, 1879.

Patrologia cursus completus: series latina, ed. J.-P. Migne, 221 vols. Paris: Migne, etc., 1841–1864.

Peter Damian. *Sermones.* In *Patrologia Latina,* 144, cols. 505–924.

Philippe de Navarre. *Les Quatre âges de l'homme.* Ed. Marcel de Fréville. Paris: Didot, 1888.

Pseudo-Albert the Great. *Mariale.* In Albertus Magnus, *Opera omnia,* ed. Auguste Borgnet and Emile Borgnet. Vol. 37, 1–362. Paris: Vivès, 1898.

Qualificación hecha por los maestros Cano y Cuevas del Catechismo [de Carranza]. In *Fray Bartolomé Carranza: Documentos históricos, VI = Audiencias III,* ed. J. Ignacio Tellechea Idígoras, 225–364. Archivo Documental Español, 33. Madrid: Real Academia de la Historia, 1981.

Raymond of Capua. *Vida y milagros de la bienaventurada Sancta Catherina de Sena, trasladada de latín en castellano por el reverendo maestro fray Antonio de la Peña.* Medina del Campo, 1569.

"Regesta romanorum pontificum pro s. ordine fratrum praedicatorum." In *Analecta Sacri Ordinis Fratrum Praedicatorum* 3 (1897–1898): 614–635.

Richard of Saint Laurent. *De laudibus B. Mariae Virginis.* In Albertus Magnus, *Opera omnia,* ed. Auguste Borgnet and Emile Borgnet. Vol. 36. Paris: Vivès, 1898.

Rodríguez del Padrón, Juan. *Obras completas.* Ed. César Hernández Alonso. Madrid: Editora Nacional, 1982.

Rupert of Deutz. *Commentaria in Canticum canticorum.* Ed. Hrabanus Haacke. Turnhout: Brepols, 1974.

———. *In Evangelium S. Joannis commentariorum Libri XIV.* In *Patrologia Latina,* 169, cols. 205–826.

Saldes, Ambrosio de. "Una versión catalana de la Regla de las Clarisas. Siglo XIV." *Estudios Franciscanos* 8 (1912): 215–223, 372–379; 9 (1912): 49–57.

Sánchez de Vercial, Clemente. *Libro de los exenplos por a.b.c.* Ed. John Esten Keller. Madrid: CSIC, 1961.

"Síguense algunas avisaciones spirituales del santo padre fray Lope." In Angel Uribe, "Nuevos escritos inéditos villacrecianos." *Archivo Ibero-Americano,* 2ª época, 34 (1974): 330–334.

Sigüenza, Fray José de. *Historia de la Orden de San Jerónimo.* Ed. Juan Catalina García. 2 vols. Nueva Biblioteca de Autores Españoles, 8 and 12. Madrid: Bailly-Baillière, 1907–1909.

Speculum humanae salvationis. Ed. J. Lutz and P. Perdrizet. 2 vols. Leipzig: Karl W. Hiersemann, 1907.

Suso, Henry. *The Exemplar, with Two German Sermons.* Ed. and trans. Frank Tobin. New York: Paulist Press, 1989.

Talavera, Hernando de. *De vestir y de calzar.* In *Escritores místicos españoles,* ed. Miguel Mir, 57–78. Nueva Biblioteca de Autores Españoles, 16. Madrid: Bailly-Baillière, 1911.

Ten Latin Schooltexts of the Later Middle Ages: Translated Selections. Trans. Ian Thomson and Louis Perraud. Lewiston, N.Y., Queenston, Can., Lampeter, Wales: Edwin Mellen Press, 1990.

Teresa of Avila. *The Collected Works of St. Teresa of Avila.* Trans. Kieran Kavanaugh and Otilio Rodríguez. 3 vols. Washington, D.C.: Institute of Carmelite Studies, 1976–1985.

———. *Conceptos del amor de Dios escritos por la beata madre Theresa de Jesús.* Ed. Gerónimo Gracián de la Madre de Dios. Brussels, 1611; facsimile reprint, Burgos, 1979.

———. *Obras completas.* Ed. Efrén de la Madre de Dios and Otger Steggink. Madrid: Editorial Católica, 1982.

Thomas Aquinas. *Catena aurea: Commentary on the Four Gospels, Collected out of the Works of the Fathers by S. Thomas Aquinas.* 4 vols. Oxford: John Henry Parker, 1841–1845.

———. *Summa theologica.* Trans. Fathers of the English Dominican Province. 3 vols. New York: Benziger Brothers, 1947–1948.

Thomas, A. H. *De oudste Constituties van de Dominicanen.* Louvain: Universiteitsbibliotheck, 1965.

Tractado muy devoto e provechoso a todos aquellos que lo bien estudiaren e acataren bien a las cosas en él contenidas. Madrid, Biblioteca Nacional, MS 5626, fols. 45^r–63^r.

"Le *Tresenario de contenplaçiones por estilo rrimado.* Texte espagnol anonyme du XVe siècle." Ed. Maximilian P. A. M. Kerkhof. In *Gesammelte Aufsätze zur Kulturgeschichte Spaniens* 31 (1984): 286–369.

Vega, Pedro de la. *Chronicorum fratrum hieronymitani ordinis.* Alcalá, 1539.

"Vetera monumenta legislativa Sacri Ordinis Praedicatorum, IV: *Liber constitutionum sororum Ordinis Praedicatorum.*" *Analecta Sacri Ordinis Fratrum Praedicatorum* 3 (1897–1898): 337–348.

Vida y fin de la bienabenturada virgen sancta Juana de la Cruz. Escorial, MS K-III-13.

"*La Vie Saint Jehan-Baptiste*": A Critical Edition of an Old French Poem of the Early Fourteenth Century. Ed. Robert L. Gieber. Tübingen: Max Niemeyer Verlag, 1978.

Villegas, Alonso de. *Adición a la tercera parte del Flos sanctorum.* Toledo, 1588.

Villena, Isabel de. *Protagonistes femenines a la "Vita Christi."* Ed. Rosanna Cantavella and Lluïsa Parra. Barcelona: LaSal, 1987.

Vita Beate Virginis Marie et Salvatoris rhythmica. Ed. Adolf Vögtlin. Tübingen: Litterarischen Verein in Stuttgart, 1888.

William of Paris. *Evangelios e epístolas con sus exposiciones en romance.* Trans. Gonzalo García de Santa María. Ed. Isak Collijn and Erik Staaff. Uppsala: Akademiska Bokhandeln, and Leipzig: Harrassowitz, 1908.

SECONDARY SOURCES

Alonso Getino, Luis G. "Centenario y Cartulario de nuestra Comunidad." *La Ciencia Tomista* 19 (1919): 5–20, 127–143, 253–272; 20 (1919): 5–21, 129–152, 265–288.

Andrés, Melquíades. *La teología española en el siglo XVI*. 2 vols. Madrid: Editorial Católica, 1976–1977.

Arco, Ricardo del. *Sepulcros de la casa real de Castilla*. Madrid: CSIC, 1954.

Arenal, Electa, and Stacey Schlau. *Untold Sisters: Hispanic Nuns in Their Own Works*. Albuquerque: University of New Mexico Press, 1989.

Astell, Ann W. *The Song of Songs in the Middle Ages*. Ithaca, N.Y., and London: Cornell University Press, 1990.

Bataillon, Marcel. *Erasmo y España*. Trans. Antonio Alatorre. Second edition. Mexico City: FCE, 1966.

Beinart, Haim. "The Judaizing Movement in the Order of San Jerónimo in Castile." In *Scripta Hierosolymitana*, VII: *Studies in History*, ed. Alexander Fuks and Israel Halpern, 167–192. Jerusalem: Magnes Press, 1961.

Beltrán de Heredia, Vicente. *Cartulario de la Universidad de Salamanca*. 6 vols. Salamanca: Universidad de Salamanca, 1970–1972.

———. *Historia de la reforma de la provincia de España (1450–1550)*. Rome: Istituto Storico Domenicano, 1939.

Berger, S. "Les Bibles castillans." *Romania* 28 (1899): 360–408, 508–567.

Berlioz, Jacques. "Il seno nel Medioevo tra erotismo e maternità." *Storia e dossier* 2:12 (1987): 40–44.

Bilinkoff, Jodi. *The Avila of Saint Teresa: Religious Reform in a Sixteenth-Century City*. Ithaca, N.Y., and London: Cornell University Press, 1989.

———. "Charisma and Controversy: The Case of María de Santo Domingo." *Archivo Dominicano* 10 (1989): 55–66.

———. "Ecstatic Text and Historical Context: The Spanish Holy Woman María de Santo Domingo (1485–1524)." Unpublished paper delivered at the Bunting Institute Colloquium Series, Radcliffe College, April 11, 1990.

———. "A Spanish Prophetess and Her Patrons: The Case of María de Santo Domingo." *Sixteenth Century Journal* 23 (1992): 21–34.

Bodenstedt, Sister Mary Immaculate. *The "Vita Christi" of Ludolphus the Carthusian*. Washington, D.C.: Catholic University of America Press, 1944.

Bonniwell, W. R. *A History of the Dominican Liturgy, 1215–1945*. Second edition. New York: Wagner, 1945.

Breckenridge, James D. " 'Et Prima Vidit': The Iconography of the Appearance of Christ to His Mother." *Art Bulletin* 39 (1957): 9–32.

Brett, Edward T. "Humbert of Romans and the Dominican Second Order." In *Cultura e istituzioni nell'Ordine Domenicano tra Medioevo e Umanesimo: Studi e testi*, 1–25. Pistoia: Memorie Domenicane, 1981.

Bynum, Caroline Walker. "The Female Body and Religious Practice in the Later Middle Ages." In *Zone 3: Fragments for a History of the Human Body*, ed. Michel Feher. 3 vols. 1:161–219. New York: Orzone, 1989.

———. *Holy Feast and Holy Fast: The Religious Significance of Food to Medieval Women*. Berkeley and Los Angeles: University of California Press, 1987.

————. *Jesus as Mother: Studies in the Spirituality of the High Middle Ages.* Berkeley and Los Angeles: University of California Press, 1982.

C. de Jesús, Sister. *Breve reseña histórica del Convento de Santo Domingo el Real de Madrid desde su fundación por el mismo santo patriarca Domingo de Guzmán año del Señor de 1218.* Santiago de Compostela: Seminario Conciliar, 1946.

Cadden, Joan. *Meanings of Sex Difference in the Middle Ages: Medicine, Science, and Culture.* Cambridge: Cambridge University Press, 1993.

Caneva, Caterina. *Botticelli: catalogo completo dei dipinti.* Florence: Cantini, 1990.

Cantera Burgos, Francisco. *Alvar García de Santa María y su familia de conversos. Historia de la judería de Burgos y de sus conversos más egregios.* Madrid: Instituto Arias Montano, 1952.

Caro Baroja, Julio. *Las formas complejas de la vida religiosa.* Madrid: Akal, 1978.

Castro, Adolfo de. "Memorias de una dama del siglo XIV y XV (de 1363 a 1412): Doña Leonor López de Córdoba." *La España Moderna* #163 (1902): 120–146; #164 (1902): 116–133.

Castro, Américo. *Aspectos del vivir hispánico.* 1949. Madrid: Alianza, 1970.

Cepeda Adán, José. "El providencialismo en los cronistas de los Reyes Católicos." *Arbor* 17 (1950): 177–190.

Chaytor, H. J. *From Script to Print: An Introduction to Medieval Vernacular Literature.* New York: October House, 1967.

Christian, William A., Jr. *Apparitions in Late Medieval and Renaissance Spain.* Princeton, N.J.: Princeton University Press, 1981.

————. *Local Religion in Sixteenth-Century Spain.* Princeton, N.J.: Princeton University Press, 1981.

Ciletti, Elena. "Patriarchal Ideology in the Renaissance Iconography of Judith." In *Refiguring Woman: Perspectives on Gender and the Italian Renaissance*, ed. Marilyn Migiel and Juliana Schiesari, 35–70. Ithaca, N.Y., and London: Cornell University Press, 1991.

Clanchy, M. T. *From Memory to Written Record, England, 1066–1307.* Cambridge, Mass.: Harvard University Press, 1979.

Coakley, John. "Friars as Confidants of Holy Women in Medieval Dominican Hagiography." In *Images of Sainthood in Medieval Europe*, ed. Renate Blumenfeld-Kosinski and Timea Szell, 222–246. Ithaca, N.Y., and London: Cornell University Press, 1991.

Coleman, Janet. *Medieval Readers and Writers, 1350–1400.* New York: Columbia University Press, 1981.

Colledge, Edmund. "*Epistola solitarii ad reges*: Alphonse of Pecha as Organizer of Birgittine and Urbanist Propaganda." *Mediaeval Studies* 18 (1956): 19–49.

Curtius, Ernst Robert. *European Literature and the Latin Middle Ages.* Trans. Willard R. Trask. New York: Harper and Row, 1963.

Derrett, J. Duncan M. *Studies in the New Testament.* Vol 1. Leiden: Brill, 1977.

Deyermond, Alan. "'El convento de dolençias': The Works of Teresa de Cartagena." *Journal of Hispanic Philology* 1 (1976): 19–29.

————. "Spain's First Women Writers." In *Women in Hispanic Literature: Icons and Fallen Idols*, ed. Beth Miller, 27–52. Berkeley and Los Angeles: University of California Press, 1983.

Dillard, Heath. *Daughters of the Reconquest: Women in Castilian Town Society, 1100–1300*. Cambridge: Cambridge University Press, 1984.

Domínguez Ruiz, José Luis. "El cardenal Cisneros y el monasterio de Santa María de la Cruz." Diss., Facultad de Derecho Canónico, Universidad Pontificia de Comillas, 1974.

Dronke, Peter. *Women Writers of the Middle Ages: A Critical Study of Texts from Perpetua (†203) to Marguerite Porete (†1310)*. Cambridge: Cambridge University Press, 1984.

Elliott, J. H. *Imperial Spain, 1469–1716*. New York: Mentor, 1963.

Estow, Clara. "Leonor López de Córdoba: Portrait of a Medieval Courtier." *Fifteenth-Century Studies* 5 (1982): 23–46.

Fernández-Armesto, Felipe. "Cardinal Cisneros as a Patron of Printing." In *God and Man in Medieval Spain: Essays in Honour of J. R. L. Highfield*, ed. Derek W. Lomax and David Mackenzie, 149–168. Warminster: Aris and Phillips, 1989.

Fita, F. "La Inquisición toledana. Relación contemporánea de los autos y autillos que celebró desde el año 1485 hasta el de 1501." *Boletín de la Real Academia de la Historia* 11 (1887): 289–322.

Flanagan, Sabina. *Hildegard of Bingen, 1098–1179: A Visionary Life*. London and New York: Routledge, 1989.

Fleming, John V. *An Introduction to the Franciscan Literature of the Middle Ages*. Chicago: Franciscan Herald Press, 1977.

Frémaux-Crouzet, Annie. "Alegato en favor de 'las mujeres e idiotas': aspectos del franciscanismo feminista en la *Glosa* de Francisco de Torres a *El Conorte* (1567–1568) de Juana de la Cruz." In *Homenaje a José Antonio Maravall*, ed. María Carmen Iglesias et al. 3 vols. 2:99–116. Madrid: Centro de Investigaciones Sociológicas, 1985.

———. "L'antiféminisme comme théologie du pouvoir chez Melchor Cano." In *Hommage à Louise Bertrand (1921–1979): Etudes ibériques et latino-américaines*, ed. Anne-Marie Couland-Maganuco and Monique Mustapha, 139–186. Paris: Les Belles Lettres, 1982.

Frugoni, Chiara. "Il linguaggio dell'iconografia e delle visioni." In *Culto dei santi, istituzioni e classi sociali in età preindustriale*, ed. Sofia Boesch Gajano and Lucia Sebastiani, 527–536. L'Aquila and Rome: Japadre, 1984.

———. "Le mistiche, le visioni e l'iconografia: Rapporti ed influssi." In *Temi e problemi nella mistica femminile trecentesca*, 137–179. Rimini: Maggioli, 1983.

García Oro, José. *El Cardenal Cisneros: Vida y empresas*. 2 vols. Madrid: Editorial Católica, 1992–1993.

García Rey, C. "La famosa priora doña Teresa de Ayala. Su correspondencia íntima con los monarcas de su tiempo." *Boletín de la Real Academia de la Historia* 96 (1930): 685–773.

González Hernández, Olegario. "Fray Hernando de Talavera. Un aspecto nuevo de su personalidad." *Hispania Sacra* 13 (1960): 143–174.

Gonzálvez Ruiz, Ramón. "El Bachiller Palma, autor de una obra desconocida en favor de los conversos." In *Simposio "Toledo Judaico."* 2 vols. 2:31–48. Toledo: Centro Universitario de Toledo, 1973?

Goodich, Michael. "The Contours of Female Piety in Later Medieval Hagiography." *Church History* 50 (1981): 20–32.

Gorissen, Friedrich. "Das Stundenbuch der Katharina von Kleve. Ein Beitrag zu seiner Datierung." *Bulletin van de Koninklijke Nederlandsche Oudheidkundige Bond* 64 (1965): 1–7.

Gougaud, L. "La prière dite de Charlemagne et les pièces apocryphes apparentées." *Revue d'Histoire Ecclésiastique* 20 (1924): 211–238.

Greenspan, Kate. "Matre Donante: The Embrace of Christ as the Virgin's Gift in the Visions of 13th-Century Italian Women." *Studia Mystica* 13:2–3 (1990): 26–37.

Grendler, Paul F. *Schooling in Renaissance Italy: Literacy and Learning, 1300–1600.* Baltimore and London: Johns Hopkins University Press, 1989.

Guilhem, Claire. "L'Inquisition et la dévaluation des discours féminins." In *L'Inquisition espagnole, XVᵉ–XIXᵉ siècle*, ed. Bartolomé Bennassar, 197–240. Paris: Hachette, 1979.

Hale, Rosemary D. "*Imitatio Mariae*: Motherhood Motifs in Devotional Memoirs." *Mystics Quarterly* 16 (1990): 193–203.

Herpoel, Sonja. "Bajo la amenaza de la inquisición: escritoras españolas en el Siglo de Oro." In *España, teatro y mujeres. Estudios dedicados a Henk Oostendorp*, ed. Martin Gosman and Hub. Hermans, 123–131. Amsterdam and Atlanta: Rodopi, 1989.

Hollander, Anne. *Seeing through Clothes.* New York: Penguin, 1988.

Hoyos, Manuel María de los. *Registro historial de la Provincia de España.* 3 vols. Madrid and Villava: Editorial OPE, 1966–1968.

Huélamo San José, Ana María. "El devocionario de la dominica Sor Constanza." *Boletín de la Asociación Española de Archiveros, Bibliotecarios, Museólogos y Documentalistas* 42:2 (1992): 133–147.

Huerga, Alvaro. "La edición cisneriana del *Tratado de la vida espiritual* y otras ediciones del siglo XVI." *Escritos del Vedat* 10 (1980): 297–313.

———. "Los pre-alumbrados y la Beata de Piedrahíta." In Fliche-Martin, *Historia de la Iglesia, vol. 17: El Renacimiento*, 523–546. Valencia: EDICEP, 1974.

———. "Un problema de la segunda escolástica: la oración mística." *Angelicum* 44 (1967): 10–59.

Hutton, Lewis J. "Teresa de Cartagena: A Study in Castilian Spirituality." *Theology Today* 12 (1955–1956): 477–483.

The Interpreter's Dictionary of the Bible. Ed. George Arthur Buttrick. 4 vols. New York and Nashville: Abingdon Press, 1962.

Jacob, Henriette s'. *Idealism and Realism: A Study of Sepulchral Symbolism.* Leiden: Brill, 1954.

Jacquart, Danielle, and Claude Thomasset. *Sexuality and Medicine in the Middle Ages.* Trans. Matthew Adamson. Princeton, N.J.: Princeton University Press, 1988.

Johnson, Penelope D. "*Mulier et monialis*: The Medieval Nun's Self-Image." *Thought* 64 (1989): 242–253.

Join-Lambert, Michel. "Marie-Madeleine: Introduction exégétique." In *Marie Madeleine dans la mystique, les arts et les lettres*, ed. Eve Duperray, 15–19. Paris: Beauchesne, 1989.

Jourdain, Charles. "Mémoire sur l'éducation des femmes au Moyen Age." *Mémoires de l'Institut National de France: Académie des Inscriptions et Belles Lettres* 28 (1874): 79–133.

Kagan, Richard L. *Students and Society in Early Modern Spain.* Baltimore: The Johns Hopkins University Press, 1974.

Keller, Carl A. "Mystical Literature." In *Mysticism and Philosophical Analysis,* ed. Steven T. Katz, 75–100. London: Sheldon Press, 1978.

Klapisch-Zuber, Christiane. "Holy Dolls: Play and Piety in Florence in the Quattrocento." In *Women, Family, and Ritual in Renaissance Italy,* trans. Lydia Cochrane, 310–329. Chicago: University of Chicago Press, 1985.

Lawrance, Jeremy N. H. *Un episodio del proto-humanismo español: Tres opúsculos de Nuño de Guzmán y Giannozzo Manetti.* Salamanca: Diputación de Salamanca, 1989.

———. "Nuño de Guzmán and Early Spanish Humanism: Some Reconsiderations." *Medium Aevum* 51 (1982): 55–85.

León Tello, Pilar. *Judíos de Toledo.* 2 vols. Madrid: CSIC, 1979.

Leroquais, V. *Les Livres d'Heures manuscrits de la Bibliothèque Nationale.* 3 vols. Paris, 1927.

———. *Les Sacramentaires et les missels manuscrits des bibliothèques publiques de France.* 3 vols. Paris, 1924.

Lewis Galanes, Adriana. "La configuración arquetipal Criador-*kourotrophos* en la obra de Santa Teresa." In *Santa Teresa y la literatura mística hispánica,* ed. Manuel Criado de Val, 93–99. Madrid: EDI-6, 1984.

Llamas Martínez, Enrique. *Santa Teresa de Jesús y la Inquisición española.* Madrid: CSIC, 1972.

Llorca, Bernardino. *La Inquisición española y los alumbrados (1509–1667).* Refundición y puesta al día de la edición de 1936. Salamanca: Universidad Pontificia, 1980.

López Estrada, Francisco. "Las mujeres escritoras en la Edad Media castellana." In *La condición de la mujer en la Edad Media,* ed. Yves-René Fonquerne and Alfonso Esteban, 9–38. Madrid: Casa de Velázquez and Universidad Complutense, 1986.

Lunas Almeida, Jesús G. *La historia del Señorío de Valdecorneja en la parte referente a Piedrahíta.* Avila: S. Martín, 1930.

McKendrick, Geraldine, and Angus MacKay. "Visionaries and Affective Spirituality during the First Half of the Sixteenth Century." In *Cultural Encounters: The Impact of the Inquisition in Spain and the New World,* ed. Mary Elizabeth Perry and Anne J. Cruz, 93–104. Berkeley and Los Angeles: University of California Press, 1991.

Mâle, Emile. *L'Art religieux de la fin du Moyen Age en France.* Third edition. Paris: Armand Colin, 1925.

———. *L'Art religieux de la fin du XVIᵉ siècle, du XVIIᵉ siècle et du XVIIIᵉ siècle.* Second edition. Paris: Armand Colin, 1951.

Marchello-Nizia, Christiane. "L'Historien et son prologue: forme littéraire et stratégies discursives." In *La Chronique et l'histoire au Moyen Age,* ed. Daniel Poirion, 13–25. Paris: Presses de l'Université de Paris-Sorbonne, [1984].

Marichal, Juan. *La voluntad de estilo.* Madrid: Revista de Occidente, 1971.

Marín Padilla, Encarnación. "Pablo Hurus, impresor de biblias en lengua castellana en el año 1478." *Anuario de Estudios Medievales* 18 (1988): 591–603.

Marino, Nancy F. "Two Spurious Chronicles of Pedro *el Cruel* and the Ambitions of His Illegitimate Successors." *La Corónica* 21:2 (1993): 1–22.

Márquez, Antonio. *Los alumbrados: Orígenes y filosofía (1525–1559)*. Second edition. Madrid: Taurus, 1980.

Martène, Edmond. *De antiquis ecclesiae ritibus libri*. 4 vols. Antwerp, 1736; facsimile reprint, Hildesheim: Georg Olms, 1967.

Matter, E. Ann. *The Voice of My Beloved: The Song of Songs in Western Medieval Christianity*. Philadelphia: University of Pennsylvania Press, 1990.

Meiss, Millard. "An Early Altarpiece from the Cathedral of Florence." *The Metropolitan Museum of Art Bulletin* 12 (1954): 302–317.

———. *Painting in Florence and Siena after the Black Death*. New York: Harper and Row, 1964.

Miles, Margaret R. *Carnal Knowing: Female Nakedness and Religious Meaning in the Christian West*. 1989. New York: Vintage, 1991.

———. *Image as Insight: Visual Understanding in Western Christianity and Secular Culture*. Boston: Beacon Press, 1985.

———. "The Virgin's One Bare Breast: Female Nudity and Religious Meaning in Tuscan Early Renaissance Culture." In *The Female Body in Western Culture: Contemporary Perspectives*, ed. Susan Rubin Suleiman, 193–208. Cambridge, Mass., and London: Harvard University Press, 1986.

Minnis, A. J. *Medieval Theory of Authorship: Scholastic Literary Attitudes in the Later Middle Ages*. Second edition. Philadelphia: University of Pennsylvania Press, 1988.

Morreale, Margherita. "Apuntes bibliográficos para la iniciación al estudio de las traducciones bíblicas medievales al castellano." *Sefarad* 20 (1960): 66–109.

———. "Las *Epístolas y evangelios* de Ambrosio Montesino, eslabón entre los romanceamientos medievales y la lectura de la Biblia en el Siglo de Oro." In *Studi in onore di Antonio Corsano*, ed. Mario Sansone, 451–463. Manduria: Lacaita, 1970.

———. "Los *Gozos* de la Virgen en el *Libro* de Juan Ruiz (II)." *Revista de Filología Española* 64 (1984): 1–69.

———. "Vernacular Scriptures in Spain." In *The Cambridge History of the Bible*, vol. 2, ed. G. W. H. Lampe, 465–491. Cambridge: Cambridge University Press, 1969.

Morris, Joan. *The Lady Was a Bishop: The Hidden History of Women with Clerical Ordination and the Jurisdiction of Bishops*. New York: Macmillan, 1973.

Murray, Robert. *Symbols of Church and Kingdom: A Study in Early Syriac Tradition*. Cambridge: Cambridge University Press, 1975.

Nader, Helen. *The Mendoza Family in the Spanish Renaissance, 1350 to 1550*. New Brunswick, N.J.: Rutgers University Press, 1979.

Newman, Barbara. *Sister of Wisdom: St. Hildegard's Theology of the Feminine*. Berkeley and Los Angeles: University of California Press, 1987.

Nieto, José C. "The Heretical Alumbrados Dexados: Isabel de la Cruz and Pedro Ruiz de Alcaraz." *Revue de Littérature Comparée* 52 (1978): 293–313.

———. *Juan de Valdés and the Origins of the Spanish and Italian Reformation*. Geneva: Droz, 1970.

Núñez, Lucio María. "Carta de una nieta del Rey D. Pedro I." *Archivo Iberoamericano* 2 (1915): 126–127.

O'Connor, Sister Mary Catharine. *The Art of Dying Well: The Development of the "Ars moriendi."* New York: Columbia University Press, 1942.

Oettel, Therese. "Una catedrática en el siglo de Isabel la Católica: Luisa (Lucía) de Medrano." *Boletín de la Real Academia de la Historia* 107 (1935): 289–368.

Omaechevarría, Ignacio. *Orígenes de la Concepción de Toledo.* Burgos: Imprenta de Aldecoa, 1976.

Ong, Walter J. *Interfaces of the Word: Studies in the Evolution of Consciousness and Culture.* Ithaca, N.Y., and London: Cornell University Press, 1977.

———. "Latin Language Study as a Renaissance Puberty Rite." In his *Rhetoric, Romance, and Technology: Studies in the Interaction of Expression and Culture,* 113–141. Ithaca, N.Y., and London: Cornell University Press, 1971.

Ornstein, Jacob. "Misogyny and Pro-feminism in Early Castilian Literature." *Modern Language Quarterly* 3 (1942): 221–234.

Ozment, Stephen E. *Mysticism and Dissent: Religious Ideology and Social Protest in the Sixteenth Century.* New Haven, Conn., and London: Yale University Press, 1973.

Panofsky, Erwin. *Problems in Titian, Mostly Iconographic.* New York: New York University Press, 1969.

———. *Tomb Sculpture: Four Lectures on Its Changing Aspects from Ancient Egypt to Bernini.* Ed. H. W. Janson. New York: Abrams, [1964].

Parkes, M. B. "The Influence of the Concepts of *Ordinatio* and *Compilatio* on the Development of the Book." In *Medieval Learning and Literature: Essays Presented to Richard William Hunt,* ed. J. J. G. Alexander and M. T. Gibson, 115–141. Oxford: Clarendon Press, 1976.

Pastor de Togneri, Reyna. "Historia de las familias en Castilla y León (siglos X–XIV) y su relación con la formación de los grandes dominios eclesiásticos." *Cuadernos de Historia de España* 43–44 (1967): 88–118.

———. "Para una historia social de la mujer hispano-medieval. Problemática y puntos de vista." In *La condición de la mujer en la Edad Media,* ed. Yves-René Fonquerne and Alfonso Esteban, 187–214. Madrid: Casa de Velázquez and Universidad Complutense, 1986.

Perdrizet, Paul. *La Vierge de Miséricorde: Etude d'un thème iconographique.* Paris: A. Fontemoing, 1908.

Phillips, John A. *Eve: The History of an Idea.* San Francisco: Harper and Row, 1984.

Pickering, F. P. *Literature and Art in the Middle Ages.* London: Macmillan, 1970.

Plummer, John. *The Hours of Catherine of Cleves: Introduction and Commentaries.* New York: George Braziller, [1966].

Pousa, Ramón J. "Catálogo de una biblioteca española del año 1331: el monasterio de San Clemente, de Toledo." *Revista de Bibliografía Nacional* 1 (1940): 48–50.

Power, Eileen. *Medieval English Nunneries, c. 1275 to 1535.* Cambridge: Cambridge University Press, 1922.

Revuelta Somalo, Josemaría. *Los jerónimos: Una orden religiosa nacida en Guadalajara.* Guadalajara: Institución Provincial de Cultura, 1982.

Rico, Francisco. *Predicación y literatura en la España medieval.* Cádiz: UNED, 1977.

Riehle, Wolfgang. *The Middle English Mystics*. Trans. Bernard Standring. London: Routledge and Kegan Paul, 1981.

Rivera Garretas, María-Milagros. "La *Admiración de las obras de Dios* de Teresa de Cartagena y la Querella de las mujeres." In *La voz del silencio, I: Fuentes directas para la historia de las mujeres (siglos VIII–XVIII)*, ed. Cristina Segura Graiño, 277–299. Madrid: Asociación Cultural Al-Mudayna, 1992.

Rodríguez Rivas, Gregorio. "La autobiografía como *exemplum*: *La arboleda de los enfermos*, de Teresa de Cartagena." In *Escritura autobiográfica*, ed. José Romera Castillo et al., 367–370. Madrid: Visor, 1993.

Russell, P. E. *The English Intervention in Spain and Portugal in the Time of Edward III and Richard II*. Oxford: Clarendon Press, 1955.

Saenger, Paul. "Books of Hours and the Reading Habits of the Later Middle Ages." *Scrittura e civiltà* 9 (1985): 239–269.

———. "Silent Reading: Its Impact on Late Medieval Script and Society." *Viator* 13 (1982): 367–414.

Sánchez Herrero, José. *Concilios provinciales y sínodos toledanos de los siglos XIV y XV*. La Laguna: Universidad de La Laguna, 1976.

Schiller, Gertrud. *Ikonographie der christlichen Kunst, IV, 2: Maria*. Gütersloh: Mohn, 1980.

Schmidtke, James A. "'Saving' by Faint Praise: St. Birgitta of Sweden, Adam Easton and Medieval Antifeminism." *American Benedictine Review* 33 (1982): 149–161.

Seidenspinner-Núñez, Dayle. "'El solo me leyó': Gendered Hermeneutics and Subversive Poetics in *Admiraçión operum Dey* of Teresa de Cartagena." *Medievalia* 15 (1993): 14–23.

Serrano y Morales, José E. *Reseña histórica en forma de diccionario de las imprentas que han existido en Valencia desde la introducción del arte tipográfico en España hasta el año 1868*. Valencia: F. Domenech, 1898–1899.

Serrano y Sanz, Manuel. *Apuntes para una biblioteca de escritoras españolas desde el año 1401 al 1833*. 2 vols. Madrid: Sucesores de Rivadeneyra, 1903–1905.

———. "Pedro Ruiz de Alcaraz, iluminado alcarreño del siglo XVI." *Revista de Archivos, Bibliotecas y Museos* 8 (1903): 1–16.

Shank, Michael H. "A Female University Student in Late Medieval Kraków." *Signs* 12 (1987): 373–380.

Sicroff, Albert A. *Los estatutos de limpieza de sangre: Controversias entre los siglos XV y XVII*. Madrid: Taurus, 1985.

Simpson, W. Sparrow. "On the Measure of the Wound in the Side of the Redeemer, Worn Anciently as a Charm, and on the Five Wounds as Represented in Art." *Journal of the British Archaeological Association* 30 (1874): 357–374.

Sinanoglou, Leah. "The Christ Child as Sacrifice: A Medieval Tradition and the Corpus Christi Plays." *Speculum* 48 (1973): 491–509.

Sinclair, Keith V. *French Devotional Texts of the Middle Ages: A Bibliographic Manuscript Guide*. Westport, Conn.: Greenwood Press, 1979.

Sitges, J. B. *Las mujeres del rey don Pedro I de Castilla*. Madrid: Sucesores de Rivadeneyra, 1910.

Soleil, Félix. *Les Heures gothiques et la littérature pieuse aux XVe et XVIe siècles*. Rouen: Augé, 1882.

Surtz, Ronald E. *The Guitar of God: Gender, Power, and Authority in the Visionary World of Mother Juana de la Cruz (1481–1534)*. Philadelphia: University of Pennsylvania Press, 1990.

———. "Image Patterns in Teresa de Cartagena's *Arboleda de los enfermos*." In *La Chispa '87. Selected Proceedings*, ed. Gilbert Paolini, 297–304. New Orleans: Tulane University, 1987.

———. *"El libro del conorte" (1509) and the Early Castilian Theater*. Barcelona: Puvill, [1982].

Torres Fontes, Juan. "La regencia de don Fernando de Antequera." *Anuario de Estudios Medievales* 1 (1964): 375–429.

Trens, Manuel. *María: Iconografía de la Virgen en el arte español*. Madrid: Plus Ultra, 1947.

Vauchez, André. "Prophétesses, visionnaires et mystiques en Occident aux derniers siècles du Moyen Age." In *Les Réformes: enracinement socio-culturel*, ed. Bernard Chevalier and Robert Sauzet, 65–72. Paris: Editions de la Maisnie, 1985.

Villalba Ruiz de Toledo, F. Javier. *El cardenal Mendoza (1428–1495)*. Madrid: Rialp, 1988.

Wailes, Stephen L. *Medieval Allegories of Jesus' Parables*. Berkeley and Los Angeles: University of California Press, 1987.

Warner, Marina. *Monuments and Maidens: The Allegory of the Female Form*. New York: Atheneum, 1985.

Weber, Alison. *Teresa of Avila and the Rhetoric of Femininity*. Princeton, N.J.: Princeton University Press, 1990.

Weinstein, Donald, and Rudolph M. Bell. *Saints and Society: The Two Worlds of Western Christendom, 1000–1700*. Chicago and London: University of Chicago Press, 1982.

Wilmart, A. *Auteurs spirituels et textes dévots du Moyen Age latin*. Paris: Bloud et Gay, 1932.

Yardley, Anne Bagnall. " 'Ful weel she soong the service dyvyne': The Cloistered Musician in the Middle Ages." In *Women Making Music: The Western Art Tradition, 1150–1950*, ed. Jane Bowers and Judith Tick, 15–38. Urbana and Chicago: University of Illinois Press, 1986.

Index

University of Pennsylvania Press
MIDDLE AGES SERIES
Edward Peters, General Editor

F. R. P. Akehurst, trans. *The* Coutumes de Beauvaisis *of Philippe de Beaumanoir*. 1992

Peter L. Allen. *The Art of Love: Amatory Fiction from Ovid to the* Romance of the Rose. 1992

David Anderson. *Before the Knight's Tale: Imitation of Classical Epic in Boccaccio's Teseida*. 1988

Benjamin Arnold. *Count and Bishop in Medieval Germany: A Study of Regional Power, 1100–1350*. 1991

Mark C. Bartusis. *The Late Byzantine Army: Arms and Society, 1204–1453*. 1992

Thomas N. Bisson, ed. *Cultures of Power: Lordship, Status, and Process in Twelfth-Century Europe*. 1995

Uta-Renate Blumenthal. *The Investiture Controversy: Church and Monarchy from the Ninth to the Twelfth Century*. 1988

Gerald A. Bond. *The Loving Subject: Desire, Eloquence, and Power in Romanesque France*. 1995

Daniel Bornstein, trans. *Dino Compagni's* Chronicle *of Florence*. 1986

Maureen Boulton. *The Song in the Story: Lyric Insertions in French Narrative Fiction, 1200–1400*. 1993

Betsy Bowden. *Chaucer Aloud: The Varieties of Textual Interpretation*. 1987

Charles R. Bowlus. *Franks, Moravians, and Magyars: The Struggle for the Middle Danube, 788–907*. 1995

James William Brodman. *Ransoming Captives in Crusader Spain: The Order of Merced on the Christian-Islamic Frontier*. 1986

Kevin Brownlee and Sylvia Huot, eds. *Rethinking the* Romance of the Rose*: Text, Image, Reception*. 1992

Matilda Tomaryn Bruckner. *Shaping Romance: Interpretation, Truth, and Closure in Twelfth-Century French Fictions*. 1993

Otto Brunner (Howard Kaminsky and James Van Horn Melton, eds. and trans.). Land *and Lordship: Structures of Governance in Medieval Austria*. 1992

Robert I. Burns, S.J., ed. *Emperor of Culture: Alfonso X the Learned of Castile and His Thirteenth-Century Renaissance*. 1990

David Burr. *Olivi and Franciscan Poverty: The Origins of the* Usus Pauper *Controversy*. 1989

David Burr. *Olivi's Peaceable Kingdom: A Reading of the Apocalypse Commentary*. 1993

Thomas Cable. *The English Alliterative Tradition*. 1991

Anthony K. Cassell and Victoria Kirkham, eds. and trans. *Diana's Hunt/Caccia di Diana: Boccaccio's First Fiction*. 1991

John C. Cavadini. *The Last Christology of the West: Adoptionism in Spain and Gaul, 785–820.* 1993

Brigitte Cazelles. *The Lady as Saint: A Collection of French Hagiographic Romances of the Thirteenth Century.* 1991

Karen Cherewatuk and Ulrike Wiethaus, eds. *Dear Sister: Medieval Women and the Epistolary Genre.* 1993

Anne L. Clark. *Elisabeth of Schönau: A Twelfth-Century Visionary.* 1992

Willene B. Clark and Meradith T. McMunn, eds. *Beasts and Birds of the Middle Ages: The Bestiary and Its Legacy.* 1989

Richard C. Dales. *The Scientific Achievement of the Middle Ages.* 1973

Charles T. Davis. *Dante's Italy and Other Essays.* 1984

William J. Dohar. *The Black Death and Pastoral Leadership: The Diocese of Hereford in the Fourteenth Century.* 1994

Katherine Fischer Drew, trans. *The Burgundian Code.* 1972

Katherine Fischer Drew, trans. *The Laws of the Salian Franks.* 1991

Katherine Fischer Drew, trans. *The Lombard Laws.* 1973

Nancy Edwards. *The Archaeology of Early Medieval Ireland.* 1990

Richard K. Emmerson and Ronald B. Herzman. *The Apocalyptic Imagination in Medieval Literature.* 1992

Theodore Evergates. *Feudal Society in Medieval France: Documents from the County of Champagne.* 1993

Felipe Fernández-Armesto. *Before Columbus: Exploration and Colonization from the Mediterranean to the Atlantic, 1229–1492.* 1987

Jerold C. Frakes. *Brides and Doom: Gender, Property, and Power in Medieval Women's Epic.* 1994

R. D. Fulk. *A History of Old English Meter.* 1992

Patrick J. Geary. *Aristocracy in Provence: The Rhône Basin at the Dawn of the Carolingian Age.* 1985

Peter Heath. *Allegory and Philosophy in Avicenna (Ibn Sînâ), with a Translation of the Book of the Prophet Muḥammad's Ascent to Heaven.* 1992

J. N. Hillgarth, ed. *Christianity and Paganism, 350–750: The Conversion of Western Europe.* 1986

Richard C. Hoffmann. *Land, Liberties, and Lordship in a Late Medieval Countryside: Agrarian Structures and Change in the Duchy of Wrocław.* 1990

Robert Hollander. *Boccaccio's Last Fiction: Il Corbaccio.* 1988

John Y. B. Hood. *Aquinas and the Jews.* 1995

Edward B. Irving, Jr. *Rereading* Beowulf. 1989

Richard A. Jackson, ed. Ordines Coronationis Franciae: *Texts and Ordines for the Coronation of Frankish and French Kings and Queens in the Middle Ages, Vol. I.* 1995

C. Stephen Jaeger. *The Envy of Angels: Cathedral Schools and Social Ideals in Medieval Europe, 950–1200.* 1994

C. Stephen Jaeger. *The Origins of Courtliness: Civilizing Trends and the Formation of Courtly Ideals, 939–1210.* 1985

Donald J. Kagay, trans. *The Usatges of Barcelona: The Fundamental Law of Catalonia.* 1994

Richard Kay. *Dante's Christian Astrology.* 1994

Ellen E. Kittell. *From* Ad Hoc *to Routine: A Case Study in Medieval Bureaucracy.* 1991

Alan C. Kors and Edward Peters, eds. *Witchcraft in Europe, 1100-1700: A Documentary History.* 1972

Barbara M. Kreutz. *Before the Normans: Southern Italy in the Ninth and Tenth Centuries.* 1992

Michael P. Kuczynski. *Prophetic Song: The Psalms as Moral Discourse in Late Medieval England.* 1995

E. Ann Matter. *The Voice of My Beloved: The Song of Songs in Western Medieval Christianity.* 1990

A. J. Minnis. *Medieval Theory of Authorship.* 1988

Lawrence Nees. *A Tainted Mantle: Hercules and the Classical Tradition at the Carolingian Court.* 1991

Lynn H. Nelson, trans. *The Chronicle of San Juan de la Peña: A Fourteenth-Century Official History of the Crown of Aragon.* 1991

Barbara Newman. *From Virile Woman to WomanChrist: Studies in Medieval Religion and Literature.* 1995

Joseph F. O'Callaghan. *The Learned King: The Reign of Alfonso X of Castile.* 1993

Odo of Tournai (Irven M. Resnick, trans.). *Two Theological Treatises:* On Original Sin *and* A Disputation with the Jew, Leo, Concerning the Advent of Christ, the Son of God. 1994

David M. Olster. *Roman Defeat, Christian Response, and the Literary Construction of the Jew.* 1994

William D. Paden, ed. *The Voice of the Trobairitz: Perspectives on the Women Troubadours.* 1989

Edward Peters. *The Magician, the Witch, and the Law.* 1982

Edward Peters, ed. *Christian Society and the Crusades, 1198–1229: Sources in Translation, including* The Capture of Damietta *by Oliver of Paderborn.* 1971

Edward Peters, ed. *The First Crusade: The* Chronicle of Fulcher of Chartres *and Other Source Materials.* 1971

Edward Peters, ed. *Heresy and Authority in Medieval Europe.* 1980

James M. Powell. *Albertanus of Brescia: The Pursuit of Happiness in the Early Thirteenth Century.* 1992

James M. Powell. *Anatomy of a Crusade, 1213–1221.* 1986

Susan A. Rabe. *Faith, Art, and Politics at Saint-Riquier: The Symbolic Vision of Angilbert.* 1995

Jean Renart (Patricia Terry and Nancy Vine Durling, trans.). *The Romance of the Rose or Guillaume de Dole.* 1993

Michael Resler, trans. Erec *by Hartmann von Aue.* 1987

Pierre Riché (Michael Idomir Allen, trans.). *The Carolingians: A Family Who Forged Europe.* 1993

Pierre Riché (Jo Ann McNamara, trans.). *Daily Life in the World of Charlemagne.* 1978

Jonathan Riley-Smith. *The First Crusade and the Idea of Crusading.* 1986

Joel T. Rosenthal. *Patriarchy and Families of Privilege in Fifteenth-Century England.* 1991

Teofilo F. Ruiz. *Crisis and Continuity: Land and Town in Late Medieval Castile*. 1994

James A. Rushing, Jr. *Images of Adventure: Ywain in the Visual Arts*. 1995

James A. Schultz. *The Knowledge of Childhood in the German Middle Ages, 1100–1350*. 1995

Pamela Sheingorn, ed. and trans. *The Book of Sainte Foy*. 1995

Robin Chapman Stacey. *The Road to Judgment: From Custom to Court in Medieval Ireland and Wales*. 1994

Sarah Stanbury. *Seeing the* Gawain-Poet: *Description and the Act of Perception*. 1992

Robert D. Stevick. *The Earliest Irish and English Bookarts: Visual and Poetic Forms Before A.D. 1000*. 1994

Thomas C. Stillinger. *The Song of Troilus: Lyric Authority in the Medieval Book*. 1992

Susan Mosher Stuard. *A State of Deference: Ragusa/Dubrovnik in the Medieval Centuries*. 1992

Susan Mosher Stuard, ed. *Women in Medieval History and Historiography*. 1987

Susan Mosher Stuard, ed. *Women in Medieval Society*. 1976

Jonathan Sumption. *The Hundred Years War: Trial by Battle*. 1992

Ronald E. Surtz. *The Guitar of God: Gender, Power, and Authority in the Visionary World of Mother Juana de la Cruz (1481–1534)*. 1990

Ronald E. Surtz. *Writing Women in Late Medieval and Early Modern Spain: The Mothers of Saint Teresa of Avila*. 1995

Del Sweeney, ed. *Agriculture in the Middle Ages*. 1995

William H. TeBrake. *A Plague of Insurrection: Popular Politics and Peasant Revolt in Flanders, 1323–1328*. 1993

Patricia Terry, trans. *Poems of the Elder Edda*. 1990

Hugh M. Thomas. *Vassals, Heiresses, Crusaders, and Thugs: The Gentry of Angevin Yorkshire, 1154–1216*. 1993

Mary F. Wack. *Lovesickness in the Middle Ages: The* Viaticum *and Its Commentaries*. 1990

Benedicta Ward. *Miracles and the Medieval Mind: Theory, Record, and Event, 1000–1215*. 1982

Suzanne Fonay Wemple. *Women in Frankish Society: Marriage and the Cloister, 500–900*. 1981

Kenneth Baxter Wolf. *Making History: The Normans and Their Historians in Eleventh-Century Italy*. 1995

Jan M. Ziolkowski. *Talking Animals: Medieval Latin Beast Poetry, 750–1150*. 1993

This book has been set in Linotron Galliard. Galliard was designed for Mergenthaler in 1978 by Matthew Carter. Galliard retains many of the features of a sixteenth-century typeface cut by Robert Granjon but has some modifications that give it a more contemporary look.

Printed on acid-free paper.